DOWNSIZING IN AMERICA

DOWNSIZING IN AMERICA

REALITY, CAUSES, AND CONSEQUENCES

WILLAM J. BAUMOL, ALAN S. BLINDER,
AND EDWARD N. WOLFF

Russell Sage Foundation • New York

The Russell Sage Foundation

The Russell Sage Foundation, one of the oldest of America's general purpose foundations, was established in 1907 by Mrs. Margaret Olivia Sage for "the improvement of social and living conditions in the United States." The Foundation seeks to fulfill this mandate by fostering the development and dissemination of knowledge about the country's political, social, and economic problems. While the Foundation endeavors to assure the accuracy and objectivity of each book it publishes, the conclusions and interpretations in Russell Sage Foundation publications are those of the authors and not of the Foundation, its Trustees, or its staff. Publication by Russell Sage, therefore, does not imply Foundation endorsement.

Library of Congress Cataloging-in-Publication Data

Baumol, William J.
  Downsizing / William J. Baumol, Alan S. Blinder, Edward N. Wolff.
    p. cm.
  Includes bibliographical references and index.
  ISBN 0-87154-094-0
  1. Downsizing of organizations—United States. 2. Organizational change—United States. 3. Industries—Size—United States. I. Blinder, Alan S. II. Wolff, Edward N. III. Title.

HD58.85 .B38 2003
338.6'4—dc21   2002036740

The paper used in this publication meets the minimum requirements of American National Standard for Information Sciences—Permanence of Paper for Printed Library Materials. ANSI Z39.48-1992.

Text design by Suzanne Nichols

RUSSELL SAGE FOUNDATION
112 East 64th Street, New York, New York 10021
10 9 8 7 6 5 4 3 2

Contents

About the Authors

William J. Baumol is professor of economics at New York University and professor emeritus and senior research economist at Princeton University.

Alan S. Blinder is the Gordon S. Rentschler Memorial Professor of Economics at Princeton University and codirector of Princeton's Center for Economic Policy Studies.

Edward N. Wolff is professor of economics at New York University and a senior scholar at the Levy Economics Institute of Bard College.

Acknowledgments

This book was a work in progress for longer than any of us wants to remember. Over that period, corporate downsizing in America went from being a hot topic to a forgotten issue, and then back to a hot topic once again. As all this happened, our intellectual debts piled up.

First and foremost, we must acknowledge the pivotal role played by Sue Anne Batey Blackman, who was a coauthor in all but name. Not only was she principally responsible for executing the study of the newspaper sample reported in chapter 2, but she also coordinated every aspect of the project efficiently and with unflagging good humor, cajoled us when necessary (which was often), corrected numerous errors, got the facts straight, and improved the prose. As always, it was a pleasure working with her.

Any three-author book that takes years to complete will involve the efforts of a number of research assistants—in this case, at New York University, Princeton University, and the Brookings Institution. We must single out the especially extensive and fine work of Celina Su and Eric Parrado. Important contributions were also made by Gauti Eggertsson, Matt Moore, Wade Pfau, and Anindita Sen. We are also happy to acknowledge the many fine suggestions we received from three anonymous but helpful reviewers.

Our secretaries at NYU and Princeton, Janeece Lewis and Kathleen Hurley, did their usual fine job of keeping track of the manuscript at many stages and "making the trains run on time."

Finally, the research reported in this book was generously and patiently supported by grants from the Russell Sage Foundation (to Baumol and Wolff) and the Rockefeller Foundation (to Blinder). We are deeply grateful. Blinder also acknowledges the support of the Brookings Institution where, on a sabbatical, a good deal of his work was done.

William J. Baumol
Alan S. Blinder
Edward N. Wolff

Chapter 1

What Is Downsizing?
An Overview

D URING THE late 1980s and, especially, the early 1990s, a wave of what was called "downsizing" swept—or allegedly swept—corporate America. Top managers of many large U.S. corporations announced both major restructurings of their businesses and sizable reductions in their workforces. Some did so repeatedly, and with gusto. Often the announcements of these two actions were linked, thereby blurring the distinction between industrial change (restructuring) and reductions in force (downsizing)—a distinction that, as we will see, is crucial.

Wall Street analysts typically greeted downsizing announcements with cheers. Such proclamations apparently were interpreted as evidence that top corporate management "got it": they understood the tough, new industrial climate in which they were working and were prepared to make their companies leaner and meaner. But investors may not have agreed with the analysts. While the evidence is not entirely one-sided, most of the studies to date have concluded that companies' announcements of downsizings (or plant closings) caused their share prices to *decrease* (on average) rather than to increase.[1] Research reported later in this book also finds little if any econometric support for the popular notion that downsizing boosted share values.

News of downsizing was naturally greeted with considerably less equanimity by workers. For them, downsizing was cause for consternation—or worse. Many lost their jobs; many more feared they would be next to get the ax. Labor turnover, which has always been high in the United States, did increase somewhat, especially for white-collar workers.[2] But the media attention lavished on downsizing may have left people believing that job insecurity had increased more than it actually had. There were stories of workers being replaced by machines, or by foreign workers, or by temporary and contingent

1

workers with few fringe benefits and little or no attachment to the firm, and so on. In general, many corporations that had traditionally prided themselves on being at least somewhat paternalistic toward their workers seemed to become more hard-nosed. Indeed, one highly critical book (Gordon 1996) characterized U.S. corporations (in its title) as "fat and mean." In sum, these were generally tough years for American workers.

Downsizing—though not *announcements* of downsizings—retreated to the back burner during the boom years of the late 1990s, when the national unemployment rate touched a thirty-year low and labor *shortages* emerged as one of management's top problems. But as the economy began to slow in the second half of 2000, and then actually to contract in 2001, the frequency of downsizing increased and public and media attention to it resurfaced. Concern with job security reclaimed its place near the top of the list of national problems. It remained there as the early stages of the economic recovery in 2002 and 2003 proved to be "jobless."

With a decade of hindsight, this seems an appropriate time to look back at and appraise the downsizing episode of the 1980s and early 1990s. If the downsizing phenomenon was real, why did it happen? Economists do not normally expect business leaders suddenly to wake up one morning believing that their previous decisions—in this case, those having to do with employment levels—are preponderantly wrong. If thousands of managers decided to downsize at more or less the same time, there must have been reasons. What, then, changed in the U.S. or world economy to foment all this industrial restructuring, labor market turmoil, and downsizing? And should we view these changes, whatever they were, as permanent features of the industrial landscape? Or were they merely transitory influences that, while requiring some painful adjustments at the time, are now largely behind us?

Then and Now: A Long Historical View

To address such questions, we begin by taking a long historical view of the U.S. economy over the last century. In subsequent analysis we will, of course, dig down deeper into the behavior of average firm size (and other measures) in individual industries, and we will focus on a much shorter time period. But since downsizing in the 1980s and early 1990s was portrayed as something new and different, it is worth starting with a simple question: In terms of the economy as a whole, was this period really different?

Figure 1.1 offers a bird's-eye view of changes in the size of the average U.S. business over the course of more than a century. It suggests that the answer may be yes—that downsizing is not just a continuation of past trends.

Figure 1.1   Average Number of Employees per U.S. Business Concern, 1885 to 1998

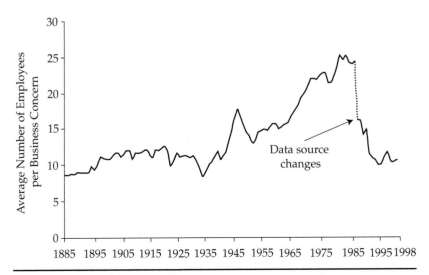

Source: Adapted from Jovanovic and Rousseau (2001), who cite *Historical Statistics of the United States, Colonial Times to 1970* (1975) and *Statistical Abstract of the United States* (various years).
Note: Beginning in 1985, the data source counts the number of business establishments instead of business firm names, resulting in a sudden drop from 24.42 to 16.29 employees per concern.

The primary data underlying this diagram unfortunately switched in 1985 from being based on the number of business *firm names* to being based on the number of business *establishments.* Since many business firms conduct their operations at more than one establishment, this switch produced a sharp break in the series between 1984 and 1985. But if we ignore that break (as we must, for it is simply a figment of the data) and ignore the sharp gyrations caused by the Great Depression (which reduced firm size for pretty obvious reasons) and World War II (which raised firm size for equally obvious reasons), a reasonably clear pattern emerges. Specifically, the size of the average American business fluctuated mostly in the range of eleven to twelve employees for roughly the first four decades of the twentieth century, then climbed steadily and markedly to a peak of about twenty-five employees over the next four decades. It then fell sharply from the early 1980s through the early 1990s before leveling off after about 1993.

In brief, what we see in figure 1.1 is a picture of increasing business size from about 1935 until about 1980, and then decreasing size from about 1980 to about 1993. In subsequent chapters, we document the fact that changes in *firm* size and changes in *establishment* size follow similar (though not quite identical) patterns. So the reversal of the historical trend that appears to have taken place in the early 1980s was probably genuine, despite the break in the data. Figure 1.1 thus suggests that the trend toward downsizing from 1980 to 1993 may indeed have been "something new"—a hypothesis that we investigate in greater detail in the coming chapters.

Figure 1.1 also suggests a second hypothesis. As we have observed, average firm size dipped sharply during the Great Contraction (1929 to 1933) and soared during the Second World War, only to fall back again thereafter. These episodes constitute what are by far the two most dramatic cyclical fluctuations of the period. But if we look closer, we can also see noticeable reductions of average firm size during the deep recessions of 1973 to 1975 and 1981 to 1983. There thus appears to be a cyclical pattern, with average firm size rising in booms and falling in recessions or depressions. This hypothesis also receives extensive attention—and strong confirmation—in this book.

Table 1.1 uses an entirely different data source and focuses on the more recent period. The American Management Association (AMA) surveys job creation, job elimination, and downsizing among its members (mainly large firms) annually. We will encounter these data again in chapter 2, where we will explain their source and nature in greater detail. Here, table 1.1 provides a quick overview of the waxing and waning of downsizing since 1988. According to the AMA survey, the year ending June 1991, which included a recession, was the worst period for downsizing in the survey's history, which began with the year ending June 1987. The data for 1990 to 1991 show that over 55 percent of the AMA's membership reported eliminating some jobs that year and that fully 79 percent of such cases were actual downsizings—that is, the number of jobs eliminated exceeded the number of new jobs created. By the 1997 survey (covering the twelve-month period ending June 1997), the macroeconomic environment had improved greatly, but 41 percent of member firms still reported some job elimination. However, in only 46 percent of these cases did total employment in the firm actually decline. In a word, job creation and destruction—the churning and restructuring of the workforce—are with us all the time. But the net balance of the two is highly cyclical.[3]

We can also see in table 1.1 that, after dissipating considerably after the mid-1990s, downsizing made a strong comeback in the most recent published survey, covering July 2000 through June 2001. The percentage of firms reporting actual downsizing (column 2), which had been at a low 21.2 percent in the year ending June 2000—roughly

Table 1.1   Downsizing Among American Management Association
Surveyed Members, 1988–1989 Through 2000–2001

Year	(1) Percentage of Gross Job Eliminators	(2) Percentage of Net Job Eliminators (Downsizers)	(3) Column 2 as a Percentage of Column 1
1988–1989	39.0	25.7	66
1989–1990	35.7	26.4	74
1990–1991	55.5	43.8	79
1991–1992	46.1	36.0	78
1992–1993	46.6	32.6	70
1993–1994	47.3	30.6	65
1994–1995	49.6	27.3	55
1995–1996	40.9	27.9	68
1996–1997	41.1	19.0	46
1997–1998	48.9	21.9	45
1998–1999	49.6	24.1	49
1999–2000	48.2	21.2	44
2000–2001	57.5	36.4	63

Source: American Management Association (various years).

matching its average over the previous four years—surged to 36.4
percent in the period 2000 to 2001. This figure is the second highest in
column 2, exceeded only by the downsizing experience during the
recession of 1990 to 1991. It seems predictable that downsizing will
receive heavy press and public attention whenever this figure is high.

The Plan of This Book

We are hardly the first economists to study downsizing. But to our
knowledge, this book is the most comprehensive treatment of the issue to date. Furthermore, as Peter Capelli (2000, 3) noted in his recent
and useful survey of research on downsizing, "There have been no
prior studies of the determinants of downsizing." Investigating those
underlying causes of downsizing is the central task of this book.

We tackle the problem from several different angles. Most of the
rest of this chapter presents six hypotheses that offer alternative and
possibly competing explanations of what may underlie the downsizing phenomenon; *observable* implications of each hypothesis are emphasized. As we seek to learn which hypotheses are supported by the
data and which are not, these six hypotheses will provide the organizational structure for the book.

Chapter 2 deals with the intense media attention that was lavished on downsizing in the 1990s. It also analyzes the experiences of a sample of mostly large firms whose downsizing announcements were reported in the newspapers. Our reason for focusing on this nonrandom newspaper sample is that very large firms tend to get lost (via top-coding, for example) in comprehensive data sets.[4] Yet these are the very firms that command public attention.

Chapter 3 then examines what basic microeconomic theory tells us about the downsizing phenomenon, emphasizing the role of changes in technology and their implications for the most efficient size of a firm in a given industry. This analysis sets the stage for our examination of the empirical evidence in the remaining chapters.

The central statistical and econometric analyses of this book are found in chapters 4 through 8. Chapter 4 is a comprehensive look at the basic facts: Has there really been downsizing in the United States since the 1980s? If so, how much? In what sectors? We show that the picture in manufacturing is very different from the picture outside manufacturing—an important point, since the vast majority of studies to date have been limited to manufacturing. Specifically, we find that downsizing is common in many manufacturing industries but rather rare outside manufacturing. In fact, what might be called *upsizing* is much closer to the norm in the retailing and service sectors—each of which employs many more workers than does manufacturing.

Having laid out the facts in detail in chapter 4, we concentrate in chapter 5 on explaining, in an econometric sense, downsizing in manufacturing. Chapter 6 then does the same for those nonmanufacturing industries for which sufficient data are available, although here the focus is on the causes of *upsizing* rather than of downsizing.

Chapter 7 returns to the manufacturing sector, which is where most of the actual downsizing occurred, and investigates a variety of possible consequences of downsizing. What happens to firms that downsize? One of the main findings of the book is that much of what has been termed "downsizing" is really industrial restructuring—that is, job churning rather than (net) job reductions. So chapter 8 turns directly to the rise in labor market turbulence and, for the only time in the book, uses data on individuals rather than on businesses.

Finally, in chapter 9 we offer a brief summary of the study's main findings and some tentative conclusions.

The Causes of Downsizing: Six Theoretical Hypotheses

Six possible explanations of downsizing have guided the empirical work of this book, especially chapters 4 through 6. Each one focuses on a single possible *cause* of downsizing and then traces its *consequences* for a firm's employment and other observable variables. Although the hypotheses are distinct, it is important to realize that they are not mutually exclusive; indeed, downsizing probably does have multiple causes. Still, it is essential to ask which of these explanations are consistent with the data and which are not. Only by doing so can we begin to understand the history of this important phenomenon, make tentative judgments on whether influences on downsizing are likely to be durable or transient, and think intelligently about the policy implications.

Some of these hypotheses raise the possibility that downsizing is not what it appears to be. First, many firms that claim to have downsized may not really have done so. Instead, they may have simply altered the *compositions* of their workforces more than their sizes. For example, some companies may have first reduced the number of less-educated or older workers or middle managers. Then, after a suitable interval required for retooling and reorganization, they may have replaced most of their former employees with others deemed more appropriate to the company's current needs.

"Downsizing" of this sort is more accurately labeled "restructuring." That relabeling does not make the consequent churning of the labor force any less important for those who pay the costs. After all, large-scale restructurings are apt to have substantial effects on productivity and can have devastating effects on the displaced workers (on the latter, see Gordon 1996; Leana and Feldman 1992; Rudolph 1998). But it does indicate that the firm in question is doing something other than shrinking.

A second possibility is that what is popularly known as downsizing may consist of reductions in the size of the typical firm accompanied by offsetting increases in the number of enterprises—leaving total *industry* employment largely unaffected. Such a scenario, like large-scale restructuring, is consistent with a large number of job terminations—lots of labor market churning, but no decrease in overall employment. In fact, as we have indicated earlier and will show in the following chapters, the evidence does not reject either of these two scenarios, neither of which should really be called downsizing (unless there is net job loss).

We proceed now to the discussion of our six hypotheses, beginning with one that certainly relates directly to genuine downsizing—that is, reductions in firm size.

Hypothesis 1: Downsizing Occurs Because Technological Change Favors Smaller Enterprises

There has long been a common presumption that technological progress favors larger firms—for example, by requiring huge investments for successful entry into the industry or by extending the range of output over which economies of scale persist. Technology of that sort certainly characterized the railroads, automobile manufacture, and earlier forms of steelmaking, for example. However, technological change can sometimes make it more efficient to operate on a *smaller* scale. Transporting freight by truck instead of by rail is one well-known example; truck transport materially decreased average firm size in the transportation industry. Mini-mills, the success story of the modern U.S. steel industry, are vastly smaller than integrated steel mills. And the recent histories of shrunken giants like GM, IBM, and AT&T indicate that mammoth size may no longer be a competitive advantage. When some people talk nowadays of the "end of mass production" in the computer age, they are emphasizing the greater relative importance of speed, flexibility, product variety, and customization.

On balance, technological change can sometimes promote larger average firm size and at other times promote smaller firms. We discuss the underlying theory in chapter 3. The influence of technology on the size of a typical enterprise presumably changes direction only gradually, but there is no reason why it should always push in the same direction. Even when the evidence shows that current technological developments predominantly favor smaller firms (at least for manufacturers), as we suggest in chapter 5, there is no clear basis on which to expect this to be a reliable portent for the future.

However, let us suppose for the moment that technological change really does favor smaller, more flexible enterprises. What should we then see in the data? One clear implication is that the distribution of firms by size should shift toward smaller firms—to the left in figure 1.2. When we look explicitly for such shifts in chapter 4, we find them in many (but certainly not all) manufacturing industries. But we do not find much evidence of shifts toward smaller firm size outside of manufacturing—in fact, the opposite shift is more common. Moreover, as we just noted, this particular version of downsizing may not imply any shrinkage in overall industry employment. Average firm size may fall, but there may be more firms.

A second empirical implication of downsizing driven by technology is that firm size should be shrinking faster in industries undergoing more rapid technological change. This implication is also testable with our industrial database. In chapters 5 and 6, we look for associations between leftward shifts of the size distribution of firms (for example, falling average firm size, as measured by employment) and various measures of technological activity, such as total factor productivity (TFP) growth, research and development (R&D) expenditures, and the employment of scientists and engineers. We find them to only a limited extent—again, chiefly in manufacturing.

Figure 1.2   The Size Distribution of Firms Under Downsizing

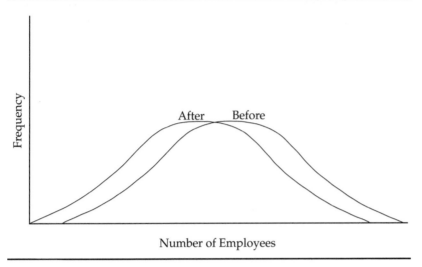

Source: Authors' configuration.

Technology can also yield more complex patterns of changes in firm size. For example, suppose new technology reduces the magnitude of sunk costs (investment costs that are required for entry) in some industries, thus decreasing the minimum efficient scale of operation in that industry, but at the same time raises sunk costs in other industries. Then we would expect to find downsizing in the one and upsizing in the other.

It is also possible that technical change in some industries makes both very small and very large firms more costly than firms of intermediate size. Computerization might have this effect, for example, by permitting greater customization and smaller production runs, on the one hand, but requiring firms to be large enough to be able to afford to buy computer technology, on the other. In that case, we would expect to find downsizing among the largest enterprises, with a countervailing trend toward upsizing among the smallest ones. In such a world, we would expect to find what is called "regression toward the mean" in the size distribution of firms, with a greater portion of firms moving toward intermediate size (as displayed in figure 1.3). Indeed, Richard E. Caves's (1998) comprehensive survey of the literature on the size distribution of firms concluded that regression toward the mean is in fact the norm—in contrast to economists' traditional belief in Gibrat's Law (which predicts ever-increasing concentration).

So, is U.S. industry evolving in the manner suggested by figure

**Figure 1.3   The Size Distribution of Firms Under Regression Toward
the Mean**

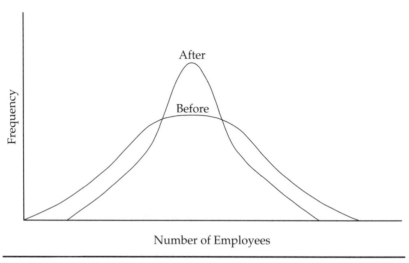

Source: Authors' configuration.

1.3? In chapters 4 and 5, we offer some evidence that regression toward the mean may indeed have happened in the manufacturing sector, but not elsewhere. Caves's (1998) conclusion turns out to have
been based mostly on studies of manufacturing—which once again
illustrates how hazardous it is to draw economywide conclusions by
looking only at manufacturing. However, if we take a broader view,
downsizing in the typical manufacturing industry coupled with *upsizing* in the typical retailing or service industry (which is roughly the
picture we find in chapters 4 and 5) can be interpreted as a kind of
economywide regression toward the mean. The reason, of course, is
that average firm size is much larger in manufacturing than in either
retailing or services. So if (larger) manufacturing companies downsize
while (smaller) nonmanufacturing companies upsize, the entire industrial structure displays regression toward the mean.

Hypothesis 2: Faster Innovation Leads to More Labor Market Churning

Our second hypothesis about downsizing also attributes this phenomenon to technical change. But here the effect stems not from
changes in the cost-minimizing size of a firm, but rather from the
pace of technological improvement itself. The essential idea is that

any product or process innovation requires alterations in the nature of the tasks that workers must perform. A speedup in the *rate* of innovation therefore implies that such changes come faster and are more dramatic. Such changes, in turn, almost certainly require more extensive reallocations of labor both within and across firms.

One important feature of this phenomenon is the unevenness with which the costs and benefits of such labor market churning are spread across the workforce. Employees who are better educated or better trained can adapt more easily to new technology and changing circumstances, while less-skilled workers are presumably less adaptable. At least, that is the usual assumption. The presumptive consequence is that highly skilled workers may actually benefit from innovation, while less-skilled workers are more likely to suffer both unemployment and wage declines when they are "downsized."

Surprisingly, the empirical literature on this issue is not entirely one-sided, perhaps because "skill" is so difficult to measure. Studies by Ann Bartel and Frank Lichtenberg (1987) and Timothy Dunne and James Schmitz (1995) offered evidence supporting the conventional wisdom that the advance of technology raises the relative demand for skilled labor. But Daniel Aaronson and Kenneth Housinger (1999) found no support for the popular notion that technology disproportionately displaces low-skilled or older workers. They did, however, find that these workers, once displaced, have a harder time finding new jobs. So, on balance, they do lose ground to higher-skilled or younger workers.

The hypothesized role of innovation as the driver of downsizing may seem at first to rest on a fortuitous relationship: technical change just happens to play a key role. But we believe otherwise. We maintain that continuing innovation is no accident and can be expected to persist in the future. Since the details of our hypothesis are somewhat novel, we will describe them step by step.

Our analysis starts with the hypothesis that the free-market mechanism creates remorseless pressures for innovation, and that these pressures are what most clearly distinguish the capitalist economy from all alternative economic systems. One major source of this pressure for continued and increasing innovative effort is the fact that the adoption of new technology, especially in the form of new products and new industrial processes, has emerged as a prime competitive weapon for firms in the major oligopolistic sectors. The result is a kind of innovation "arms race" that can literally be a matter of life or death for the participants. And like other arms races, it becomes what has been called a "Red-Queen game" because, in terms of market position, the participants find themselves forced to keep running in

Figure 1.4   Real U.S. Private R&D Expenditures, 1953 to 1998

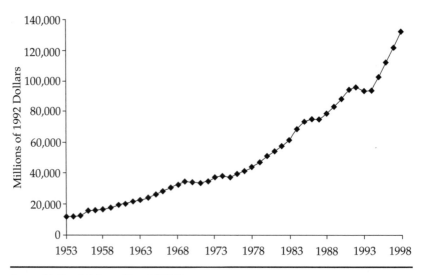

Source: National Science Board (2000).

order to stand still (see Khalil 1997, 411–15; Baumol 2002). In such a situation, no player dares to fall behind, and many may seek ways to pull ahead of their rivals.

This sort of rivalry is clearly a recipe for increasing investment in R&D and for innovative activities more generally. And the evidence is that real private outlays on R&D have indeed risen substantially and fairly persistently over the postwar period—although the period of sharpest rise has not always coincided with peaks in downsizing. Figure 1.4 shows that the increase in private industry R&D expenditures from 1953 to 1998 was dramatic. In dollars of constant purchasing power, industry funding nearly quadrupled between 1970 and 1998, increasing from about $34 billion to nearly $133 billion. The latter sum amounted to about 70 percent of the nation's R&D expenditures in 1998. As a percentage of real GDP, real R&D expenditures rose from about 1.5 percent in 1953 to almost 3 percent in 1964, and these expenditures have been mostly in the 2.5 to 3.0 percent range ever since.

Several features of the innovation process bear directly on our second hypothesis about downsizing. First, while innovation has contributed spectacularly to the growth of labor productivity, historical evidence decisively rejects the popular view that rising productivity leads to long-term growth in unemployment. Luddites (both nineteenth-century and modern) notwithstanding, the evidence shows that, while innovation does indeed destroy certain jobs, it also stimulates demand for new products—which creates new jobs. And history teaches us that the the creation of new jobs always overwhelms the destruction of old jobs by a huge margin. For example, productivity in the United States has increased more than elevenfold since 1870, meaning that employment could have been reduced by more than 90 percent without any loss in per-capita output (see Maddison 2001). Yet the unemployment rate in this country shows no long-term upward trend. The same point applies to foreign competition (which we discuss in the context of the next hypothesis about downsizing). In the long run, any loss of jobs to foreign competitors may well be offset by increased purchases by foreigners.

A second feature of the innovation process is that faster technological change increases the frequency with which plant and equipment needs to be replaced. By accelerating the replacement of capital, it presumably also adds to the amount of labor-market churning and hence to the rate of frictional unemployment. This process manifests itself in a transitory link between the rate of innovation and the length of unemployment spells—a link that is apparent in the data (see Baumol and Wolff 1999).

Third, as already suggested, moving labor from obsolete plants to state-of-the-art facilities typically entails more than mere geographic relocation. More often than not, it requires either retraining existing workers or replacing them with others who are better able to use the new technology. Such changes are therefore disadvantageous to those whom it is particularly difficult or costly to retrain (for example, the poorly educated) or who offer bleak prospects for recovery of the firm's investments in retraining (for example, older workers). In this way, innovation may leave a permanent—or at least a very long-lasting—imprint on relative wages and the distribution of income, depressing the wages of unskilled and less-educated workers relative to those with more skill and education. But such phenomena, socially troubling as they may be, should not be called downsizing.

Fourth, technologically driven restructurings, with their consequent churning of the workforce, should be expected to continue indefinitely. The mechanism that forces firms to focus on innovation as the primary instrument of competition leads us to expect no slowdown in the stream of innovations. Indeed, as we have noted, the arms-race attribute of competition in innovation may even force investment in R&D to accelerate. Of course, both the rate of successful innovation and its impact on the economy will display fluctuations. But we would surely not want to repeat the misdiagnosis of Charles H. Duell, commissioner of U.S. patents, who in 1899 said, "Everything that can be invented has been invented," and, in his shortsightedness, recommended that the patent office be shut down (Federal Reserve Bank of Dallas 1996b, 5).

A critical question about the future therefore arises: Will the technologically based handicap now apparently besetting less-skilled workers last forever? Perhaps not, for history suggests that new technology typically follows an evolutionary pattern: it tends to be complicated and relatively difficult to use at first, but becomes simpler and more "user-friendly" later on (see, for example, Rosenberg 1982, 6–8, 62–70). Early innovations are apt to require the specialized skills of educated workers, who are needed both to improve and to operate the new product or process. This enhanced demand for skills clearly hurts unskilled, and presumably inflexible, labor. The later stages of the innovation process, however, may work in favor of such workers, who find the new technology becoming easier to use as it matures.

While that is a hopeful thought, at least two influences push in the opposite direction. First, more technically advanced products that are simpler to use are ordinarily more complex beneath the surface. An automobile without a crank is easier to drive, but it has a starter mechanism that needs to be maintained by trained mechanics. A modern personal computer is more user-friendly than its predecessors, but only the most able specialists can penetrate the complex software that makes it run. If this pattern is typical, even the later stages of innovation may favor skilled labor. Second, suppose industrial processes really do become simpler as technology matures. In that case, formerly skilled jobs may metamorphose into unskilled ones and migrate to less developed countries, where wages are much lower. For example, much of the less complex work involving computer programming and code writing is now conducted in countries such as India, and the resulting products are brought quickly and cheaply back to the United States.

These two economic mechanisms suggest that the term "downsizing" may be a misnomer for the phenomenon explained by our second hypothesis (the rate of innovation affects the reallocation of labor). What is really taking place in these cases is a systematic *change in the composition* of the typical firm's labor force rather than a *cut in its size*. This phenomenon is better labeled "churning" or "restructuring" than downsizing.

Finally, let us ask whether the evidence is consistent with a hypothesis that attributes downsizing to the workforce adjustments necessitated by rapid technological change. Since total factor productivity growth (a commonly used measure of technological progress) during the prime downsizing period (the late 1980s and the early 1990s) was rising faster in manufacturing than outside of manufacturing, the hypothesis clearly suggests that downsizing should be found mainly in the manufacturing sector and in those nonmanufacturing industries that were experiencing rapid technological change (such as computer software, telecommunications, and finance). As we demonstrate in chapters 4 and 5, this prediction seems to be borne out in the data: downsizing is found mainly in manufacturing industries, and within the manufacturing sector, industries with the most rapid gains in total factor productivity appear to have downsized the most. But the evidence for the latter finding is weak, as we shall see.

However, as noted earlier, what appears to have happened in manufacturing is not universal downsizing, but rather something closer to regression toward the mean: many of the largest manufacturing firms reduced the number of their employees and many of the smaller firms expanded their labor forces. Thus, the evidence may well be compatible with the technological story of our second hypothesis: that there is both downsizing (in some places) and general restructuring and churning.

Another basic premise of hypothesis 2 is that more-educated labor can be reallocated more easily than less-educated labor. If so, both the length of unemployment spells and the wage loss after job displacement should be smaller for more-educated workers, as appears to be true. For example, Steven Hipple (1999, 20) examined data for the years 1981 to 1996 from the U.S. Department of Labor's Displaced Workers Surveys (DWS). He found that "job losers with more schooling spent considerably less time without work than their counterparts with less education," and that more-educated displaced workers experienced much smaller earnings losses. Similarly, Henry Farber (2001, 14, 21), who looked at the DWS data for 1981 to 1999, reported that more-educated job losers suffered smaller earnings declines, on average, than workers with less education, and had higher post-displacement employment probabilities.

Our second hypothesis about downsizing focuses attention on the overall extent of job restructuring within industries. Did such restructurings accelerate during the 1980s? Is the degree of job restructuring greater in industries with more rapid rates of technological activity— or with more exposure to imports (a factor we consider in discussing the third hypothesis)? In chapter 7, we make use of the raw occupational data for each industry to construct measures of changes in job composition over time and relate such changes to technology and to changes in firm size. We find only modest statistical associations.

Most obviously, the theory predicts widening skill differentials in wages, which have certainly occurred. This fact has been extensively documented elsewhere, so we do not attempt to expand the evidence in this book.[5]

Hypothesis 3: Foreign Competition Compels Domestic Industry to Downsize by Trimming "Fat"

Our third hypothesis attributes downsizing to the intensification of foreign competition, whether actual or threatened. It comes in two versions, one of which is actually a variant of our second hypothesis. In this version, increased competition from abroad—or perhaps simply greater cross-border economic activity—changes relative demands and supplies in the U.S. market; those changes, in turn, require some firms and industries to contract while others expand. From there, the story is almost the same as in the second hypothesis. The basic story may be more one of churning than of literal downsizing.

In fact, the availability of cheaper foreign products can be viewed as analogous to technological progress: both increase the value of the outputs that the U.S. economy can obtain from a given quantity of inputs, and both are likely to require significant industrial change. Furthermore, increased globalization is fundamentally rooted in technological advance: reduced transportation costs, faster telecommunications, and the like are among the primary drivers of increased trade.

According to this third hypothesis, the United States and other industrial economies have grown increasingly vulnerable to import competition as trade barriers have fallen, as new technology has been adopted by other countries, and, perhaps, as educational standards have risen in a number of former Third World countries. The growth of international trade is truly impressive. Angus Maddison (1995, 38) estimates that since 1820 world exports as a percentage of world GDP have grown thirteenfold; the percentage in the United States alone has tripled since 1950. And this growth accelerated markedly after 1973, when the Bretton Woods system of fixed exchange rates ended.

All this foreign competition, the story goes, has forced American firms to reduce what economists call "X-inefficiency"—in plain English, to trim the "fat" from their operations (see Leibenstein 1966). And they have often accomplished this slimming down by cutting the dispensable portions of their labor forces. The argument is that certain, presumably large, firms used to have (or perhaps still have) more labor than they need to produce the desired level of output—excess that they subsequently shed (or are shedding) under pressure from foreign competitors. The prototypical case may be the U.S. auto industry in the 1960s and early 1970s, which was widely viewed as "fat and lazy" before the one-two punch of Japanese competition and the OPEC oil embargo.[6] The industry is now both leaner and meaner, and Japanese competition is probably a major reason why.

The second version of the foreign competition argument—the one more frequently found in the academic literature—emphasizes the pressure that low-wage labor abroad puts on U.S. labor markets, especially on markets for unskilled labor. Like the story of skill-biased technical progress that underpins our second hypothesis (that faster innovation leads to more reallocation of labor), the notion that workers in poor countries (the "South") pose a threat to low-skilled workers in rich countries (the "North") has been widely offered as an explanation for rising wage inequality in the industrial countries. But it may also lead firms to rid themselves of excess domestic labor—that is, to downsize in the United States. The hypothesis itself is controversial, whether offered as an explanation of declining wages or of declining employment.[7] Yet, because it has been discussed and debated so extensively, it may be useful to consider some of its observable implications.

In this version, downsizing is allegedly caused by intensified competition. If this is so, the inference seems obvious: the phenomenon should be most severe where the intensification of competition is greatest. While journalistic accounts regularly advance this idea, there is much less academic evidence, perhaps because it is not easy to measure the intensity of competition.[8] Falling profit margins are one indication that a particular industry is facing greater competition, but profits are influenced by myriad other factors as well. Lower profitability would therefore be a poor statistical proxy for stiffer competition. Nor is greater *foreign* competition the only source (nor even the main source) of greater competition in most industries.

To the extent that increased international competition is the driving force, we should perhaps find a positive correlation between downsizing and the share of imports (and maybe even the share of exports) in an industry's output. And as we will see in chapters 4 and 5, there is considerable evidence in support of this view. There are several pitfalls here, however. For example, the theory of contestable markets emphasizes that *potential* competition can sometimes be nearly as effective as *actual* competition in keeping profits down. Hence, profits can be depressed by growing foreign competitiveness even if the foreign market share is low and remains so.

Regardless of the underlying cause, it would appear that the "trimming fat" hypothesis has a clear empirical implication: downsizing should raise the *average* productivity of labor substantially—after all, when a firm rids itself of redundant labor, its labor input should be reduced without reducing output. This implication appears at least partly testable in a cross-section of firms: labor productivity should rise faster in industries that displace relatively more workers. We test this hypothesis in chapter 7. Like earlier work on the effects of downsizing on productivity, our findings do not provide much support for the frequent assertion that downsizing produces sharp gains in productivity.[9]

The implications for profits, however, are less clear. As we have mentioned, intensified competition should reduce profitability, all other things being equal. On the other hand, shedding of excess labor should increase profitability. To complicate things further, profits are heavily influenced by, for example, cyclical conditions, which must be controlled for in any empirical test.[10] We will, of course, look at the implications of downsizing for profitability. But relating what we find (generally, an increase in profitability after downsizing) to any particular theory of downsizing is rather difficult.

Hypothesis 4: Downsizing Occurs When Capital Is Substituted for Labor

Another possible explanation for downsizing is that firms are shedding labor because they are adopting new production technologies that employ relatively less labor and relatively more capital. In this case, the total output of a typical firm does not fall, but employment falls and capital usage rises as firms substitute more capital for less labor.

In the early years of the great capital spending boom of the 1990s (approximately 1992 to 1994), there was indeed much written in the financial press suggesting that the surge in investment was motivated more by the desire to replace labor with capital than by any desire to expand capacity. However, this talk all but disappeared during the growth spurt between 1996 and 2000, when firms were scrambling for labor and the unemployment rate fell to a thirty-year low. Moreover, the U.S. Federal Reserve Board's index of industrial production shows a marked acceleration of the growth of industrial capacity throughout this period—indicating that firms were indeed building new productive capacity, not just replacing labor with capital. For example, the estimated compound annual growth rate of total industrial capacity (not capacity *utilization*) from December 1995 to December 2000 was 5.2 percent—well above the 3.0 percent growth rate over the previous five-year period.

But let us suppose for the moment that capital-labor substitution does indeed underlie downsizing. Why might this be so? Standard economic theory looks to the prices of the various inputs used in the production process to explain optimal factor proportions: in other words, given technology, firms should decide to use more of one factor of production (say, capital) relative to another (say, labor) when the *relative* price of the first factor falls. A rise in the capital-labor ratio should therefore be prompted by a rise in the ratio of labor compensation to the cost of capital. But in fact, real wages were certainly not growing rapidly during what were apparently the prime downsizing years, 1985 to 1993. Indeed, real wages even lagged behind sluggish labor productivity. For example, the U.S. Bureau of Labor Statistics reported that real compensation per hour in the nonfarm business sector advanced at a mere 0.8 percent annual rate over those eight years, while labor productivity grew at an annual rate of 1.5 percent. That comparison hardly suggests that rapidly escalating wages were forcing firms to find ways to economize on labor.[11]

However, the cost of capital probably did fall substantially from the early 1980s until at least 2000 (and probably beyond). In 2000, the stock market was much higher and real interest rates were slightly lower than they were around 1985. So labor costs may have risen faster than capital costs even though wages were barely creeping up. An empirical comparison of real compensation per hour with the (real) cost of capital may well shed light on this issue. We investigate the relative behavior of wages and profits in manufacturing in chapter 7, where we turn up a fascinating and potentially important finding: downsizing typically squeezes wages and raises profits.

Another possibility harkens back to the skill-biased technical progress of the second hypothesis, in which the advent of new technology reduces demand for less-skilled and less-educated workers. Most attention has been given recently to the notion that technical change over the last twenty years or so has shifted optimal input proportions away from unskilled labor and toward skilled labor. But suppose capital is both a *complement* to skilled labor (computers require literate and numerate workers) and a *substitute* for unskilled labor (machines replace brawn) (see Griliches 1969, 465–68). In that case, skill-biased technical progress would also promote capital deepening.

Hypothesis 5: Downsizing Is a Consequence of the Breakdown of the Social Contract Between Labor and Capital

A quite different explanation of the genesis of downsizing hypothesizes a sea change in the relationship between labor and capital in America. This story shares common elements with the parts of our third hypothesis that focus on trimming fat. However, it emphasizes the "fat" embodied in high *wages* rather than in redundant labor. The hypothesis comes in two variants.

According to the first variant, firms and their shareholders have become less generous toward or less solicitous of labor. Whereas previously at least the larger corporations entered into a kind of paternalistic "social contract" with their workers—one that involved considerable job security and the sharing of any excess profits—capital has unilaterally broken that contract and demanded more of the spoils for itself. Labor is thus faced with a Hobbesian choice between lower wages and fewer jobs, the latter being used as a threat to achieve the former (see Gordon 1996).

The second, and related, variant of the social-contract hypothesis envisions a change in the nature of corporate shareholding: the historically more patient, relationship-oriented stockholders (such as company insiders) have given way to more impatient, return-oriented stockholders (such as mutual fund managers who must show quarterly results). For example, the percentage of corporate stock held directly by individuals dropped from 85.6 percent in 1960 to 41.1 percent in 1998, while the percentage held by pension and mutual funds soared from 7.5 percent to 42.2 percent (New York Stock Exchange 2000, 34). This second variant can possibly explain the first: more activist shareholders may have demanded that company management focus on "creating shareholder value"—to the detriment of labor and other stakeholders, if necessary.

If, indeed, the social contract has been rewritten in this way, we can think of several possible causes. One is the intensification of competition, whether domestic or foreign, that we have already discussed. A second explanation would attribute the change to the fact that the nature of shareholding has shifted toward large (especially institutional) shareholders who give less weight to stakeholders—such as the firm's workers—and are more focused on the bottom line.

A third possible cause—but one that is likely to make economists uneasy—can simply be called the "discovery of error." Discovering that they are not minimizing costs, firms may be mending their ways. This hypothesis, of course, raises some obvious questions: Why were firms not optimizing in the first place? What makes them realize their errors now? Until those questions are answered, it is hard to know how to test this hypothesis—or how to distinguish it from the idea that downsizing is just the latest management fad. One possible indicator is the prediction that more downsizing will occur among high-cost producers because they have the most to gain by mending their ways. However, as noted earlier, studies by Martin Neil Baily, Eric Bartelsman, and John Haltiwanger (1996a) and others on the effects of downsizing on productivity do not provide much support for the notion that downsizing has typically led to large productivity gains. Nor do our own findings in chapter 7 point in that direction.

Finally, an attitudinal change associated with the country's political shift to the right may have played a role. That shift, in turn, may be ascribable in part to the success of economists' teachings. We economists have been persuasive. The free-market message has gotten through. Economic life is now imitating economic theory as never before.[12] One consequence of this "economics-ization" of America has been the elevation of shareholder value to primacy among a firm's possible goals, to the exclusion of the interests of stakeholders. Thus, for example, labor is increasingly viewed as "just another commodity" whose price and conditions of employment are determined by supply-demand conditions and nothing else. Needless to say, this is a highly speculative hypothesis, not easily amenable to statistical testing.

Regardless of the cause, how would we know whether the social-contract hypothesis is valid? One source of potential evidence begins with several studies published in the late 1980s that documented sizable and persistent interindustry wage differentials (see Dickens and Katz 1987; Krueger and Summers 1987, 1988). These studies found that some industries tend to pay all their workers—and not just the occupational groups in short supply—more than other industries do. Several hypotheses were advanced to explain this phenomenon, but one in particular was and has remained convincing. Suppose managers and owners of large, profitable firms were inclined to share the largesse with other stakeholders—in particular, with their workers. And suppose further that only certain industries had such largesse to distribute, perhaps because only they enjoyed market power. Then employees fortunate enough to work in these industries would enjoy higher wages across the board.

The question is: Have such supernormal wages been squeezed or eliminated? The answer appears to be that the interindustry wage differentials observed in the 1980s persisted into the 1990s, but they appear to have shrunk a bit. For example, Alan Krueger (1998) found from Current Population Survey (CPS) wage data that, after controlling for differences in the educational attainment and experience of their workforces, the interindustry wage distribution became less dispersed over the decade from 1983 to 1993. This evidence is vaguely consistent with the hypothesis that the social contract has been amended in ways that reduce labor's rents.

Another source of evidence is aggregate data on the division of business income among the factors of production. If the owners of capital become more aggressive about pursuing profits—and are successful at it—then factor shares should shift toward profits and away from labor compensation. The available historical data series on factor shares appear to contain some crude evidence in support of this hypothesis: the share of corporate profits in national income rose in the 1990s—from 9.1 percent in 1992 to 10.8 percent in 1999—while the share of employee compensation declined by about the same amount over the same seven-year period, from 73.0 percent to 71.1

percent.[13] But care must be taken in interpreting such numbers because profits are extremely cyclical. Corporate profits as a share of national income dropped all the way back to 9.0 percent in the weaker economy of 2001.

A more reliable industry-level test of the explanation of the shift in factor shares would begin by noting that the shift should be greater in industries in which the forces of competition have increased and the power of labor has declined. One way to test such a hypothesis is to use our industry database to relate capital's (or labor's) share within an industry to, among other things, the unionization rate, the degree of import penetration, and the concentration ratio. This will be done statistically in chapter 7. Returning to explanations of downsizing (rather than to explanations of the decline in labor's share), we may expect to find downsizing more prevalent where unions are weaker (another implication we test in chapters 5 and 6, without finding much support for it).

Incidentally, the hypothesis that downsizing is based on a change in the social contract has a fascinating implication for the level of stock prices. If profitability is raised permanently (a big if), the stock market should enjoy a transition period—perhaps lasting for several years—during which price appreciation is extraordinarily high. That is just what seemed to be happening, of course, as stock prices soared from 1995 to their extraordinary peak in 2000. But permanently higher profitability may not have been the only reason, nor even the main reason. Many observers of the stock market, for example, believed then (and some still believe now) that investors were willing to accept a lower risk premium for holding equity than they had previously demanded.[14] If so, that would enduringly (if not permanently) elevate equilibrium price-earnings ratios. Others insisted, with some foresight, that stocks were (and perhaps still are) seriously overvalued and were bound to fall (see, for example, Shiller 2000). We will refrain here from entering the debate over the proper valuation of common stocks.

Downsizing based on a breakdown of the social contract clearly carries rather doleful implications for the labor market: real wages should fall and job insecurity should rise. But the fall in employment should be transitory; in this scenario, job insecurity is a way to discipline the workforce. Once workers have been properly disciplined, the economy will have adjusted to the new "rules of the game," with rents squeezed out of real wages. Then labor should have become (permanently) cheaper, and the optimal capital-labor ratio should fall.

What about productivity? In the standard neoclassical view, if downsizing is all about the redistribution of rents, its implications for productivity should be nil. It is just that capital should capture more of the rent, and labor less. In fact, as we have noted, there is precious little evidence that downsizing systematically enhances productivity.

There is, however, another view, one reminiscent of the Japanese model of labor-management relations. Under George Akerlof's (1982) gift-exchange model, cooperation between a firm and its workers yields a productivity bonus that pays for these "rents" through a mutually beneficial exchange of gifts: firms offer better compensation packages and working conditions than the Darwinian marketplace dictates, and workers reciprocate by working harder and more efficiently. Theories that emphasize the efficiency gains from well-developed "internal labor markets" have similar implications. If the rents in big companies stem from efficient gift-exchange or internal labor markets, rather than from inefficient slack, then unilateral attempts by capital to expropriate these rents will destroy them and thus will reduce productivity and profitability. This is a place where, once again, studies of the effects of downsizing on productivity, such as those of Baily, Bartelsman, and Haltiwanger (1996b) and the American Management Association surveys, are relevant. And these sources do not suggest that downsizing has been systematically associated with exceptionally rapid gains in productivity.

Hypothesis 6: Downsizing Amounts to the "Blue-Collarization" of White-Collar Labor

Job instability in the United States (and in other countries) has always been high. Millions of workers lose their jobs each month. (Of course, in most months a slightly larger number acquire jobs.) But one new feature of contemporary labor markets may be that more white-collar workers are now experiencing the degree of job instability that has long been the lot of blue-collar workers. On this view, by the way, *perceptions* of the rise in job insecurity may have been far worse in the 1980s and early 1990s than the objective reality because job instability was then hitting the class of people whom journalists knew personally—and hence was being reported more often in the media.[15]

If it is true that white-collar workers are increasingly being treated like blue-collar workers, the cause is far from clear. Perhaps the phenomenon is a manifestation of the effort to root out X-inefficiency, as in our "fat-trimming" third hypothesis: companies discovered that they had too much middle management and took steps to slim down. If so, we must again ask: Why did they not discover this sooner?

An alternative, and perhaps more plausible, answer is that modern communications and computing technology are gradually eliminating the need for several layers of management. If so, this would be yet another form of "skill-biased technical progress"—but now technology would be biased against highly skilled employees rather than in their favor. It is one possible explanation for regression toward the mean.

Yet a third explanation could be a change in attitudes, which would be reminiscent of our fifth hypothesis (breakdown of the social contract between labor and capital). Managers—especially those with long job tenure—used to be important stakeholders whom firms would shelter from adversity, even at the expense of profits. Now that firms are more single-mindedly devoted to maximizing shareholder value, they must be more ruthless about trimming the managerial ranks.

If this theory of downsizing has validity, we would expect to find the increase in job instability concentrated among white-collar workers, not blue-collar workers. Findings from studies of the Displaced Workers Surveys provide clear support for this view. Specifically, in comparing the periods 1981 to 1982 and 1991 to 1992, Jennifer Gardner (1995) found that the incidence of job loss *increased* among white-collar workers but *decreased* among blue-collar workers. (The overall rates of job loss were similar in the two periods.) Similarly, Henry Farber (1997, 77) found substantial increases in the rate of job loss for managers over the periods 1987 to 1989, 1989 to 1991, and 1991 to 1993, and then some decline from 1993 to 1995.

These six hypotheses on downsizing, with which we began our research for this book, were elucidated before we had accumulated any systematic evidence on the subject (though we were not, of course, innocent of the claims and findings of others). Some of the hypotheses are "soft" and almost sociological—like the breakdown in the social contract. Others, like capital-labor substitution, are strictly neoclassical. These disparate hypotheses have partially overlapping, partially differing implications for a number of observable variables. Some of their implications can be tested using existing data, and some cannot. (We perform some of the relevant tests in subsequent chapters.) To give the reader a kind of Baedeker's guide to what is to come, we conclude this chapter by offering a quick summary of our major findings—including some that go beyond the six hypotheses and that we had not anticipated.

What Is to Come: A Preview of Major Findings

Chapter 2, an examination of the popular press accounts of downsizing, contains quite a few surprises, at least for us. We had expected the journalists' reporting to be exaggerated and to have missed many if not most of the subtleties. But in fact, we found them to be surprisingly accurate. For example, journalists unearthed the fact that many reported cases of "downsizing" were actually restructurings *without* net reductions in force. In our statistical analysis of a sample of newspaper articles, we find that roughly 55 percent of announced "downsizings" did not in fact reduce the company's total employment. As a matter of fact, in a substantial portion of the cases in the sample, firms ended up with workforces larger than those they had prior to the downsizing announcement. The newspaper sample also provides our first hint of regression toward the mean in firm size as measured by employment—a hint that is subsequently verified (at least for manufacturing) in chapter 5.

In chapter 3, we look at what basic microeconomic theory can tell us about the determinants of firm size. Our conclusion is that technology *must* drive average firm size in the long run, but that demand can play a large role in the short run. As we shall see, looking at the data through this particular theoretical prism suggests that short-run influences (demand, for example) must dominate what we observe in the available data.

Chapter 4 is an exhaustive statistical analysis of the basic facts about downsizing (or upsizing), based mainly on a previously unexploited data source: the U.S. Commerce Department's Enterprise Statistics. We find not only that firm size did typically shrink in manufacturing industries during the "downsizing period" (1987 to 1992), as the media reports suggested, but that this is actually an old story. The U.S. manufacturing sector has been downsizing, on average, since about 1967 (but not before that). Outside of manufacturing, however, we find little evidence of downsizing. In fact, upsizing is the norm.

Why the sharp difference between manufacturing and nonmanufacturing? In chapter 4, we offer preliminary evidence for an extremely simple model: fast-growing industries (like retailing and most services) tend to upsize, while slow-growing or shrinking industries (like many manufacturing industries) tend to downsize. This is hardly a subtle thought. But analysis in subsequent chapters offers rather strong support for this finding, which, incidentally, is not one of the hypotheses with which our study began.

Chapter 5 focuses on the causes of downsizing in manufacturing, the one sector where downsizing has in fact been prevalent. We find that interindustry shifts—that is, workers moving from industries in which the typical firm is larger to industries in which it is smaller—account for essentially *none* of the observed downsizing in the U.S. manufacturing sector. The entire story plays out within industries, and hence is attributable to declining firm size in many manufacturing industries. We also find some evidence for regression toward the mean, but we find no such evidence outside of manufacturing.

Turning to the original six hypotheses, we find only very limited support for hypotheses 1 and 2 (technologically driven downsizing): more R&D spending does seem to lead to more downsizing, but faster total factor productivity growth does not. However, the data offer substantial statistical support for hypothesis 3—which emphasizes the role of international trade—including an ancillary finding that lower profitability leads to more downsizing. But there is essentially no evidence in favor of hypothesis 4 (substitution of capital for labor). As we have emphasized, hypothesis 5 (breakdown of the social contract) is slippery and very hard to test econometrically. But consistent with one of its seeming implications, we find that the more unionized industries tend to downsize *more*, not less.

Finally, it is worth noting that the results for manufacturing differ only slightly depending on whether we use data on firms or data on establishments. This reassuring finding is repeated in chapter 6's analysis of the (limited amount of) data that are available for non-manufacturing industries.

Chapter 6 repeats and reinforces the finding of chapter 5 that the most important determinant of changes in firm size, at least in the short run, is the change in industrywide employment—which we interpret as an indicator of the strength of product demand. We also find openness, especially import intensity, to exert significant influence on *up*sizing. But none of three other possible influences—total factor productivity, capital intensity, and unionization—seem to matter much.

Since we find that genuine downsizing is largely restricted to manufacturing, it is on that sector that we focus when we turn to an investigation of the *consequences* of downsizing in chapter 7. Our findings are both clear and fascinating. Firms that downsize appear, on average, to increase their *profits* but not their *productivity*. How is that possible?

We may safely assume that the act of downsizing does not raise the prices at which firms can sell their outputs. After all, buyers do not care about the size of the average firm in the industry. Hence, downsizing must on average reduce unit costs of production—presumably unit labor costs. But since we, like others who have studied the question, find that productivity does *not* generally rise when firms downsize, that must mean that wages typically fall (compared to wages at firms that do not downsize). In short, downsizing in U.S. manufacturing appears to have been largely a way to squeeze labor. That finding conforms nicely with hypothesis 5 (breakdown of the social contract), although we certainly cannot demonstrate that a changing social contract is the reason for the wage squeeze. Curiously, however, we also find that downsizers are *not* generally rewarded by the stock market, despite the increase in their profits.[16]

Since much of what is commonly called downsizing actually turns out to be labor-market churning resulting from industrial restructuring, we turn in chapter 8 to turbulence in the labor market and look at it from the point of view of individuals. The greater churning during the downsizing period is apparent in these microdata. We find that labor did indeed shift around more—both by occupation and by industry—in the years from 1981 through 1992 than in the earlier 1969 to 1980 period. Unsurprisingly, younger workers changed occupation and industry more frequently than did older workers. Men also changed more frequently than did women.

Finally, in chapter 9 we present a short and somewhat interpretative summary of our findings.

Chapter 2

Downsizing and the Press: Perception and Reality

ONE OF the purposes of our research was to determine the degree to which the reality of downsizing differs from what people generally believe it to be. To that end, it was patently necessary to investigate not only the hard facts of downsizing but also the popular views. We were not in a position to carry out a survey of these popular beliefs, but we could and did study one of their primary sources. Public perceptions of the downsizing phenomenon probably derive to a significant extent from what people read in newspapers. Newspaper stories on this subject have abounded, and we therefore turned to those accounts to try to infer whether there are marked differences between the perception and the reality of downsizing.

Study of newspaper reports on downsizing offered one other significant benefit. For obvious reasons, the newspaper stories could be expected to focus on the nation's largest and best-known enterprises. And indeed, these large firms play a very significant role in the economy. Yet it is difficult to find out much about them as a group from the generally available government and business statistics, in which large firms are usually lost in the broad categories (such as firms with more than one thousand employees) into which the statistical data are organized. By sampling newspaper reporting on downsizing, we hoped to get a glimpse of this extreme upper tail of the distribution of business firms—the Fortune 500 and the runners-up to this group.[1]

For these purposes, we conducted an electronic search for the word "downsizing" in the archives of two newspapers that were most likely to deal with the subject extensively, the *New York Times* and the *Wall Street Journal*, for the years 1993 through 1997.[2] We also chose these newspapers because of their reputations for accuracy and objectivity, and these years because they seemed to be the ones during which downsizing was most intensely reported. The search turned up approximately 1,700 newspaper articles, ranging from brief descriptions of anticipated employee dismissals from individual firms to wide-ranging, multipart series on the downsizing phenomenon.[3] We read each story carefully, compiled a list of the companies that were reported to be downsizing, and then compared the newspaper reports with information about each firm's actual employment levels. This chapter describes what we found.

A Preliminary Overview of Our Findings

We had several expectations, at least some of which turned out to be baseless. First, we expected that many newspaper stories on downsizing would conclude, incorrectly, that dismissals by firms would contribute to unemployment problems for the economy. We also thought that "human interest" stories would predominate and that they would focus nearly exclusively on the distress of those who had lost their jobs, rather than on those whom the downsizing firms continued to employ. We expected that the newspapers would accept downsizing for what it appeared to be—preponderantly, if not universally, a reduction in the size of a company's labor force—even though the reality was considerably different, as we will see. Finally, we thought that stories on the subject would decline in frequency as the period of unprecedented prosperity continued and unemployment in the economy fell to unexpected levels.

To examine these and other issues related to downsizing, we constructed our "newspaper sample," comprising 133 firms (whittled down from the nearly 300 company names encountered in our two-newspaper search). These were the companies that were reported during the five years from 1993 to 1997 to have undergone downsizing, and for which the data required for our analysis were available.[4] Of course, we make no pretense that this represents anything like a properly drawn random sample. Our newspaper sample is examined here for only two very limited purposes. The first is to describe the type of downsizing information that was most generally and effectively communicated to the public, while also providing some further information on the actual behavior of the types of firms reported by the press as "downsizers." The second purpose is to use the sample to derive some additional hypotheses that are subjected to more legitimate tests in later chapters. For example, it was our newspaper sample that first led us to recognize that a significant proportion of the self-designated downsizers turned out to be "upsizers" in reality. In addition, it was the newspaper sample that first suggested the possibility that the sizes of company labor forces may be moving toward the middle of their earlier range, with the largest firms tending to grow smaller and the smallest firms tending to grow larger. As the reader will find in chapter 4, this actually turned out to be true in the manufacturing sector of the economy.

To investigate the firms in our newspaper sample, we relied mainly on Standard & Poor's Compustat database, which provides the pertinent information about individual firms' employment levels.[5] For comparison, we also looked at data collected by the American Management Association and the job placement firm Challenger, Gray & Christmas, among others.

The journalists reporting for the *New York Times* and the *Wall Street Journal* performed very well and provided little ground for criticism by economists. In those stories that we read, the newspaper coverage generally avoided the fallacy of composition, meaning that they did not conclude from the many announcements of labor-force reductions by individual firms that, taken together, these were likely to increase economywide unemployment. Second, while there were, quite appropriately, many stories about the terrible consequences for those who lost their jobs, there were also interesting reports on those who had met the problems by becoming entrepreneurs and assuming the risks and hardships such ventures entail. In addition, these reporters focused particularly on the morale problems created for those who were not fired and the resulting difficulties for both the persons directly involved and their employers. Third, the journalists smoked out the least obvious side of the downsizing phenomenon: the fact that a number of firms that were ostensibly downsizing turned out to have "upsized," or at least to have replaced those who left with about an equal number of new employees, presumably individuals better suited to the firm's changing needs. It should be noted at once that such upsizing and churning of the labor force was hardly the exception for the companies covered in our newspaper sample; indeed, of our 133 firms, all of which had announced downsizing programs, 55 percent ended up in 1998 with a labor force no smaller than in 1990. Finally, despite protracted prosperity, the evidence did not consistently indicate that there had been a substantial decline in the number of firms making downsizing announcements.

The chapter notes one other surprising phenomenon. The group of firms that were upsizing or churning does not seem to have been selected fortuitously. Indeed, we will see that there was a marked pattern in our newspaper sample, with the largest firms the more frequent downsizers and the smallest firms the more frequent upsizers. In another context this pattern has been referred to as regression to the mean, with the entities in question driven from both extremes toward the center. However, it should be noted that the newspaper sample is heavily biased toward manufacturing, since it is the manufacturing firms that are often among the largest and best known and whose downsizing announcements are most likely to be noticed by the press. And manufacturing in the United States generally did undergo a pattern of regression toward the mean during this period, in terms of firm size. The same is true in our sample, where manufacturing firms taken alone behaved quite similarly to the entire newspaper sample.

Composition of the Newspaper Sample

The full list of firms encountered in our newspaper search is reported in the appendix to this book. As already noted, the sample is composed primarily of manufacturing firms, which account for about 61 percent of the companies. Next come insurance and finance firms at about 16 percent, and retail and miscellaneous services are third at about 7 percent. Table 2.1 presents the data for what may be referred to as the gross sample, consisting of the 292 firms named in downsizing stories in the newspapers during the period studied, including those firms we eventually dropped from the final sample because in-

Table 2.1   Firms Encountered in Newspaper Search of Downsizing
             Articles, 1993 Through 1997

Industry	Number (Percentage of Total)
Insurance and finance	48 (16.4)
Telecommunications	15 (5.1)
Airlines	9 (3.1)
Oil and gas	10 (3.4)
Utilities	5 (1.7)
Manufacturing	179 (61.5)
Metals manufacturing and mining	7 (2.4)
Aerospace	22 (7.5)
Foods, beverages, and tobacco	26 (9.0)
Computers, electronics, electrical, and software	28 (9.6)
Pharmaceuticals	13 (4.5)
Autos, other vehicles, vehicle parts	19 (6.5)
Miscellaneous manufacturing	64 (22.0)
Railroads	5 (1.7)
Retail and miscellaneous services	21 (7.2)
Total	292

Source: Authors' compilation.
Note: Newspapers searched were the New York Times and the Wall Street Journal. Totals may not add up exactly because of rounding.

sufficient Compustat information was available about them. The labor forces in the final sample of 133 firms ranged from under 1,000 to more than 500,000 employees.

Volume of Downsizing and the Business Cycle

Before reporting what our analysis of the newspaper sample showed, we first provide some background on downsizing among all American firms and its trend in the past decade. Our purpose is to determine whether downsizing is simply a reflection of the stage of the business cycle—specifically, whether it occurs predominantly during recession as one manifestation of the growing unemployment or the lag in job creation that characterizes such periods. The available data, particularly those for the 1990s, tell somewhat inconsistent stories. Here it must be recalled that the 1990s began with a period of recession and slow recovery that gave way, by the middle of the decade, to an extremely prosperous era.

One source of data on the total number of firms reporting downsizing in the United States is the annual information gathered by Challenger, Gray & Christmas, a Chicago executive outplacement firm (which finds jobs for laid-off executives, often as a service offered by the firm that is laying them off). Since 1989 the firm has compiled an informal data set of job-cut announcements in daily newspapers, other news media, and state labor office news releases (see figures 2.1 and 2.2).[6] We see that, in this sample, the number of reported cases of downsizing rose in the early 1990s, as would be expected, and then moderated somewhat during the middle of the decade. But downsizing rose again at the end of the decade, even before the onset of the recession of 2001. With the beginning of the new century and its business slowdown, downsizing increased substantially.[7]

There is another data source that is based on newspaper reports. Henry Farber and Kevin Hallock (1999) searched for the words "layoff," "laid off," "downsize," "downsizing," and "plant closing" in ten years (1985 to 1995) of abstracts of *Wall Street Journal* articles in Pro Quest's "Newspaper Abstracts." Figure 2.3, which is their plot of the number of articles they found, shows an explosion of reporting in the early 1990s that tailed off through 1995. They also looked through the *Wall Street Journal Index* for announcements of reductions in force (RIFs) by Fortune 500 firms over a twenty-eight-year period beginning in 1970. These data are presented in figure 2.4, with the number of RIFs plotted on the left axis and the civilian unemployment rate on the right axis; both show a declining trend after the early 1990s.[8] Our own observations are somewhat different. When we revisited our

Figure 2.1   Permanent Job Cuts Announced by U.S. Corporations, 1989 to 2002

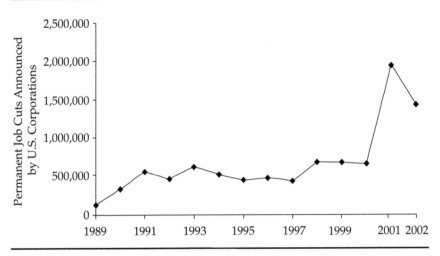

Source: Challenger, Gray, & Christmas, Inc. (various years).

newspaper search, running a quick count of downsizing stories in the *Wall Street Journal* and *New York Times* archives for the period 1990 to 2002, we found that, although stories on downsizing continued to appear with regularity, the frequency dropped dramatically, as indicated in figure 2.5.

Downsizing data are also collected by the American Management Association, a trade organization with more than ten thousand corporate members.[9] The AMA has surveyed its members' human resource managers on downsizing and other staffing issues since 1986. Indeed, the changing titles of these surveys over the years are of interest in themselves, as they mirror the ups and downs of the downsizing phenomenon. In 1989 the survey was called *Downsizing and Outplacement.* The title changed to *Survey on Downsizing* in 1990, and to *Survey on Downsizing and Assistance to Displaced Workers* from 1991 through 1995. By 1996 it had become *Survey on Downsizing, Job Elimination, and Job Creation.* In 1997 downsizing took a back seat (*Survey on Corporate Job Creation, Job Elimination, and Downsizing*), and the term disappeared altogether in 1998, 1999, and 2000 with *Survey on Staffing and Structure* and in the 2001 *Staffing Survey.*

Figure 2.6, based on the AMA's data, indicates that the number of companies reporting some job eliminations continues to be significant, while the number of actual downsizers—firms reporting *net* workforce reductions—declined after the beginning of the 1990s, then

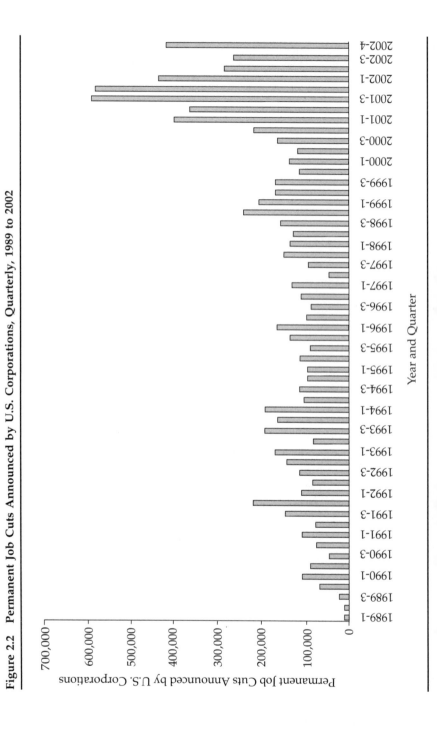

Figure 2.2 Permanent Job Cuts Announced by U.S. Corporations, Quarterly, 1989 to 2002

Figure 2.3   Number of *Wall Street Journal* Articles with Selected Words and Word Combinations Related to Job Loss, 1985 to 1995

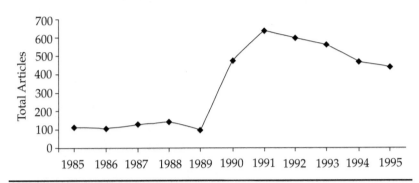

Source: Adapted from Farber and Hallock (1999).
Note: Articles included the following words: "layoff," "laid off," "downsize," "plant closing," or "downsizing." These articles need not relate to any specific firm.

Figure 2.4   Frequency of All Job Loss Announcements, by Year, 1970 to 2000 (With Civilian Unemployment Rate)

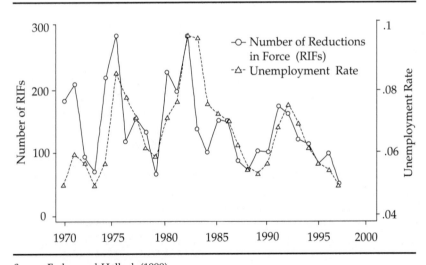

Source: Farber and Hallock (1999).

Figure 2.5   Follow-Up 1990 to 2002 Newspaper Search for *New York Times* and *Wall Street Journal* Articles with the Word "Downsizing"

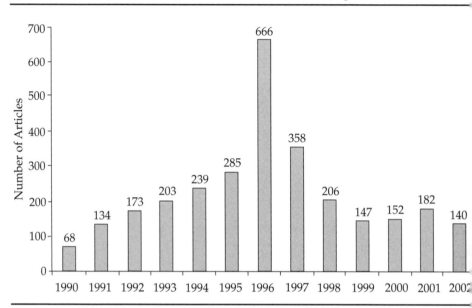

Sources: Lexis-Nexis Academic search engine (*www.lexis-nexis.com*) and Dow Jones Interactive (*http:,nrstg2p.djnr.com*).
Note: Articles in which downsizing is used in other contexts (for example, downsizing of automobil dimensions) are not counted here.

ticked up with the new decade's economic slowdown (with most companies still creating more jobs than they eliminate). The figure also shows that, for the AMA member corporations that reported net workforce reductions, the average percentage of the reduction held fairly steady at around 10 percent throughout the 1990s and into 2000. We multiplied these two percentages (the percentage of AMA firms reporting a net workforce reduction times their average percentage net reduction) to get the average net workforce reduction in the whole sample of member companies responding to the survey—a number that declined from a high of 5 percent in 1990 to 1991 to between 2 and 3 percent in the years after 1994 (see table 2.2).

Finally, the official government statistics from the U.S. Bureau of Labor Statistics' Displaced Worker Surveys are presented in figure 2.7, reproduced from Farber's (2003) study of these data.[10] We see, in particular, that three-year job-loss rates rose much more sharply from the 1987–1989 period to the 1989–1991 period than did the unemployment rate. And between the periods 1991 to 1993 and 1993 to 1995, job-loss rates moved upward again—despite a strong economy

Figure 2.6 American Management Association Surveys of Labor-Force Changes Among Its Members, 1986 to 2001

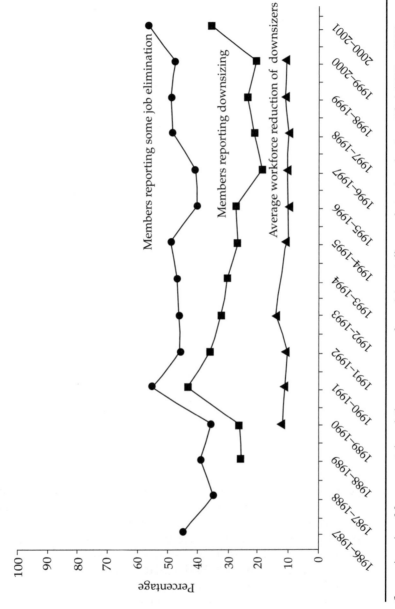

Source: American Management Association, surveys on downsizing, staffing, and structure (various titles) (1986 to 2001).

Table 2.2   American Management Association Surveys on Labor-Force
Changes Among Its Members, 1986 Through 2001

Year[a]	(1) Firms Reporting Some Job Elimination	(2) Firms Reporting Net Workforce Reduction (Downsizing)	(3) Average Percentage Net Workforce Reduction in Firms Reporting Net Workforce Reduction	(4) Average Percentage Net Workforce Reduction in All Respondents (Column 2 × Column 3)
1986–1987	45.0%	—	—	—
1987–1988	35.0	—	—	—
1988–1989	39.0	25.7%	—	—
1989–1990	35.7	26.4	12.0%	3.2%
1990–1991	55.5	43.8	11.4	5.0
1991–1992	46.1	36.0	10.5	3.8
1992–1993	46.6	32.6	13.9	4.5
1993–1994	47.3	30.6	—	—
1994–1995	49.6	27.3	10.2	2.8
1995–1996	40.9	27.9	10.4	2.9
1996–1997	41.1	19.0	10.7	2.0
1997–1998	48.9	21.9	10.5	2.3
1998–1999	49.6	24.1	11.4	2.7
1999–2000	48.2	21.2	11.1	2.4
2000–2001	57.5	36.4	—	—

Source: American Management Association, surveys on downsizing, staffing, and structure (various titles) (1986 to 2001).
[a]The twelve months ending in June (when surveys were conducted).
— Not available.

and robust labor market. Then, beginning in the 1995 to 1997 period, overall job-loss rates declined substantially and by the 1997 to 1999 period were back down to their late-1980s level. In the most recent period, 1999 to 2001, job-loss rates have risen sharply again, reflecting the recession that commenced in 2001. Farber concludes, "While job-loss rates have a strong cyclical component, the rates did not decline as early or as much as might have been expected in the 1990s given the sustained expansion" (Farber 2003, 32).

Thus, there is some disagreement among these sources about the behavior of reported downsizing during the recent period of extraordinary business prosperity. Preliminary evidence does indicate that the severe economic slowdown that began near the onset of the twenty-first century already has been accompanied by substantial downsizing and may well continue to be. This mixed evidence leaves us with the uncertain conclusion that both actual and publicly per-

Figure 2.7   Three-Year Job-Loss Rate (and Unemployment Rate), 1981–1983 to 1999–2001

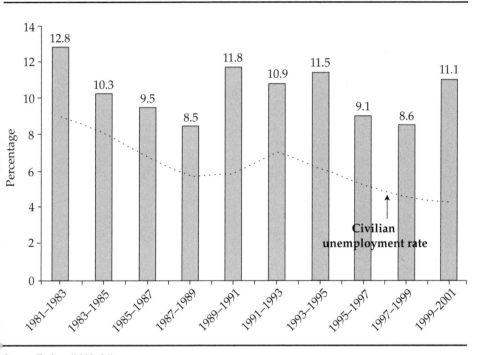

Source: Farber (2003, 36).
Note: Three-year job-loss rates calculated using data from the Displaced Worker Surveys carried out by the U.S. Census Bureau for the Bureau of Labor Statistics.

ceived downsizing seem often to follow the state of the economy and to follow the expectable pattern. This association, however, does not appear to be dependable and without exceptions.[11]

Downsizing or Upsizing?

As we saw in figure 2.6, in the American Management Association's most recent corporate staffing survey, close to 60 percent of the respondents reported some job eliminations over the twelve months ending in June 2001.[12] But did all of these companies make good on their word? Did they indeed end up leaner and meaner? There are, of course, other possibilities. Changes in market conditions can force a firm's actions to be very different from its plans. Alternatively, dismissals may be a way of getting rid of employees no longer deemed to suit the needs of the enterprise or to make way for the hiring of

Figure 2.8   E.I. Du Pont de Nemours Labor-Force Changes, 1979 to 1998

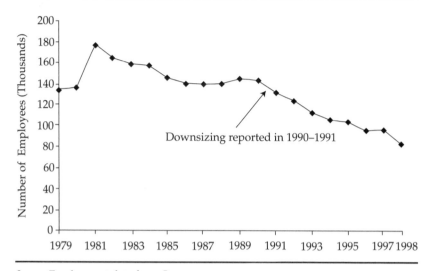

Source: Employment data from Compustat.
Note: SIC: 2820 Manufacturing: plastics materials and synthetics.

new employees better adapted to the requirements of the firm's place in the new economy. And indeed, as we have already seen in figure 2.6, there were significantly fewer AMA companies reporting actual net workforce reductions than those reporting job eliminations.

To examine this issue further, we constructed a time-series graph of employment for each of the 133 firms in our 1993 through 1997 newspaper sample. It became clear that many firms did reduce their labor forces after their downsizing was announced. But a substantial number ended up with a labor force roughly the same size, and even more firms had labor forces *larger* than before the announcement.[13] Figures 2.8 through 2.11 show some typical examples of the patterns encountered. Figure 2.8 indicates that Du Pont's workforce did indeed decline materially after its downsizing announcements in 1990 and 1991. In contrast, figure 2.9 shows that Bristol-Myers Squibb churned its labor force, ending in 1998—after a temporary decline when its 1994 to 1995 downsizing announcement was made—with about as many jobs as it offered in 1989. Figure 2.10 shows a case of marked upsizing: Alcoa's labor force has risen more than 60 percent since its reported 1990 to 1991 downsizing. Finally, figure 2.11 shows Alliant Techsystems to be a mixed case that is not easily classified.

Of the 133 newspaper-sample firms, only 45 percent turned out to be downsizers (employment levels decreased more than 10 percent

Figure 2.9   Bristol-Myers Squibb Labor-Force Changes, 1979 to 1998

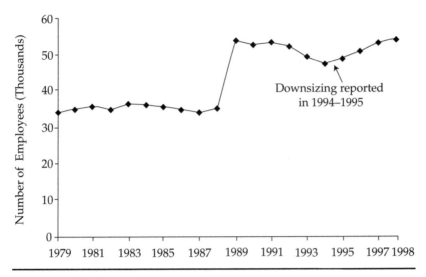

Source: Employment data from Compustat.
Note: SIC: 2834 Manufacturing: pharmaceutical preparations.

Figure 2.10   Alcoa, Inc. Labor-Force Changes, 1979 to 1998

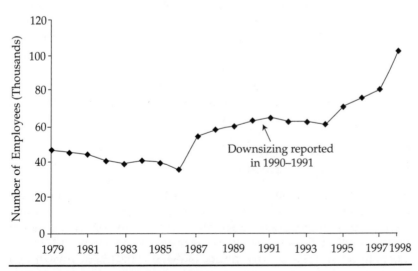

Source: Employment data from Compustat.
Note: SIC: 3350 Manufacturing: nonferrous rolling and drawing.

Figure 2.11   Alliant Techsystems Labor-Force Changes, 1990 to 1998

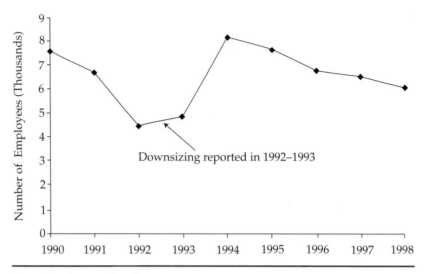

Source: Employment data from Compustat.
Note: SIC: 3480 Manufacturing: ordnance and accessories, n.e.c.

between 1990 and 1998); 11 percent manifested approximate con-
stancy in the number of jobs they provided (less than a 10 percent
change in employment level); and 44 percent were upsizers (employment levels increased more than 10 percent). Dividing these firms by
U.S. Standard Industrial Classification (SIC) code into one-digit industries, the percentage of firms downsizing in each industry category is shown in table 2.3. We see that the share of downsizers was
above 50 percent in only two sectors: transportation/public utilities
and services other than wholesale and retail trade, finance, and real
estate. Clearly, more and more firms are reporting that they are eliminating jobs, but because they have increased hiring, they have not
ended up with a smaller labor force.

Regression Toward the Mean in
Our Newspaper Sample

Next we turn to the question of whether the sizes of the labor forces
in our newspaper sample were regressing toward the mean (for other
relevant data on the subject, see Hart and Oulton 2001). The newspaper sample naturally was biased toward well-known and, hence,
larger firms. To seek out differences of behavior between smaller and
larger firms within this group, we ranked the firms from smallest to
largest according to their employment size in 1990, then looked at

Table 2.3 Downsizers, Upsizers, and "Unchanged Employment" Firms in 133-Firm Downsizing Newspaper Sample, by One-Digit SIC Code, 1990 to 1998

SIC Code	Number of Firms in Industry Sample	Number of Down-sizers in Industry Sample	Down-sizers as Percent-age of Industry Sample	Number of Upsizers in Industry Sample	Upsizers as Percent-age of Industry Sample	Number of Un-changed Firms in Industry Sample	Un-changed Firms as Percent-age of Industry Sample	Number of Churners in Industry Sample	Churners as Percent-age of Industry Sample
1—Mining and construction	2	1	50	1	50	0	0	1	50
2 and 3—Manufacturing	89	41	46	36	40	12	13	48	54
4—Transportation and public utilities	16	9	56	5	31	2	13	7	44
5—Wholesale and retail trade	6	3	50	3	50	0	0	3	50
6—Finance, insurance, and real estate	15	3	20	11	73	1	7	12	80
7, 8, and 9—Services	5	3	60	2	40	0	0	2	40
Total	133	60	45	58	44	15	11	73	55
"Other" (categories 1, 5, 7, 8, 9)	13	7	54	6	46	0	0	6	46

Source: Authors' calculations using Compustat employment data.
Note: Unchanged employment is defined as less than a 10 percent change in employment between 1990 and 1998. Churners are defined as firms whose labor force either remained unchanged or increased since the date of the reported downsizing.

Figure 2.12   Changes in Employment Levels at 133 Newspaper-Sample Companies (Ranked by 1990 Employment Size), 1990 to 1998

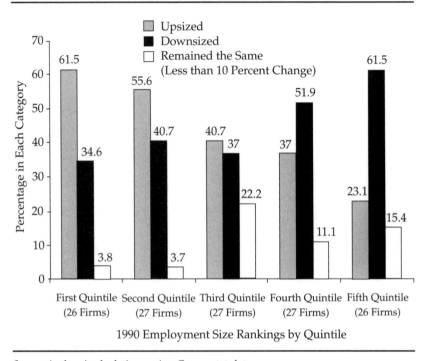

First Quintile   Second Quintile   Third Quintile   Fourth Quintile   Fifth Quintile
(26 Firms)   (27 Firms)   (27 Firms)   (27 Firms)   (26 Firms)

1990 Employment Size Rankings by Quintile

Source: Authors' calculations using Compustat data.

their employment sizes in 1998. The results, shown in figure 2.12, indicate that downsizing occurred more frequently than churning (which meant that a firm either upsized or ended up at about the same size) among the largest firms. In the upper quintile of the 133-firm group, 62 percent reduced their labor force, while 15 percent ended up the same size and 23 percent upsized. Among the smallest firms in the sample, the reverse was true: in the lowest quintile, 62 percent underwent upsizing and 4 percent were not substantially changed; only 35 percent downsized. In the middle quintile, 41 percent upsized, 37 percent downsized, and 22 percent were, roughly, unchanged.

As we noted earlier, our sample was heavily biased toward manufacturing (61 percent of the original 292 firms encountered in the newspaper search and 67 percent of the final 133-firm sample). U.S. manufacturing generally has undergone a pattern of movement toward the mean in terms of firm size in the period since World War II. The same is true in our 133-firm sample: looking at the 89 manufacturing firms alone, we obtain a pattern quite similar to the sample as

**Figure 2.13   Changes in Employment Levels at Eighty-Nine
Newspaper-Sample Manufacturing Companies (Ranked by
1990 Employment Size), 1990 to 1998**

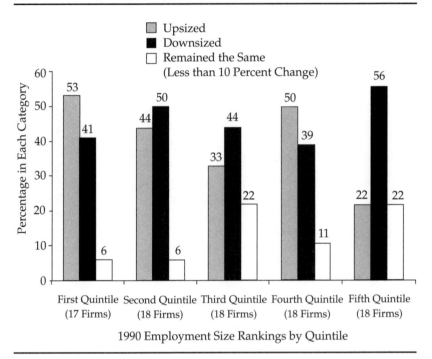

Source: Authors' calculations using Compustat data.

a whole, but a bit *less* pronounced. Figure 2.13 indicates that among
the manufacturing firms in the highest quintile of our sample, downsizers were the most numerous (56 percent), while in the lowest quintile it was the upsizers who were ahead (53 percent). In the middle
quintile, downsizers still led, at 44 percent. However, they were well
behind the combination of upsizers and those that remained the same
(55 percent). This is also a pattern of regression toward the mean: in
the group with the largest firms, far more were reducing their labor
force than were increasing it or holding it steady. The reverse was
true of the smaller firms, while the intermediate group was more
equally divided between those that downsized and those that did not.

In chapter 4, we will see the extent to which the story holds for the
full set of American firms and not just for the newspaper sample. But
before that, in chapter 3 we will offer some hypotheses and theoretical analysis that can help to explain this phenomenon. Since we find
that regression toward the mean did occur in significant segments of
the economy, while in the remainder upsizing generally predomi-

nated over downsizing, two things are certainly clear: the downsizing movement is not quite what it appeared to be, and there is much to be explained that was not immediately obvious.

The Newspaper Accounts of Downsizing

Some excerpts from the newspaper stories will show what sorts of information were provided to the public. These excerpts are also taken from the *New York Times* and the *Wall Street Journal*. Our discussion is divided according to several of the topics on which the journalists focused.

Explanations of Downsizing

The conjectures offered by many articles about the causes of downsizing held few surprises: the prime influences, they indicated, were foreign competition, technological change, and competitive pressures that had forced elimination of corporate "fat." Later in the book we discuss what we have been able to determine from the theory and the data about the causes of downsizing. But here we simply offer some examples of journalists' conclusions on the subject.

> Millions of American workers are embarking on a journey of insecurity, and professional and highly skilled employees are not exempt. All are affected by the unprecedented confluence of four trends. Global competition is transferring both high- and low-paying jobs overseas. Automation, which has boosted productivity but eroded the manufacturing job base for decades, now is penetrating the service sector. Major industries such as banking, construction, aerospace and defense are shrinking, perhaps permanently. And cost-conscious companies are turning to a contingent work force—part-timers, temporaries, contract labor—to avoid soaring fringe benefits and to increase profits. (*Wall Street Journal*, March 10, 1993, A1)

> The economy is growing and American companies are prospering, but announcements of job cuts this year are more numerous than ever. . . . Advances in technology are allowing companies to produce much more with fewer employees. With price increases hard to get, companies increasingly maintain profits by slicing labor costs. And job shedding has become fashionable—the mark of a good manager. (*New York Times*, March 22, 1994, 1)

> GM's push to become competitive comes down to a tough equation: Simpler products and Japanese-style manufacturing equals fewer workers. . . . [For example, last April] assembly of steering columns for GM's Pontiac Grand Am and its sister cars began on a new production line

that was designed with the help of UAW production employees. The line makes it easier for them to install parts. The Grand Am's new steering column also has a simpler design, with about 30% fewer parts than its predecessor had. The result: 14 workers can assemble 1,000 steering columns a day, about 71 columns per worker. That is more than three times the productivity of an older, mass-production line 50 feet away. And even though the new line's machinery cost 30% to 40% less than that on the old line, the quality of the columns it produces is roughly seven times higher. (*Wall Street Journal*, June 23, 1993, A1)

The Unprecedented Vulnerability of White-Collar Employees

Many of the newspaper articles drew attention to the fact that, for the first time, employment uncertainty now faced white-collar workers, who previously had been far less vulnerable to dismissal than blue-collar employees.

Managers, supervisors, professionals and technicians accounted for more than half of the eliminated jobs for the first time. . . . Eastman Kodak Co. may typify the growing prevalence of white-collar job cuts. Last month . . . [it] said it would cut 10,000 jobs . . . expected to come heavily from the ranks of professional workers and middle managers. (*Wall Street Journal*, September 24, 1993, A2)

WAYNE, PA.— . . . It was a weekday in this affluent suburb on Philadelphia's Main Line. Mr. Parker had recently lost his job at IBM. . . . Cloistered inside his six-bedroom colonial, Mr. Parker sat running off resumes on a laser printer. Hearing a loud crash, he rushed outside— and found three male neighbors already there on the curb. ". . . we gawked at each other, as if to say, 'So it's two in the afternoon and you aren't at the office, either!'" (*Wall Street Journal*, September 20, 1993, A1)

Productivity-related job losses are expected to be especially heavy in the service industries. That's terrible news for millions of clerical workers, supervisors, and middle managers in service companies and for workers who perform support functions at manufacturers. (*Wall Street Journal*, March 16, 1993, A1)

These observations are borne out in government and industry statistics. Farber's (2003) examination of evidence from the 1981 to 2001 Displaced Workers Surveys found that there has been a secular increase in the job loss rates of college-educated workers from the early 1990s forward (though the least educated workers continue to have the highest rates of job loss). And American Management Association surveys found that in 1992 (for the first time in the survey's seven-year history), a majority of the jobs eliminated by its member corporations belonged not to hourly workers (who accounted for 45 percent of job cuts) but to supervisors (15 percent), middle managers (19 percent), and professionals or technicians (20 percent). Through the rest of the decade, most years saw salaried workers accounting for about half of reported job eliminations (American Management Association, various years; see also Capelli et al. 1997).

Other Groups Vulnerable to Dismissal

The newspaper journalists repeatedly indicated to readers that, in addition to newly vulnerable white-collar workers, other groups of workers were disproportionately singled out for downsizing, including unskilled workers, older employees, and women (see also, for example, Bartel and Lichtenberg 1987; Farber 1997; Gardner 1995; Pietrykowski 1999; Polsky 1999; Rodriguez and Zavodny 2000).

> Many aging baby boomers have already been casualties of corporate retrenchment. They know that "over the hill" gets younger every year and that job survival depends on out-hustling the hungriest young co-worker. But even the most vital can't escape being part of a demographic bulge in a stripped-down workplace, and most economists envision underemployment for many of them: being cut loose from a corporate berth and taking a new, lesser job at lower pay; or trading a full-time paycheck for the vagaries of self-employment. . . . "The pressures on companies to reduce staff will continue into the next decade," says Lawrence Mishel, executive director at the Economic Policy Institute. . . . "Older white-collar workers will be increasingly vulnerable, and there will be more people in marginalized employment situations." (Wall Street Journal, October 31, 1995, B1)

> The reason Connecticut ranks so high in the number of businesses being opened by women is directly related to downsizing in the insurance and military industries in the state. Many of the people who lost jobs were in middle management positions and many of those people were women. (New York Times, August 1, 1993, 1)

> Staff cuts and management overhauls have given companies opportunities to save money by unloading workers whose personal circumstances, they think, may require special attention. New mothers . . . are especially likely targets. . . . During an economic downturn, employers can mask pregnancy discrimination as layoffs and downsizing which makes it harder to prove the underlying discriminatory motivation. (New York Times, January 2, 1993, 1)

> "The group facing the greatest hardship," says Richard Freeman, a Harvard labor economist, "is middle-aged men without college degrees who had union jobs and were earning more than a competitive wage." . . . Corporations will tend to keep their better workers and discharge

the less skilled or those with poorer work habits, the people most likely to lose their jobs are the ones who will have the hardest time finding reemployment. (*Wall Street Journal*, March 16, 1993, A1)

Government statistics generally agree with these assessments, confirming that older, more-educated, white-collar workers have experienced increases in joblessness, but some researchers emphasize that less-skilled workers are still bearing the brunt of job loss. Lori Kletzer (1998, 122), for instance, examined the 1992 Displaced Workers Survey and concluded that, "despite the changing image of [job] displacement toward white-collar jobs, it is still an experience that affects blue-collar goods-producing workers disproportionately" (see also Hall 1995). Farber (2003) reported that college-educated displaced workers are more likely to find reemployment than high school–educated workers, men are more likely to find reemployment than women, and whites are more likely to find reemployment than nonwhites.

The Hardships of Dismissed Employees

Many stories described the personal tribulations of dismissed workers (on this subject, see also Downs 1995; Gottlieb and Conkling 1995; Hellgren and Sverke 2001; King 1996; Leana and Feldman 1992; and Rudolph 1998). Several pointed to the special problems resulting from the firing of both spouses in a family.[14]

> Diane Smith already was sobbing when a supervisor told her that she would lose her job this month as an administrative analyst for International Business Machines Corp. in East Fishkill, N.Y. Five minutes earlier, her husband, George Smith, had gotten the same bad news from IBM. He is an import coordinator at a facility in nearby Poughkeepsie. Together, the Smiths make about $75,000 a year. IBM "knows we both worked there," says Mrs. Smith, bitterly. "They know they are wiping out a total family's income here." . . . The Smiths' harsh situation is hardly unique. (*Wall Street Journal*, May 7, 1993, B1)

> With two cars in the garage and a swing set in the backyard, Craig Miller and his family fell easily into the suburban rhythms of Johnson County. He was a sheet-metal worker for TWA. His middle-class status was stamped on the pay stub: $15.65 an hour. . . . But the airline was troubled, and it laid off Mr. Miller in the summer of 1992. When he began to search for another job, he quickly learned the market value of a blue-collar worker with a strong back and a good work ethic but few special skills: about $5 an hour. . . . In the months after TWA laid off several hundred workers like Mr. Miller, some marriages collapsed. Alcohol took a toll. And union officials say perhaps a dozen men peered

into the bleakness of the future and committed suicide. (*New York Times,* March 11, 1994, 1)

The struggle to stay in the middle class exacts a high price. Husbands live 1,000 miles from their families because that is where a job is. A highly skilled machinist, confronting the fact that this layoff is permanent, goes without health insurance for his family. (From "The Downsizing of America" [seven-part series], *New York Times,* March 8, 1996, 31)

Like more than 43 million others over the past two decades, Douglas E. Owens was downsized, unemployed, rented out, and basically left to survive by his wits. His resume went out to hundreds of companies and his feet walked miles of carpet in and out of interviews after he was cast out of the cradle-to-grave corporate world that he had inhabited for 23 years. Unlike many others still grappling with the uncertainty of today's labor market, Mr. Owens, 50, has a real job again. More importantly, he knows he probably won't keep it. . . . Nationally, temporary work [has moved] from a $16 billion to a $31 billion industry from 1990 to 1995. (*New York Times,* February 16, 1997, 6)

Morale and Other Problems of Retained Employees

Several of the newspaper accounts called attention to an important phenomenon that is often overlooked: the effect of downsizing on the morale *and performance* of those who are not dismissed. The reports indicated that the effects on such individuals are often strikingly traumatic, affecting sleep, general attitude, and ability to perform on the job. A number of these employees reported marked inability to carry out their work, in contrast to their performance before downsizing took place. It may well be surmised that this sort of effect may help to account for the reported failure of downsizing, in many cases, to increase productivity.

After nearly a decade of frantic cost-cutting, the downside of downsizing is beginning to take its toll: Decimated sales staffs turn in lousy numbers. "Survivor syndrome" takes hold, and overburdened staffers just go through the motions of working. New-product ideas languish. Risk-taking dwindles because the culture of cost-cutting emphasizes the certainties of cutting costs over the uncertainties—and expense—of trying something new. (*Wall Street Journal,* July 5, 1995, A1)

[An American Management Association survey] highlights the stress corporate restructuring brings to the workplace and shows how employer efforts to save money through job cuts may be undermined by rising disability costs. . . . According to the survey . . . about 38% of employers that cut jobs from 1990 to 1995 saw an increase in psychiatric and substance-abuse claims, compared with 29% of firms that didn't cut jobs. A similar gap also appeared for heart and blood-pressure claims, with 19% of job-cutting firms reporting an increase compared with 13% of firms that didn't cut employment. (*Wall Street Journal*, November 21, 1996, A2)

Long after a major downsizing, employees who remain at the company often suffer from . . . "layoff survivor sickness"—a syndrome characterized by anger, depression, fear, guilt, risk aversion, vulnerability, powerlessness and loss of motivation. (*Wall Street Journal*, July 21, 1997, A22)

Though the morale issue is clearly significant, it appears to be declining, possibly because employees are becoming habituated to the new labor market, with its increased uncertainties. By 2000, in a much tighter job market, the American Management Association found that less than one-third of its member companies reported morale problems after job cuts, down from a high of 89 percent of companies that reported declining morale following job eliminations in 1994.

Job Search Assistance by Firms for Dismissed Employees

Whether as an act of altruism, out of concern for the morale of continuing employees, or to avoid unfavorable publicity, some firms undertook active measures to help the workers who were being dismissed in finding new jobs and in other ways, as described in the following newspaper story:

Managers have been trained to help employees cope with their emotions. None were unceremoniously escorted out the door or stripped of their company identification. Instead, they were encouraged to use a new resource center set up in Parsippany to help them find new jobs. And they have full use of the center for as long as it takes to find another job. . . . Workshops by an outside management consultant . . . include everything from resume writing to burnishing one's professional image and negotiating a salary. . . . Hoping to take advantage of the upswing, AT&T is placing advertisements recommending its former employees. (*New York Times*, August 28, 1994, New Jersey section, 1)

The trend in the number of firms offering reemployment help to their displaced workers seems to have changed over the period studied. The AMA *Staffing and Structure Surveys* found that the share of companies offering outplacement assistance grew steadily in the early 1990s, peaking at 84 percent in 1994, and then steadily declined to 64 percent in 1997–98, the same level as that in 1989 (American Management Association 1998, 8).

Dismissed Workers Turn to Entrepreneurship

One favorable consequence of downsizing for the economy seems to have been its stimulation of entrepreneurship. A number of those who lost their jobs were driven to start new firms, often as consultants on the activity in which they had recently been engaged as employees.

> People in their 20s and early 30s, sometimes called Generation X, are particularly drawn to self-employment, partly because they want to avoid the perils of corporate downsizing. (*Wall Street Journal,* March 19, 1997, B2)

> With so many people starting their own businesses, or doing work from home offices, the demand is strong in a state like New Jersey, where corporate downsizing in recent years has turned tens of thousands of people into entrepreneurs. (*New York Times,* October 19, 1997, New Jersey section, 1)

The evidence indicates that the United States has been leading the industrial world by a considerable margin in the number of new firms recently established, and some economists ascribe to this phenomenon much of the superiority of American productivity growth in the 1990s over that in Europe and Japan. However, it is highly plausible that causation here went the other way: that the boom in the United States, which was not matched in Europe or the Far East, stimulated superior firm creation. Yet even in earlier periods the United States was the more entrepreneurial economy, leading most other economies in the relative frequency of formation of new firms.[15]

Failure to Achieve Substantially Increased Productivity

As indicated earlier, the effect of downsizing on productivity was often quite disappointing, something that did not escape the journalists. (for evidence on this subject in addition to that provided later in this book, see, for example, Collins and Harris 1999; Krepps and Candell 1997).

> The continuing "downsizing" phenomenon is prompting new worries that many cuts are ill-considered and even inappropriate. . . . That concern is underscored by a new analysis of manufacturing productivity at 140,000 factories that employed a total of about 12.7 million people during the 1980s. The analysis, done for the Center for Economic Study at the Census Bureau [Baily, Bartelsman, and Haltiwanger (1996a)] found that, while 55% of productivity gains came at factories where the work force fell over the 10 years studied, the other 45% of gains came at

plants with growing employment—and whose total output more than doubled over the period.

"Most major corporate downsizings have failed to produce what was expected," says Peter Scott-Morgan, associate director of Arthur D. Little and author of *The Unwritten Rules of the Game,* a new management study. "A conspiracy of silence has grown around disappointing results of many corporate overhauls," he says, adding, "In future, the degree of failure will become even more extreme, because current cuts are becoming far broader in scope." (*Wall Street Journal,* June 7, 1994, A2)

There have been some broader studies of the productivity consequences of downsizing. The Federal Reserve Bank of Dallas (1996a, 8) examined a small sample of top corporate job cutters in the 1990s and found that, "after adjusting for inflation, the collective output of all 10 firms [between 1990 and 1995] was down 9.7 percent. The companies used 34.4 percent fewer workers, however, so output per worker surged nearly 25 percent, or 5 percent a year."[16] The Baily, Bartelsman, and Haltiwanger study (1996a, 259–78) mentioned above reported mixed productivity effects of downsizing: some firms achieved gains and others did not. The 1994 AMA *Survey on Downsizing and Assistance to Displaced Workers* (American Management Association 1994, 7) found that, after downsizing, the goals of increased profits and greater productivity are often unrealized: "Overall, only 51 percent of companies reporting workforce reductions since January 1989 reported an increase in operating profits after the cuts. . . . Productivity gains [were] . . . even more elusive. Among all firms reporting reductions, only a third said productivity increased; nearly 30 percent said it declined." But by 1999, half of job-eliminating firms reported improved worker productivity, according to the summary of key findings from the AMA *Survey on Staffing and Structure* (American Management Association 1999, 7). In the next section, we will see that a significant proportion of downsizing firms in our newspaper sample did increase their productivity compared to the national average.

Investor Approval of Downsizing

Despite the apparently mixed performance of downsizing as a stimulus to productivity growth within the firms that undertook it, downsizing announcements, according to the newspaper reports, led to increases in security prices (see also Abowd, Milkovich, and Hannon 1990; Abraham 1999; Caves and Krepps 1993; Hallock 1998; Worrell, Davidson, and Sharma 1991).

While selective investors can use many different guideposts to pick companies, one yardstick sounds a very familiar theme: downsizing and similar cost-cutting maneuvers. Of course, many companies have already improved profits by laying off workers or otherwise revamping. But more are on the way. (*New York Times*, February 9, 1997, 4)

> The Eastman Kodak Company drastically raised the company's planned number of job eliminations to 16,600 yesterday, saying the 10,000 figure announced only a month ago was just an estimate and that managers had since found more positions they could cut. . . . The extra job cuts seemed to provide some optimism to skeptical investors. Yesterday, [Kodak] shares rose 2.5 percent despite a broad downturn in the stock market. (*New York Times*, December 19, 1997, D1)

In contrast to this conventional wisdom, Farber and Hallock (1999, 1, 20) found that announcements of so-called reductions in force led to small *negative* effects on share prices rather than increasing them. Nonetheless, they also reported "clear evidence that the distribution of stock market reactions has shifted to the right," that is, had become less negative, between 1970 and 1997. They surmised that a plausible explanation for this change is an increase in the share of RIFs designed to improve efficiency relative to the RIFs in response to decreases in product demand. The Federal Reserve Bank of Dallas (1996a, 4) reported: "More often than not, the wisdom in the hard-nosed decision to downsize wins approval on Wall Street as companies become more profitable and stock prices rise. Indeed, stock price gains among [the ten top corporate downsizers] averaged over 130 percent from 1990 to 1995, as compared with only 86 percent for the S&P 500 companies overall." Other researchers, however, have concluded that the stock market reaction to news of layoffs and downsizing was generally negative (see, for example, Hallock 1998, 711–23), though firms that include restructuring in their downsizing plans tend to show stock price improvements (for a description of the numerous studies in this area, see Capelli 2000). As we will see later in the chapter, stock prices of most of the downsizing firms in our newspaper sample underperformed the Standard & Poor's 500 stock index.

Upsizing, Not Downsizing

Quite a few of the journalists writing news stories on corporate workforce changes were *not* misled by the fact that the firms in question were announcing downsizing programs. Some accounts noted the frequency with which those firms were actually—perhaps with some lag—upsizing or simply replacing current staff with other employees.

> Corporate downsizing is losing some of its sting. Not only are businesses laying off fewer people, they're creating nearly as many jobs as they shed. . . . For example, MCI Communications Corp. has said it will lay off about 3,000 employees, or 7.1 percent of its 42,000-person work force, by the end of 1995. . . . But MCI is still hiring in other areas. . . .

Fewer businesses foresee cutbacks so severe that their work forces actually will shrink despite expanded hiring. (*Wall Street Journal,* October 23, 1995, A2)

Despite continued layoffs and corporate restructuring that resulted in approximately 250,000 job cuts since January, the nation's demand for managers is booming . . . says Ken Goldstein, an economist with the Conference Board. . . . Big layoff announcements and gloomy downsizing stories continue to make the front pages of some major newspapers, "but for every AT&T, there's also an MCI," says Michael Useem, business professor at the Wharton School of the University of Pennsylvania. "And for every Kmart, there's a Wal-Mart." He notes that while AT&T has cut thousands of jobs in recent years, MCI Communications Corp. has grown to 50,000 employees, from only 12,000 a decade ago. "That job growth doesn't usually make the papers," he notes. A similar trend is occurring in the retail industry, where chains such as Wal-Mart Stores Inc. are expanding ranks even as companies such as Kmart Corp. scale back. . . . Although [IBM] has recently shed thousands of jobs in its core computer manufacturing and sales units, its computer services unit, which offers outsourcing and consulting work, has hired 10,000 workers so far this year and intends to hire another 5,000 by year's end. (*Wall Street Journal,* September 26, 1996, A2)

Downsizing is not an illness but a symptom of one of the most profound transformations ever in our economy. . . . All told, we have emerged as the world's strongest, most resilient and most competitive economy. . . . The American economic success story has always entailed shedding unneeded jobs while creating more productive ones. . . . [For example,] even after repeated "downsizing," employment in the telecommunications industry is higher today than ever. (*New York Times,* October 16, 1996, 17)

The United States is not downsizing. It is upsizing. . . . Of course, cutbacks at large companies like AT&T are painful. But the overall job market may actually be more stable than earlier in the post war period. . . . Of course, deep anxiety exists. But the change in the economy is what is causing the problem: Jobs have moved from Fortune 500 companies to small business, the engine of expansion. And women, who have won almost two of every three new jobs in the last 30 years, have displaced men, especially older men. (*New York Times,* March 25, 1996, 15)

Other Developments in Our Newspaper-Sample Firms Relative to the National Average

Finally, we examined our newspaper-sample firms to see what we could infer about the effects of their downsizing decisions (or at least their downsizing *announcements*) on their subsequent performance.

Figure 2.14   Capital Investment: Change in Assets per Employee in 106
Newspaper-Sample Firms, 1990 to 1998, as Compared to the
29 Percent National Average Increase

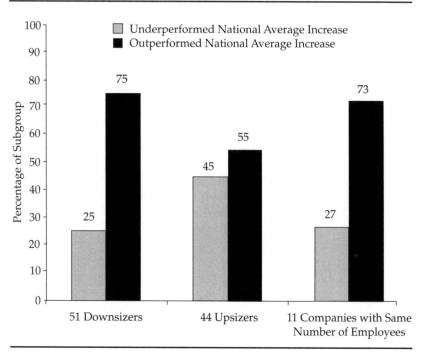

Sources: For firms, Compustat data 4 (current assets) and data 29 (employees); for U.S.
average, total nonresidential private fixed assets per employed civilian worker.
Note: Data not available for banks or property and casualty companies.

This part of the study is only suggestive at best, because it makes no
attempt to compare directly the "before and after" performances of
the individual firms in question. While desirable, such a direct comparison was not feasible because the downsizing announcements
were made at different times, meaning that the market conditions
they faced were not the same. In addition, there was no systematic
correspondence between the date of the announcement, the date at
which workforce reductions actually began, and the patterns by
which reductions were spread over time.

Thus, instead of trying to see how the performance of each firm
before its downsizing announcement differed from that in the period
following it, we measured five economic performance indicators—
capital investment, productivity growth, profitability growth, stock
price, and output—for the entire sample of firms between 1990 (selected as a pre-downsizing date) and 1998 (selected as a post-down-
sizing date). (Recall that our newspaper search encompassed the

Figure 2.15   Productivity Growth at 133 Newspaper-Sample Firms, 1990 to 1998, as Compared to the 16 Percent National Average Increase

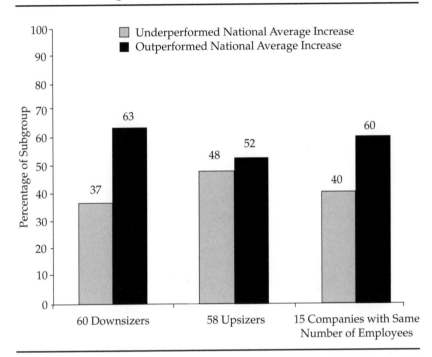

Sources: For firms, Compustat data 12 (net sales) and data 29 (employees); for U.S. average, GDP per employed person.

years 1993 through 1997.) We then compared the performance of the firms in the newspaper sample with corresponding figures for the U.S. economy as a whole, as reported by official data sources such as the U.S. Department of Labor's Bureau of Labor Statistics, the U.S. Department of Commerce's Bureau of Economic Analysis, the U.S. Bureau of the Census's *Statistical Abstract of the United States,* and the Council of Economic Advisers' *Economic Report of the President.* To obtain some suggestive observations about the effects of actual downsizing as distinguished from mere announcements of such programs, we divided the firms in the newspaper sample into downsizers, upsizers, and those whose labor-force size changed very little. (Remember, all the firms in the sample claimed to be downsizers.) The results of this comparison are reported in figures 2.14 through 2.18.

One might have guessed that firms that actually downsized were led to do so by significantly poorer performance in terms of such attributes as productivity growth than firms that upsized. Yet generally, with one significant exception, the results show surprisingly little

Figure 2.16   Profitability Growth of 127 Newspaper-Sample Firms, 1990 to 1998, as Compared to the 67 Percent National Average Increase in Corporate Profits

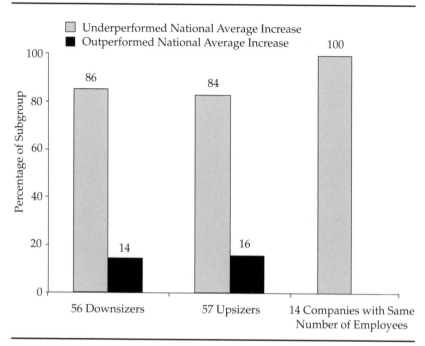

Sources: Firm profits measured by ratio of income (Compustat data 13: operating income before depreciation) to sales (Compustat data 12: net sales) and compared to U.S. corporate profits with inventory valuation and without capital consumption adjustment.

qualitative difference in performance among these three groups. That is, the behavior and accomplishments of firms that ended up with enlarged labor forces were not substantially different from those that actually reduced the number of their employees. Figure 2.14 shows that the majority of firms in each of the three samples—75 percent of downsizing firms, 73 percent of "unchanged-employment" firms, and 55 percent of upsizing firms—outperformed the national average increase in capital investment, which was 29 percent over the eight-year period. This can be interpreted to mean that workers in these firms ended up with an increase in quantity or quality of plant and equipment greater than the national average. Such a change can represent an attempt to counteract, at least in part, any impediment to output growth resulting from workforce reductions. In addition, this change ought to have led to a relative productivity growth advantage for

Figure 2.17   Stock Price Performance of 127 Newspaper-Sample Firms, 1990 to 1998, as Compared to the 224 Percent Increase in Standard & Poor's 500 Stock Index

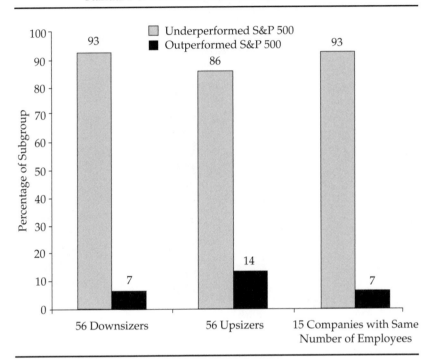

Sources: For firms, Compustat data 24 (stock price at close); for Standard and Poor's Composite Index of 500 Stocks, see U.S. Bureau of the Census (2000).

these firms, since better equipment should enhance the productivity of the labor force. Figure 2.15 is consistent with this observation, showing that at least 60 percent of both downsizing and unchanged-employment firms outperformed the economy's 16 percent increase in productivity between 1990 and 1998, while 52 percent of upsizing firms did so.

Nevertheless, the relative profit record of the firms in the newspaper sample hardly matched the growth in comparative productivity. As we see in figure 2.16, in each subgroup more than 80 percent of the firms underperformed the 67 percent national average increase in profitability. And predictably, the stock market reacted correspondingly: the stock prices of more than 93 percent of downsizers, 86 percent of upsizers, and 93 percent of the unchanged-employment group underperformed the 224 percent increase in Standard and Poor's 500 stock index between 1990 and 1998 (see figure 2.17). Thus, like Farber

Figure 2.18   Output Growth for 133 Newspaper-Sample Firms, 1990 to 1998, as Compared to the 31 Percent Increase in U.S. Nonfarm Business-Sector GDP

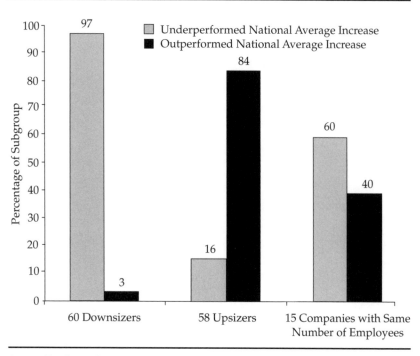

Sources: For firms, Compustat data 12 (net sales); for U.S. nonfarm business sector GDP, see U.S. Bureau of the Census (2000).

and Hallock (1999), but unlike the conventional wisdom, we conclude that downsizing announcements did not generally raise stock prices. Of course, it is possible that the stock prices of the firms in the sample would have fallen even further if they had not announced downsizing programs. And the fact that their stock prices lagged cannot be taken to indicate that their initial downsizing programs had little or no effect.

So far, these figures for our newspaper-sample companies show virtually no qualitative differences between the record of the downsizers and that of the upsizers, though upsizers did worse than downsizers in terms of capital investment and productivity growth, and slightly better in terms of profits and stock prices. But matters are very different when we come to output growth. Figure 2.18 shows that virtually all of the downsizers (97 percent) underperformed the

31 percent national average increase in output, while the upsizers did virtually the opposite: 84 percent of upsizing firms outdid the national average increase.

These changes, of course, are hardly surprising, since curtailment of the labor force can be expected to impede growth in production, and increases in employment per firm should enhance it. However, the magnitude of the difference is very large. It also suggests that the direction of causation may have been from sales volume to employment rather than the reverse: firms with growing markets may have been induced to upsize in order to meet rising demand. It suggests also that the observed changes in the size of the firms' labor forces were dictated more by short-run market conditions than by longer-term technological influences. The latter would have led upsizing firms to "churn" their employees, replacing those less easily adaptable to evolving technological demands with other workers better suited to the new technology.

Conclusions About the Journalists' Insights

Since this chapter's evidence was unavoidably somewhat haphazard and it consequently permitted nothing like a rigorous analysis, we can offer only our own impressions and evaluation of the performance of the journalists who wrote about downsizing. Though we found some errors in the newspaper stories—for example, the somewhat premature announcement of the end of downsizing—journalists generally went beyond reporting the superficial and obvious. They discovered and reported much of what was *really* going on. They were particularly observant in their recognition of the upsizing and churning of the labor force that went on side by side with downsizing. They also recognized that even firms that had announced sensational job reductions were apt, before long, to join the ranks of the upsizers, and occasionally they observed that true downsizing was to be found preponderantly among the larger firms.

These journalists also provided important information that went beyond anything that could be gleaned from the numerical data alone. Occasionally they suggested that some employers were callous and quick to fire loyal workers with little regard for the resulting loss in human capital. But they also reported the special efforts undertaken by some of the downsizing firms to help displaced workers get new jobs and assist them in other ways. The human interest stories about the hardships of those who had lost their jobs were no less important for being predictable. But in reporting on the near-paralysis that beset some of the employees who were not among the dismissed, journal-

ists showed their readers a face of downsizing that is patently significant, but not generally recognized. Thus, the newspapers can be cred-
ited with the accuracy of their accounts and the insights they provided.

In the chapters that follow, careful consideration of the pertinent
economic theory and more systematic analysis of the available data
will offer us more representative information about actual labor-force
changes, their sources, and their implications for the general welfare.
We therefore postpone our conclusions on the underlying economic
issues for later discussion.

Chapter 3

Theoretical Underpinnings
of Downsizing

T AKEN LITERALLY, downsizing means simply that a firm's labor
force is growing smaller, and as we have seen, there are many
reasons why this can happen.[1] In this chapter, we suggest that
two phenomena in particular can be expected to lead to recurring
changes in the size of a firm's workforce. Moreover, they are the obvious two causes of such change: the state of market demand and
technical progress.

Two Fundamental Influences on Downsizing

It does not require specialized training in economics to guess that lack
of demand for a company's products will lead it to cut back on jobs.
And recognition of a connection between innovation and the number
of jobs is hardly new. The Luddites' destruction of machines in the
nineteenth century in an effort to preserve jobs constitutes only one
example. As we will see, empirical data and systematic analysis support at least part of these suppositions. But the way in which these
two influences work turns out to be quite different and more subtle
than what seems commonly to be supposed.

In emphasizing the primacy of the influence of market demand
and technological change, we do not claim that nothing else affects
downsizing. Indeed, the six hypotheses outlined in chapter 1 should
make it clear that there may be much more to the matter. Downsizing
can even be induced by developments that must be interpreted as
historical accidents, or by nonrecurrent and transitory causes. What is
special about the two influences we focus on here—and ultimately
throughout the book—is that they can be expected not only to persist
but also to elicit job-cutting behavior periodically, whether in the typi-

cal business firm in a particular sector of the economy or in the economy as a whole.

Downsizing in the Short Run: The Role of Product Demand

Market demand and technological change influence a firm's downsizing behavior quite differently. Market demand can be expected to make its influence felt quite quickly, but its effects can also be expected to be rather transitory, lasting a few months or, at most, a few years. In contrast, downsizing elicited by technical change does not normally occur overnight, but once a firm has downsized, the change can typically be expected to endure for years or even decades. Thus, we suggest that the state of demand is the primary short-run determinant of downsizing activity, while the state of technology is the fundamental long-run influence.

The beginning of the tale is a downturn of demand, such as occurs when the economy is hit by recession or an industry's major product falls out of fashion. What happens in such cases is quite clear. The business firms in that industry find themselves short of funds and are forced to cut back wherever they can—on advertising expenditures, on consulting fees, on construction costs, and, of course, on their wage payments. Particularly where enforceable wage agreements are in place, this last sort of saving must take the form of job cuts. In chapter 4, we will see that the statistical evidence supports this account of how downsizing typically occurs in the short run. Indeed, so far as the statistical data are concerned, there seems to be no influence as important as that of declining product demand. We argue, however, that if what has so far been described is not accompanied by significant technical change in the industry, the downsizing cannot be expected to last, *even if there has been no recovery in demand conditions.* That is the surprising part of the sequence of events involved in downsizing, and one that is not generally recognized.

The Fundamental Long-Run Influence of Competition, Technology, and Cost

The reason lack of demand cannot by itself hold down the size of a firm's labor force is that if the firm was of efficient size before workers were laid off, its reduced size is apt to be *inefficient.* And one of the prime attributes of competition is that it does not tolerate inefficiency. If firm A produces widgets at a cost of twenty-five dollars per widget while rival firm B can do it for fifteen dollars, then firm A had better shape up or it will find itself faced with firm B prices that it cannot match. Firm A can expect to face declining sales and market share, and ultimately it will be driven out of the market altogether.

Although the modern economy does have some pockets of monopoly and many places where competition is weak, market pressures nevertheless generally retain considerable power and influence. Inefficiency can even serve as a potent threat to any monopoly power that a firm may enjoy, because inefficiency may lure new and more efficient rivals into the market, thus effectively undermining the monopoly power of the incumbent enterprise. Thus, while effective competition is hardly universal in our economy, it is neither so weak nor so rare as to tolerate substantial inefficiency for very long.

If downsizing brings the size of a firm's labor force below the level required for efficiency, competitive pressures will eventually force the firm to reverse its hiring stance. Those pressures will mandate a larger labor force, even if demand for the industry's product has not been restored. But how can the firm afford to hire without the demand increase to back up the job expansion? The answer is that there will be an increase of demand for the product *of the firm* even if the demand for the entire industry—for all of its firms together—remains low. Some of the firms in the industry simply will be unable to cover their wage bills, and though they may resist demise for a while, hoping that business conditions will improve, when that does not happen they will be driven out of business, leaving a reduced number of firms to share the limited industry sales of its product. Even though there has been no expansion in industry sales, each of the surviving firms will thus be able to sell enough of this limited volume to justify employment of the number of workers required for efficiency within the firm. The industry will end up with fewer firms and fewer workers in total, but each surviving firm will return to the labor-force size required for minimum product cost.

An example will make the story clear. Consider an industry with twenty firms, each of which has an assembly line that requires one hundred workers to operate efficiently. Suppose sales volume falls in half, and so each firm tries to cut its workforce correspondingly. With each assembly line understaffed, breakdowns become more frequent, a growing percentage of products are rejected because they do not pass inspection, and other sources of inefficiency arise. A firm that holds out and refuses to cut its labor force, or one that rehires to full strength, can produce at lower cost than its downsizing rivals and will drive some of them out of business. Other surviving firms will be forced to follow a pattern of rehiring, which will drive still more rivals from the market. This process will not stop until the number of firms in the industry has fallen from the original twenty down to ten survivors, each with the one hundred workers required for efficient operation.

The bottom line is that falling industry demand does indeed drive

Figure 3.1   Average Number of Employees per Firm, by Industry, 1992

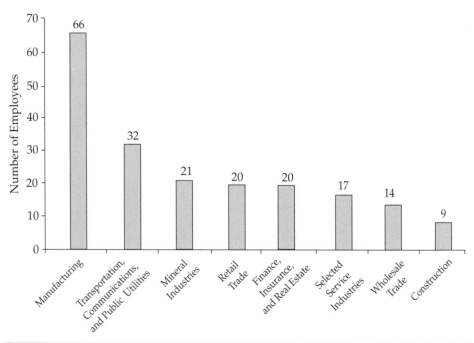

Source: Authors' calculations using data from U.S. Bureau of the Census, Enterprise Statistics (1992).

firms to downsize. But if the power of competition is sufficient, that state of affairs cannot endure. In the long run, declining demand causes the firms in the industry to become *fewer*. It does not enable them to continue to be *smaller*.

Straightforward (if unsystematic) observation generally supports this story. Firm size does differ markedly by industry, and the difference is long-lasting and seems to correspond well to technological requirements. Farms are consistently smaller than automobile manufacturers, trucking firms generally have fewer employees than railroads, and so on. Figure 3.1 provides a fuller description of differences in the number of employees per firm by economic sector. These differences persist through periods of prosperity and recession. Technological requirements seem to be the only plausible explanation.[2]

How Technical Change Can Lead to Downsizing

So far we have discussed how technology can prevent downsizing from enduring, but we have not offered any support for our earlier assertion that it can also lead to downsizing in the long run. The reason is simple. When technology changes, sometimes bigger becomes better, but sometimes the reverse is true: smaller can become more beautiful. The transportation industry offers a striking example. In the nineteenth century, when railroads replaced animal-drawn vehicles as well as much of water transportation, the average firm size in the industry increased dramatically, perhaps even enough to increase the average firm size in the economy as a whole. An eighteenth-century proprietorship in the transport business could operate with a horse and wagon and one or two employees, but no railroad could be run with so small a staff. This upsizing was imposed by the change in technology.

But technological change can also do the reverse, and transportation once more offers a striking example. After the Second World War and completion of the interstate highway system in the United States, truck transportation captured a considerable portion of the business formerly enjoyed by the railroads, and the average labor-force size of freight transportation firms dropped precipitately. This sharp downsizing, once again, was the result of technical change: the emergence of efficient motor vehicles and the construction of the highways that the vehicles need for effective operation.

The railroad example shows that the connection between downsizing and technological change is a real-life phenomenon, not just a theoretical notion. The influence of widespread technological changes also seems more plausible than industry demand conditions or mere coincidence in explaining certain developments that span many industries. In a more recent example, the nearly simultaneous fall from preeminence of many business giants in different industries—General Motors, IBM, AT&T, and U.S. Steel, for example—seems to fit such an explanation. Of course, all of these firms continue to be giants, but their relative position is no longer what it was.

The Difficulty of Statistically Testing the Role of Technological Change

In chapter 4, we examine the relevant statistics and show that they offer strong support for the influence of market demand on downsizing. But paradoxically, technological change, which we claim, on theoretical grounds, is likely to be the most powerful influence on firm size in the long run, by its very nature seriously impedes the *statistical* testing of that hypothesis.

There are two fundamental problems with statistical testing of technical change. We can confidently conclude that technical change modifies the size of the labor force of a typical firm, but as we have seen, the change can go either way. Sometimes a firm's labor force will expand, sometimes it will contract, and sometimes it will remain the same. The fact that labor-force size can change in either direction—or not at all—poses a serious obstacle to statistical testing. In contrast, a one-way assertion is simple to test. To test the assertion, "Increased rainfall expands umbrella sales," for instance, one simply collects data on umbrella sales volume and amount of rain—say, by month over a ten-year period—and calculates whether sales always grow larger every time rainfall is more abundant. But what can one do statistically with the statement, "Technological change modifies firm size over the long run *in one direction or the other, or possibly not at all*"?

A second and equally daunting problem stems from the fact that no one knows how to measure the speed or quantity of technical change. By definition, each such change results in a product different from any that preceded it. Any aggregate measure therefore entails an "apples-oranges" comparison par excellence. We have been unable to find any good measures of the quantity and speed of technical change because by its very nature it fights measurement and even a good definition. But if we cannot measure it, how can we hope to study its effects statistically? We are left with no choice but to rely primarily on theoretical analysis of the sort that follows for the test of our conclusion.

Technological Change and Labor-Force Churning That Looks Like Downsizing

The purpose of this chapter is to investigate not only reductions in the labor forces of individual firms but also *churnings* of the labor force—that is, reduction in the number of jobs offered to one group of workers and their immediate or subsequent replacement by another group. Churning is clearly very different from true downsizing, but it can easily be mistaken for downsizing, particularly when the time lag in replacement is substantial. We should not reject in advance the possibility that job churning is really what is going on when downsizing in an economy seems to be substantial and at times even pervasive. Such churning, we argue, can also plausibly be ascribed to the nature and speed of technical change. New technology may sometimes reduce a firm's need for unskilled workers, and it can simultaneously require workers with technological training and advanced education who can cope with the demands of more sophisticated equipment. This need for better skills plainly can lead to churning—unskilled personnel are replaced by skilled personnel—with no net reduction of jobs in the firm. But the loss of jobs by some of the affected workers may attract the most attention and give the appearance of downsizing.

The churning effect of technological change can also take more subtle forms. For example, if the new equipment in which the technical change is embodied has reached a degree of sophistication that makes it quite user-friendly, the firm may need *fewer* workers with intermediate levels of skill but more of both low-skilled personnel (to operate the user-friendly equipment) and highly skilled personnel (to service, inspect, and improve the equipment). The basic story is the same: one type of worker is replaced by another type, and the overall number of employees in the firm stays the same.

In sum, we see that technological change can lead to either downsizing or churning.

Models of Determination of Firm Size

Since a downsizing simply amounts to adoption of a smaller firm size, an explanation must analyze what determines the size of the firm. We therefore turn to a basic model of the determination of the size of the firm in the long run in a competitive market.

Competition and Technological Imperatives: The Cost-Based Model of Firm Size

Our basic conclusion, as already noted, is that in an industry subject to strong competitive forces, a firm's labor-force size is driven primarily by the state of technology. In an industry characterized by substantial competition, single-product firms, and a U-shaped average cost curve (with its lowest point at the least-cost level of output for the firm), every firm's output must be close to that lowest point of the curve. Moreover, a firm's input mix is also dictated mechanistically by the cost-minimization requirement. Thus, any pervasive downsizing that is not relatively transitory must be ascribed either to the weakness of competitive forces in the industry or to the changes in technology that have reduced the cost-minimizing firm size.

These conclusions raise a number of questions that this chapter addresses. First, the argument would seem to imply that all firms in a competitive industry tend to be very similar in size. Yet we know that in the most competitive of industries—for example, farming and clothing manufacturing—the sizes of the largest firms are a substantial multiple of the sizes of the smallest. How do we reconcile this with the hypothesis that firm size is determined by the state of technology?

Second, if technology is the primary determinant of firm size, measured in terms of a firm's level of employment, we should expect downsizing to be the result of competitive forces forcing industries to adapt to some significant technical developments. Yet some of the industries most substantially affected by technological change are oligopolistic: there are only a few firms in the industry, and many of them are suspected to possess market power (the ability to maintain prices well above competitive levels). How does this scenario comport with an analysis in which competition plays a key role?

Third, the competition that is surely pertinent is obviously not perfect competition, for the reasons just mentioned. More fundamentally, the very assumption of perfect competition renders the concept inapplicable to the determination of firm size, since such an assumption requires that all firms be minuscule to begin with. Therefore, the question is: What form of competition, if not perfect competition, is pertinent to the analysis of downsizing?

And finally, the key role claimed for competition needs a bit of explanation. Even a theoretically pure monopoly has a substantial efficiency incentive. Indeed, given its output, maximization of the profits of a pure monopoly requires that the cost it incurs in supplying that output be kept to a minimum. Why, then, can competition be claimed to be the key to the efficiency analysis of downsizing?

The consequence for firm size of the proposition that effective competition precludes inefficiency is that, given the vector of industry output quantities selected by the market, determination of the sizes of the outputs and the input quantities of the individual firms becomes, in principle, a straightforward and mechanical minimization computation. Of course, in practice that is not nearly as simple as it sounds. Few firms in reality know their cost functions in anything like the requisite detail or with the necessary accuracy of approximation. And if the relationships are sufficiently complex, the calculation of the minimizing values of the variables can be far from straightforward. Still, as we will see, the matter is often considerably less complicated than these remarks suggest, and some clear general observations are possible. Moreover, we will find that while demand conditions clearly play a crucial part in selection of the industry's output vector, in long-run equilibrium their influence on the size of a firm turns out to be, at least in theory, far more modest than might have been suspected.

All this is shown quite clearly, if somewhat misleadingly, by the most elementary model of the output of the firm.[3] This model assumes that the industry produces a single homogeneous product; that the firms have average and marginal cost curves that are well defined and U-shaped; and that rent payments to more efficient inputs make the average costs inclusive of rents identical for all of the firms. It is also assumed that there is a well-defined demand curve of normal shape for the industry.

Let y_m represent the cost-minimizing output of the firm—an output level that is identical for all of the industry's firms, given the assumption that they all have identical cost curves. At the equilibrium price, p, let the quantity of output demanded from the industry be $Y(p)$. First, we have the following result:

Proposition 1   If $Y(p)/y_m = n$ is an integer, then the efficiency property of long-run equilibrium requires the industry's output to be produced by n firms, each producing AC-minimizing output y_m. If there is a shift in the industry demand curve—say, one that moves the demand curve to the right, but the increased n remains an integer—then the number of firms, n, producing the industry output will increase, but the size of each firm will remain absolutely unchanged.

Proof of this result is trivial, and its outlines need only be indicated. Assume that, contrary to the proposition, firm j produces quantity y_j, which is not equal to y_m. Then there must be at least one other firm that is also not producing y_m, since otherwise total output could not add up to the quantity demanded, which is by assumption an integer multiple of y_m. The simplest case is that in which one firm is producing less than the quantity that minimizes average cost and another firm is producing more. Then the total cost of the industry's market-clearing output could obviously be reduced if the first firm were to increase its output and the second were to reduce it by the same amount. Hence, the assumed outputs of these two firms must constitute an inefficiency and are therefore incompatible with long-run equilibrium. A similar argument can be applied to any other pattern of deviations from the cost-minimizing output level by any firms in the industry.

Where $Y(p)/y_m = n$—the ratio of industry quantity demanded at price p to the average cost-minimizing output—is not an integer, then only a minor modification of our previous result is required. We have:

Proposition 2   Where n is not an integer, the industry output in an efficient equilibrium will be produced by a number of firms no less than $n - 1$ and no greater than $n + 1$.

The proof by contradiction is also straightforward, and once again, it will only be sketched. Let us focus on the upper bound upon the number of firms. There is obviously an integer, n^*, with $n < n^* < n + 1$. Consider a possible equilibrium with industry output Y in which the number of firms is $n^{**} > n + 1$. Then the average output of the firm at price p will be $Y/n^{**} < Y/n^* < Y/n$. Since the average cost curves are assumed to be U-shaped, we must have $AC(Y/n^{**}) > AC(Y/n^*) > AC(Y/n) = ACmin$. Thus, the number of firms n^{**} cannot be compatible with cost minimization.

The implication of proposition 2 is that the *average* output of the firms will be close to y_m. Moreover, we see next that competitive market forces will push the outputs of *all* of the firms to close proximity to the output that minimizes average cost. Indeed, we have:

Proposition 3   If the marginal cost curves of all the firms are (also) identical and U-shaped (that is, the second derivative of total cost is positive everywhere in the relevant range), then where industry output is not an integer multiple of y_m, efficiency requires the output of every firm to deviate equally from its AC-minimizing level.

Proof   Let industry output be $(n+v)y_m$, with n an integer and $0 < v < 1$. By proposition 2, the number of firms must be either n or n + 1. If there are n firms in the industry, and each firm produces $y_m + (v/n)y_m$, this clearly yields the industry output. But suppose firm j produces more than this amount. Then, given industry output, there must be another firm, i, which produces less than this quantity. In that case, rising marginal cost means that the marginal cost of j must be greater than that of i, and this clearly is incompatible with cost minimization. A similar argument applies in the case where the number of firms is n + 1.

Corollary   Efficiency requires the deviation of the output of the firm from the AC-minimizing output to be a decreasing function of the number of firms in the industry.

Proof   The preceding discussion indicates that the deviation is $(v/n)y_m$ (or it is equal in absolute value to $y_m[1 - v]/[n + 1]$). Either of these is obviously a decreasing function of n.

Propositions 1 through 3 indicate for this simple model how little effect demand *may* have on the size of a firm dictated by the efficiency requirement of competition, and the corollary places an explicit bound on this influence. Shifts in demand largely affect the number of firms in a single-product industry with U-shaped average cost curves of its firms, but demand does not affect their size, except to the extent that shifts lead to an industry output that deviates from an integer multiple of y_m. Competition forces firms to remain near their cost-minimizing output level. In particular, where the number of firms in the industry is large, the effect of demand on firm size must be negligible—at most, it must yield a deviation close to $(1/n)y_m$ in the case where v in the proof of the corollary approaches its maximum value, unity.

We will see that only in the simple model with which we have dealt so far is demand assigned such a negligible role in the determination of firm size. Nevertheless, considerable validity remains for the conclusion most directly pertinent to our analysis: in competitive industries, if we observe any substantial and enduring changes in the size of the outputs of their firms, or in the magnitude of their labor forces, we should expect changes in technology to play a critical role in the change.

Efficiency and Heterogeneity in Firm Sizes

Propositions 1 and 3 are not quite realistic as they stand. They imply that efficiency requires all firms in an industry to be equal in size, but casual observation confirms that in reality firm sizes *within* an industry do vary, sometimes considerably. The explanation is that the equal-size feature of our results is simply a consequence of the simplifying assumptions adopted so far. The argument has used three premises: that all firms in the industry have identical average-cost curves; that these curves are U-shaped; and that the firms in question supply only a single product. Abandonment of any one of these assumptions permits considerable heterogeneity in firm size, without undermining our main conclusion that technology determines firm size uniquely under competitive conditions. Let us consider these premises in turn.

Interfirm Differences in Cost Curves   The premise that all the firms in an industry have identical average cost curves was justified by the argument that differences in (nonrent) costs from one firm to another are ascribable to differences in the quality and performance of their inputs. But according to the standard argument, under competition the gains from superior efficiencies of this sort will be captured in the prices of the responsible inputs in the form of efficiency rents. So far as the firm is concerned, such a rent payment is no different from any other cost, and so, once rent is included, the interfirm cost differences will be eliminated.

But this argument is not quite right as it stands. Even if all efficiency rents go to the inputs responsible for a firm's superior performance, all firms in an industry will have the same minimum average cost. But that minimum for firm v can easily occur at an output different from that for firm w that supplies the same product. For example, firm v may have a labor force particularly skilled in dealing with a small number of units of product, while in firm w the labor force may be more attuned to mass production. Although each may have the same minimum average cost, that cost will be attained by firm v at a lower output than it is by firm w. The preceding propositions require only minor modification to take such diversity into account, and they do not materially affect the technological determination of the sizes of firms in long-run equilibrium.

U-Shaped Versus Flat-Bottomed Average Cost Curves   Much of the preclusion of differences in firm size can also be attributed to the assumption that the average cost curves are perfectly U-shaped. Empirical evidence and business experience indicate, however, that in reality flat-bottomed average cost curves are reasonably common, perhaps much more so than average cost curves with unique minima.[4] A flat-bottomed AC curve is one in which, after an initial declining segment, the average costs level off and remain horizontal for a considerable range of output before beginning to go back uphill. In such a case, efficient firms can vary in size between the lowest output in the horizontal portion of the AC curve (the point of *minimum efficient scale*) and the largest output in this range (*maximum efficient scale*). This range can, of course, be substantial. And where it is large, the size of a firm and its labor force plainly are influenced by the demand for its product. Thus, when technological influences have a range of neutrality in terms of efficient firm size, demand becomes the determining influence. We have what can perhaps be interpreted as a lexicographical ordering of determinants of firm size, with technology assuming the primary role and demand taking over only where technology does not impose a unique equilibrium magnitude.

Multiproduct Firms   The range of firm size compatible with equilibrium grows larger still when we consider multiproduct enterprises that, over some ranges of outputs and product lines, benefit from economies of scale and scope (for a fuller discussion of some of these size variants, see Baumol, Panzar, and Willig 1988, ch. 5). Here it is important to note that virtually all, if not all, firms in reality supply a number of products; at the least, their principal product is carried in different sizes, colors, and so on. Thus, a multiproduct analysis is applicable to them. But in the multiproduct case, it can be shown that the sizes of the firms in an efficient industry configuration can vary quite substantially.[5] It can be efficient for some firms to specialize in a small number of products, seeking to produce the amounts of these few items called for by efficient scale, while others that are characterized by wide diversification benefit appropriately from economies of scope.

The relationships are illustrated in figure 3.2, which represents the situation in a two-product industry. The axes measure the quantities of the two products, y_1 and y_2. The point labeled Y(p) represents the industry output vector, and the output vectors of the firms in the industry can be indicated by different points in the graph (not shown), whose vector sum must be Y(p).

The counterpart in this model of a U-shaped average cost curve in the single-product case is what has been called "U-shaped ray average cost" (see Baumol and Fischer 1978). That is, consider any ray, such as 0w, that clearly represents all vectors of the two outputs in which the output proportion remains constant and equal to the slope of 0w. Then, with constant output proportions, we can define an un-

Figure 3.2   Firm Size Determination in a Multiproduct Industry

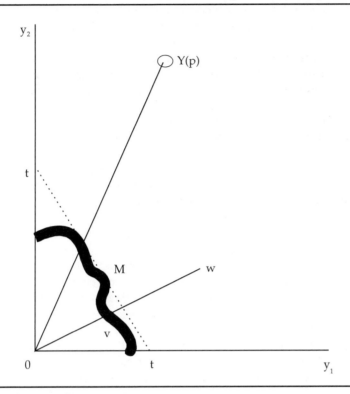

Source: Authors' configuration.

ambiguous measure of the quantity of output and, correspondingly, a measure of average cost along that ray. If, proceeding from the origin along this ray, this ray average cost first declines, then reaches a minimum, and thereafter begins to rise, we have a case of U-shaped ray average cost. Suppose the point of minimum ray average cost along the ray occurs at point v, where 0w intersects the heavy curve, M. Repeating this process for all other rays, we obtain the (possibly irregular) curve M, which is the locus of the minima of all the ray average costs.

It should be clear that efficiency requires the firm to be located not too far from the M locus. But this can occur on the axes, where firms specialize in only one product, or in the center of the graph, where the firm's production is quite unspecialized. Moreover, efficiency is not incompatible with the location of some multiproduct firms' output vectors at a considerable distance from the M locus. For example, draw the lowest supporting hyperplane, tt, to the region on and below the M locus, and also draw in a hyperplane 2tt (not shown), parallel to and twice as far from the origin as tt. Then it can be shown that any output vector for a firm that lies between M and 2tt need not be inefficient.

The argument is analogous to that for the single-product case in the previous section, where, if market equilibrium requires industry output equal to $y_m + v$, with y_m the output that minimizes average cost and $0 < v < y_m$, then, depending on the shape of the cost curves, it plainly may sometimes be more efficient for the entire output to be produced by a single firm, or alternatively, for a second firm to share in supply of the output. Thus, even in the single-product case, where equilibrium output exceeds the amount that minimizes AC but is less than twice that amount, we cannot say in general whether one larger or two smaller firms will be the more efficient arrangement. So there will be a zone of output level in which the optimal size of a firm cannot be determined from the magnitude of y_m.

The same is true in the multiproduct case depicted in figure 3.2. There the hyperplane 2tt parallel to supporting hyperplane tt for the M locus plays the role analogous to the output level $2y_m$ for the single-product case. Any point between M and 2tt may represent an efficient output vector for one of the multiproduct firms.[6] Of course, in any particular case the set of multiproduct firms that, together, produce the industry's output most efficiently may be uniquely determined, but such a unique solution may well entail a set of firms whose output vectors are represented by points scattered throughout the region surrounding the M locus that has just been described.

Thus, our analysis is not incompatible with the reality of the dispersion of firm sizes within industries. But in showing this we may seem to have proved too much. We seem to have demonstrated that there is little that is universal about the firm size results of the very simple model with which we began. We have, however, shown a great deal. Nothing said here has questioned the fundamental conclusion that in a highly competitive market a firm's size and its level of employment of labor must satisfy the efficiency requirement that, in long-run equilibrium, the distribution of firm sizes must be such as to produce the industry output vector at minimum cost. And there is no reason to assume that this cost-minimizing configuration of firm sizes is not unique, even though it may entail a considerable dispersion of firm sizes. Competitive forces, if sufficiently powerful, should drive the actual vector of firm sizes toward that cost-minimizing configuration. This observation also confirms the key role of technology in such circumstances. It supports the inference that if widespread downsizing is in fact occurring, we must consider technical change that reduces the efficient size of the labor force as one of the possible explanations, perhaps even as the one that is most plausible. Certainly where competition is effective this must be so in the long run.

Second, we have shown that in a competitive market, determination of firm size offers only a secondary role to demand. This is so because the equilibrium sizes of the firms in the market are to be calculated from the requirements of minimum cost of production of the industry output in the given state of technology. Yet demand does clearly play a role in the determination of the industry output vector, though that determination is likely to have a greater effect on the number of firms in the industry than on their size, except for the range of outputs corresponding to minimum average cost in a flat-bottomed average cost curve or its counterpart in a multiproduct industry. Finally, we have provided some qualitative indication of the influences that affect the cost-minimizing size of a firm and the way its analysis can be approached.

Competition, of course, is crucial for the relevance of the analysis, and we turn to this subject presently. First, however, it is important to consider whether the theoretical result at which we have just arrived is consistent with the statistical evidence provided in later chapters.

The Empirical Results and the Cost Curve Analysis

Our theory must be adapted to two primary results of our data analysis in the following chapters: there have been sectors, such as retailing, in which the size of firms, measured in terms of number of employees, has been increasing substantially; and in some parts of the economy, notably in manufacturing, both the largest and the smallest firms have been moving toward an intermediate size. Let us consider these developments in terms of our model.

If we assume that competition is fully effective, then in the sense of the comparative statics of the move from one long-run equilibrium to another, there is only one possible explanation for the growth in the size of retailing firms. Technology must have evolved in a way that makes larger retailing firms relatively more economical than they were before. For an imaginary single-product retailer whose average cost curve is flat-bottomed, the situation must have changed in the manner described in figure 3.3. Here we see that the average cost curve has shifted toward the right, from thinner curve AC1 to thicker curve AC2, with the minimum efficient scale increasing from the abscissa of R to that of r.

Similarly, the regression toward the mean of firms in manufacturing industries very plausibly may have been technology-driven. The obvious picture for the single-product firm is shown in figure 3.4. Here the evolution from initial average cost curve AC1 to subsequent curve AC2 entails a (relative) rise in the tails and a (relative) lowering

Figure 3.3   The Long-Run Retailing Parable

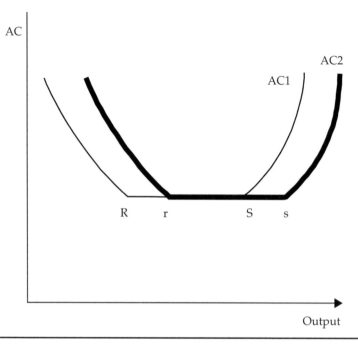

Source: Authors' configuration.

of the central portions of the curve, giving midsize firms a greater advantage than they possessed previously in comparison with larger and smaller enterprises. But that is not the critical development. Rather, it is the narrowing of the efficient range from RS to rs, which means that the range of firm sizes that are viable in the long run has narrowed.

One can create a story that imparts plausibility to the shifts in figures 3.3 and 3.4 by emphasizing the explosion of information technology (computers, the Internet, and attendant technological developments). For example, one can argue that such developments have reduced the advantages of mass production: because long production runs and a corresponding degree of standardization are no longer required, the degree of superiority of larger manufacturing firms is reduced.[7] There is much evidence that computerization has greatly reduced the minimum economically viable length of production run on the assembly line of some products. It is now far cheaper, relatively, to switch from one set of product specifications—color, size, and other variants—to another. It has also become less costly to tailor

Figure 3.4   The Long-Run Manufacturing Parable

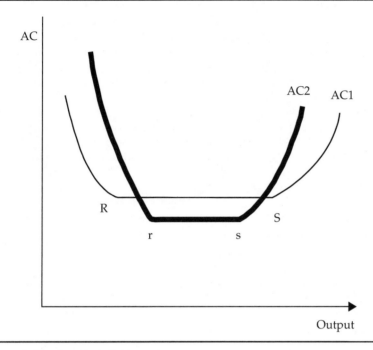

Source: Authors' configuration.

the product to fit the specifications desired by the individual consumer. This can undermine, or at least greatly moderate, the cost advantages of mass production, thus handicapping the largest firms in
the manufacturing industries relative to where they had stood before.
But so-called built-to-order production methods are also becoming
more common in large manufacturing firms (for example, Dell Computer and the automobile manufacturer Renault) and may even lead
to "mass customization"—individualized production on a mass scale
(see *The Economist* 2001).

At the same time, information technology has apparently cut the
costs of the communication, coordination, and record-keeping needed
to manage larger enterprises. This is already a disadvantage of large
firm size in most industries, so the fall in this cost difference may be
widespread. As a result, smaller firms may lose this source of cost
advantage while remaining subject to all of the other cost handicaps
of smaller enterprises. In this story, this shift in cost advantages is
why the smallest firms became scarcer in retailing and elsewhere. The
reality of this scenario is suggested by accounts such as that in the

2001 *Economic Report of the President* (Council of Economic Advisers 2001, 121–25):

> The trucking industry is using [information technology] to better serve its customers' logistics needs. . . . To track and dispatch trucks efficiently, they use sophisticated locating technology, such as the satellite-based global positioning system; real-time traffic, weather, and road construction information; computers on board the trucks themselves; complex software and algorithms; and supporting hardware to organize customers and loads. . . . [In banking, digital imaging technology] has freed employees from having to record check amounts manually, lowered transactions costs by eliminating the need to move checks physically, and allowed banks to reorganize their workflow around a more extensive division of labor.

The crucial fact here is that powerful computers can now be purchased at prices that are trivial for most business firms, and their use nowadays is usually not very costly or complicated. The fall in computer technology prices and costs from their very high levels only a few decades ago itself contributes a competitive advantage to firms of smaller and intermediate size.[8] Here another observation is relevant. Large firms (many of them with outputs exceeding those of a considerable number of small countries) are generally run as planned economies. That is, even though they operate in a market economy, internally they tend to be centrally directed. Despite sporadic attempts at decentralization and pseudo-profit system rules for the different divisions of the large enterprises, managements of these large firms tend to control outputs, investments, prices, and other decisions through top-down bureaucratic processes rather than anything resembling market forces. It seems plausible that the resulting efficiency costs are greater, the larger the size of the firm. Growing competition, including competition from abroad, has arguably made such inefficiencies a more serious business handicap and may well have harmed large firms more than small ones.[9]

On the other hand, in retailing, the contribution of the computer to record-keeping, ordering, and inventory control may well have raised the minimum efficient scale of firms and establishments. Here the suggestive illustration is the rise of large chains with large establishments (Wal-Mart, Home Depot, Barnes and Noble, and all the giant-sized supermarkets, to name a few) and the decline in the number of "mom and pop" stores.

The Role of Competition and Its Pertinent Form

Up to this point the form of competition used in our theoretical analysis has deliberately been left vague. As already indicated, perfect competition will not do for analysis of firm size, because its very definition requires that firms be small and so assumes away the issue. Moreover, many of the firms for which the issue of downsizing arises are much too large for consistency with that definition.

The standard of comparison that our analysis will use throughout is behavior in an effectively competitive market, which will be defined here as the hypothetical state of perfect contestability, with its perfect freedom of entry and exit. In a perfectly contestable market, firms need not be small; they can be of any size permitted by demand and the structure of costs. Moreover, the contestable markets model permits direct analysis of the economic determinants of firm size. It does so by means of the theorem that in such a hypothetical market, as in the case of perfect competition (a special case of perfect contestability), there cannot be any inefficiency in (long-run) equilibrium. Hence, the sizes of an industry's firms will be those necessary to turn out the industry's output at minimum cost. It is this theorem that transforms the problem into what is, at least in principle, a tractable mathematical calculation, given the state of technology and the accompanying production function.

The discussion has stressed the crucial role of competition in compelling firms to adapt the size of their labor force to the dictates of technology. Yet we must not overlook the fact that technology and cost minimization are clearly also relevant for less competitive market forms. The theory tells us that even a pure monopoly will seek to minimize the cost of whatever output it selects, if its objective is profit maximization. Thus, cost minimization, and hence the state of technology, also plays a significant role in determining the size of the monopolist's labor force. However, strategic considerations can also be an important influence, particularly in oligopolistic markets. For example, as game theory has brought to our attention, the size of a firm's output capacity may be significantly affected by the desire to discourage entry, and the resulting output and level of employment may well drive the firm far from the cost-minimizing levels. Moreover, in oligopolistic markets, firms can pursue goals other than profit maximization and engage in wasteful expenditure because the means to discipline management are imperfect and agency problems can arise when the goals of management and ownership are imperfectly compatible.

It is only the absence of barriers to entry—that is, of costs that must be borne by an entrant but not by an incumbent—that can be relied on to force even an oligopolistic industry to minimize the cost of the industry output vector. And that is why we turn to the concept of contestability as the basis for our competitive analysis.

Nevertheless, we can argue intuitively, and on the basis of casual empiricism, that in the long run in a market economy competitive forces universally exercise their effects in a rough and ready way. Even in a market with substantial entry barriers, extremely wasteful practices by incumbents or extremely excessive prices and profits can make the effort to overcome the entry barriers attractive. The mere threat that this can happen generally induces even firms with market power to avoid dramatically wasteful behavior. That is presumably why automobile producers and airplane manufacturers operate firms and establishments whose size seems to correspond roughly to the efficiency conditions dictated by technology. More generally, the differences among industries in the size of their typical firm does seem to correspond roughly to their technological requirements, as has already been noted.

Firm Size Versus Size of Establishment

We emphasized earlier—and will continue to stress throughout the book—the importance of distinguishing between the size of a firm and the size of an establishment. It is clear, for example, that large firms can be composed of many small establishments. Thus, in terms of number of employees, Wal-Mart is the largest firm in the United States. Yet, while its individual stores are large establishments for what is standard in retailing activity, their individual labor forces are very small compared to that of a Boeing airplane manufacturing plant. Moreover, there is nothing that prevents a firm from growing in size while the size of its establishments declines, or the reverse.

Our discussion of technological influences on firm size most immediately applies to the size of establishments rather than the size of firms. The optimal size of an assembly line is an attribute of the establishment rather than the firm. The role of technological determinants in fixing the size of firms is a bit less easily grasped intuitively than is the corresponding relationship to size of establishment.

Yet in principle, there is no difference between the two. For this purpose, the firm should be viewed as the provider of a variety of services to its establishments: for example, purchasing of supplies, advertising, or serving as a guarantor of quality. And it is the cost function—that is, the technology in the broadest sense—that determines the firm's minimum efficient scale in carrying out these tasks. Economies of scale and scope can arise in the activities of the firm in serving its establishments and can determine the maximum number of establishments the firm can serve efficiently. Here too technological change in communication and computation can play a profound role. They certainly affect the cost of advertisement and the choice of media used for the purpose. They also affect the cost of whatever coordination is required among the activities of a firm's establishments.

Thus, there is no difference in principle between the types of variables that determine the size of firms and those that determine the size of establishments. Of course, these choices can be interdependent, whether made deliberately and consciously in a process of managerial planning or as an evolving response to market forces. Here it is important to emphasize, however, that while the size of firms and the size of establishments are arguably determined, at least in the long run, by similar forces, those forces may not always move them in the same direction. New technology may, for example, increase the relative efficiency of larger establishments while at the same time reducing that of larger firms. So one cannot simply conclude that, because firms and establishments are both governed by the same sorts of variables, if the data show establishment size to be growing in some industry or some sector of the economy, the same must be true of the size of firms in that industry.

The bottom line is that, where competition is effective, in the case of the firm and the establishment alike, theory leads us to look at technological developments to see whether downsizing is to be expected and to determine what it really implies for the size of a firm's labor force.

Models of Churning and Remarks on the Role of International Trade

Technical change has been emphasized as a direct determination of firm size. We will see next that there is also reason to expect an indirect influence of technology, through the influence of such change on the volume and character of international trade and specialization.

Speed of Technical Change and Labor Force Churning

Next we examine further the influences that lead to churning of the labor force. We provide a theoretical link between the speed of innovation and the cost-minimizing composition of the labor force. We argue that whether or not the new techniques require different skills, the speedup of the process of innovation by itself will lead to changes in the types of worker a firm can most efficiently employ, resulting in some churning of the labor force. The rate of technical progress clearly increases the relative cost of employing a person whom it is relatively expensive to retrain or who is less likely to provide an incremental revenue product sufficient to repay the cost of retraining. The enhanced relative price of hiring such workers leads to substitution for their services: they are replaced with higher-paid workers whose retraining cost is not so high. This is shown in the nearly obvious result:

Proposition 4   In a competitive economy, a rise in the speed of technical change that increases the frequency of plant redesign and retooling will lead to a relative decrease in the employment of less-
educated workers whose wage is relatively low but whose relative
retraining cost is thus increased.

For simplicity, we aggregate all production into a single output
whose quantity is y. We also assume that all workers fall into one of
two classes, less educated and better educated. We then carry out a
standard comparative-statics analysis to determine the effects of a
change in the parameter that measures the rate of technical change (as
indicated by the frequency of plant retooling) on the relative employment of the two classes of labor. The following notation is used:

w = the annual wage of a less-educated worker

h = the length of time between plant retoolings

k = the cost of retraining a less-educated worker

w^* = the annual wage of a better-educated worker

k^* = the cost of retraining a better-educated worker

v = the number of less-educated workers employed

v^* = the number of better-educated workers employed

y = $F(v,v^*)$: the production function

H = the horizon, which can, if desired, be assumed to be infinite

i = the rate of interest used for discounting

Then, the present value of the cost of production of y is

$$C = f(H)\,(wv + w^*v^*) + g(h)\,(kv + k^*v^*) \qquad (3.1)$$

where $f(H) = \Sigma_{t=0}^{H} [1/(1 + i)]^t$, which is constant in our calculation,
and $g(h) = \Sigma_{t=0}^{H/h} [1/(1 + i)]^{ht}$ or writing $R = [1/(1+i)]^h$, $= [1 -
R^{(H+h)/h}]/(1 - R)$.

This last expression can be shown to be a decreasing function of h,
the time between plant retoolings, that is:

$$g'(h) < 0 \qquad (3.2)$$

which means, simply (see equation 3.1), that an increase in the rate of
innovation, which reduces h (the length of time between plant retoolings), increases the present value of the stream of retraining costs.

We also assume, for reasons already explained, that:

$$w < w^*, k > k^*, \text{ and } F_v < F_{v^*}, \qquad (3.3)$$

where a subscript represents the partial derivative with respect to the indicated variable, and the last inequality, of course, means that the marginal product of skilled labor is greater than that of unskilled labor.

Our problem is to minimize C, subject to y = constant, yielding the Lagrangian

$$L(v,v^*,v) = f(H)(wv + w^*v^*) + g(h)(kv + k^*v^*) + s[F(v,v^*) - y]$$
(3.4)

in which s is the Lagrange multiplier. We have the first-order minimum conditions

$$fw + g(h)k + sF_v = 0$$
$$fw^* + g(h)k^* + sF_{v^*} = 0$$
$$F(v,v^*) = y$$
(3.5)

The second-order conditions include the requirement that D, the bordered hessian of the system, and its principal minors, D_{ii}, have the same sign, so

$$D_{ii} D > 0.$$
(3.6)

To determine the comparative-statics effect of a change in the frequency of technical change on employment of less-educated workers—that is, the effect of a change in the value of the parameter h on v—we set the total differentials of the three first-order conditions equal to 0:

$$sF_{vv}dv + sF_{vv^*}dv^* + F_vds = -g'kdh$$
$$sF_{v^*v}dv + sF_{v^*v^*}dv^* + F_{v^*}ds = -g'k^*dh$$
$$sF_vdv + sF_{v^*}dv^* = 0.$$
(3.7)

First, we note that $D_{11} = -F_{v^*}^2 < 0$, so that, by equation 3.6, D < 0. Next, dividing equation 3.7 through by dh and solving for dv/dh, we obtain:

$$dv/dh = \begin{vmatrix} -g'k & sF_{vv^*} & F_v \\ -g'k^* & sF_{v^*v^*} & F_{v^*} \\ 0 & F_{v^*} & 0 \end{vmatrix} /D$$

$$= [g'kF_{v^*}^2 - g'k^* F_v F_{v^*}]/D$$
$$= [F_{v^*}g'(kF_{v^*} - k^* F_v)]/D > 0,$$
(3.8)

where the direction of the inequality follows from equations 3.2 and 3.3 and $D < 0$. Specifically, equation 3.8 tells us that a rise in the length of the time interval between plant retoolings—that is, a ceteris paribus slowdown in technical progress—increases the employment of the less-educated workers. Exactly the same line of argument shows that it reduces the employment of better-educated workers; the same result can be obtained directly from equation 3.8 and the last line in equation 3.7. The reverse holds, of course, for a speedup of technical progress. This completes the proof of proposition 4.[10]

Note again that this result was obtained considering only changes in total retraining cost relative to wages for the better-educated and less-educated workers resulting from increased or decreased frequency of technical changes, as indicated by h. This result is probably strengthened by such supplementary influences as the likelihood that more rapid technical change will increase the level of skill and education needed by workers, thereby reducing the relative marginal product of the less-educated.

Something like proposition 4 holds not only for less-educated workers but also, with one exacerbating difference, for older workers as well (for discussions of the evidence on the types of workers affected, see Allen, Clark, and Scheiber 1999; Bartel and Lichtenberg 1987; Farber 1997; Gardner 1995; Polsky 1999; Rodriguez and Zavodny 2000). Like the less-educated, older workers too may be harder to retrain than young, educated workers, because they may have become set in their ways and because their education, far in the past, may be less helpful in adapting to the latest technical developments. In addition, because older workers are closer to retirement age, they offer the employer a briefer stream of incremental revenues with which to recoup the sunk costs of their retraining (Becker 1975). As a result, an employer's prospects for recouping those training costs will be dimmer for its older employees, enhancing its incentive to replace them with younger, educated workers when technical progress accelerates.[11]

So changes in the *rapidity* of technical change can modify substantially the cost-minimizing composition of the affected firm's labor force. That change, in turn, can lead to the replacement of one group of workers with another, giving a rather misleading appearance of downsizing as the firm sheds the types of workers it no longer wants to employ. In contrast, if changes in the workforce are driven by modification in the requirements of cost minimization stemming from changed technology, true downsizing may result. But that is not the only possible result of such a technology-governed scenario. For example, as we have seen, the latest generation of technology may make both very large and very small size less efficient, relatively speaking, than they were before. If so, the nature of that technical change will drive the size of firms to move toward the mean. In that case we could still expect to find that larger firms are driven to actual downsizing—that is, to net reductions in the number of persons they employ. Since it is the larger firms that attract the most public attention, the result may be an impression that downsizing is universal. But such a trend need not lead to an increase in unemployment in the industry, because even as the largest firms become smaller, there may well be an offsetting rise in the number of enterprises in the field.

Foreign Competition, Input Prices, and Firm Size

In the economic literature, the influence of *technology* on a firm's demand for labor is usually distinguished from the role of *foreign competition* (on the role of foreign competition, see, for example, Bernard et al. 2000; Borjas and Ramey 1995; Wood 1994, 1995). There are arguments about the relative influence of these two factors on the availability of jobs and the level of wages. However, we argue here that technology and foreign competition are inextricably intertwined, and that their interconnection is an important part of the analysis. We have stressed the significance of competition in ensuring the influence of technology on the size of a firm's labor force. Increasingly, that competition comes from foreign sources. The automobile industry is just one dramatic illustration of this development. The U.S. auto market, once almost the exclusive province of a small number of domestic manufacturers, now faces the effective competition of imports from more than a half-dozen foreign countries, as well as cars manufactured in the United States by foreign-owned firms.

The growth of such competition is itself highly dramatic. As we noted in chapter 1, the *share* of exports in world GDP has risen more than thirteenfold in the last two hundred years (Maddison 1995, 38). Considering how rapidly GDP itself has increased over this period, we can conclude that the absolute value of exports has exploded. Angus Maddison estimates (in constant 1990 dollars) that world GDP in 1820 was $695 billion and had increased to $27,995 billion by 1992 (a 40-fold increase); the value of world exports was $7 billion in 1820 and $3,786 billion in 1992 (a 541-fold increase). Thus, trade is increasingly the source of the competition that enforces the influence of technology on the size of a firm and its labor force.

But the relationship is also mutual. The growth of foreign trade and foreign competition is itself ascribable primarily to innovations that have revolutionized transportation and communication. These innovations have sped up the transport of physical product around the globe from a period of months to a day or two, and the communication of information to virtually an instant. They have reduced the real cost of transportation to a small fraction of its previous levels and changed transportation itself from an incredibly perilous activity to one that is among the economy's safest.[12] Since the eighteenth century, the steam engine, metal hulls, radio communication, satellite location processes, and a host of other innovations have clearly revolutionized transportation and communication, bringing substantial foreign competition even into the service industries, from many of which it was almost totally absent until quite recently.

We may note that the interdependence of trade and innovation goes even further. Increasingly, innovation has become a prime competitive weapon: producers try to fight off their rivals with the aid of improved products and processes. The increased intensity of foreign competition has surely contributed to the pace of innovation in this way. And the increased facility of communication has, in turn, helped to speed technology transfer from one country to another. Information about innovations is disseminated throughout the world almost instantly in fields in which technology-exchange agreements between firms are widespread. And even in the absence of such friendly transfers, it is estimated that information about most innovations is spread throughout the industrialized countries within a year or two of their introduction (see Maddison 1995).

International competition does not influence the size of a firm's labor force simply by enforcing cost minimization. As we have just argued, it also influences relative input prices and thereby determines whether capital will be substituted for labor, for example, or whether skilled labor will be substituted for unskilled. The magnitude of the wage effects of enhanced competition from abroad is a subject very much in dispute, both on theoretical grounds and in light of the results of different methods of econometric analysis of the available data. This is not the place to discuss these issues in detail. However, it may be useful to offer a few remarks on the implications for downsizing of the effects of trade competition on patterns of input prices.

Clearly, if foreign competition primarily serves to reduce wages in industrialized countries without influencing the cost of capital substantially, it should lead to substitution of labor for capital and we would expect to observe the reverse of downsizing. Firms whose outputs are relatively stationary should tend to increase the size of their labor forces. Foreign competition could lead to downsizing only if it led firms to increase their labor forces by moving plants from domestic to foreign locations where labor is still cheaper than at home. This could entail the downsizing of the firm, but not of the establishment, if firms are induced to export primarily their plants that make heaviest use of labor.

On the other hand, suppose that foreign competition primarily affects input prices by decreasing the number of unskilled domestic workers demanded at a given level of wages for the unskilled, and that it has the reverse effect on the demand function and wages of skilled labor. This may be another explanation for the empirical observation that downsizing is to a substantial degree a churning phenomenon, which in the end restructures the labor force without necessarily producing any substantial effects on its overall size.

The Theory of Downsizing and the Six Hypotheses on Downsizing

How much light have the theoretical models of this chapter shed on the validity of the six hypotheses we proposed in chapter 1 as candidate explanations for downsizing? The answer, in brief, is that we believe these models have provided strong theoretical support for two of the hypotheses, offered suggestive comments favoring another, had only peripheral relevance for two others, and contributed nothing of relevance to the remaining one. In addition, the discussion has suggested that a primary role is played by a seventh influence that may have been implied in our six initial conjectures but was certainly not featured in them.

Our first hypothesis was that downsizing can occur when technical change favors smaller enterprises. Clearly, our theoretical models have been consistent with this view. Although pure theory cannot constitute proof of a hypothesis about the real world, it can impart a substantial degree of plausibility to a hypothesis and, at the very least, constitutes a demonstration of its internal consistency.

The same can be said about the second hypothesis, the possibility that much of what appears to be downsizing may simply be the most visible manifestation of churning, that is, a replacement—stimulated by rapidity of technical change—of one group of employees by another. This proposition was also tested theoretically and explicitly in the analysis reported in this chapter.

The third hypothesis, that growing foreign competition may induce downsizing by requiring firms to trim any "fat" in their labor force, received some informal support in this chapter. But while the observations offered here are suggestive and do seem to favor the hypothesis, they offer little more of any relevance.

Any claims for illumination derived from the analysis of this chapter about the remaining hypotheses must surely be modest indeed. This discussion has been marginally pertinent to the fourth hypothesis, that downsizing has been a consequence of the substitution of capital for labor, and the sixth hypothesis, that downsizing entails the "blue-collarization" of the tasks of white-collar workers. The rele-

vance of this chapter's theoretical models is their focus on the technical change that surely must be involved in any capital-labor substitution or the substitution of one type of labor for another. But the light
shed by the models does not seem to extend beyond this, nor does it
even begin to reach the fifth hypothesis, that downsizing can be attributed to, or was at least stimulated by, a breakdown of an implicit
social contract between employers and employees.

Arguably more significant than these negative results is the hypothesis put forward early in this chapter—that a primary short-run
role in downsizing must be ascribed to declining demand for the relevant products, that is, those that the affected workers were employed
in producing. But it must be recognized that the hypothesis did not
emerge from the theory, and indeed, it has received little analytical
underpinning here. A theoretical model would no doubt focus on the
high cost of and impediments to the rapid exit of firms from an industry facing declining demand for its products and uncertainty about
whether that demand will recover. Firms would be tempted to try to
stay in business until they had met their short-run spending commit-
ments. This economic reality would cause firms to resist exit from the
industry and certainly to postpone any such exit so long as there was
hope for the future. So, in the short run firms typically respond to
declining product demand by reducing their labor force, even if that
reduction brings them below the cost-minimizing number of employees.

The product-demand hypothesis surely requires further examination, which will be provided in the analysis of statistical data in chapter 4.[13]

Conclusions

This chapter has offered some theoretical foundation for the empirical
materials that follow. The range of hypotheses at issue and the complexity of their interactions have prevented an exhaustive examination of all elements of the downsizing issue, and much of the chapter's discussion is unavoidably unsystematic. However, it does leave
us with a pair of hypotheses that, if valid, show us the way to a
unifying overview of the determinants of downsizing.

We have concluded that in the short run the market conditions that
face a firm are the primary determinants of its hiring and firing decisions, so that downsizing is primarily a response to declining demand
for its products. In the long run, however, the story is quite different.
The imperfect but powerful competitive forces that arguably pervade
the economy automatically impose severe punishment on an enterprise that operates inefficiently. The result is that the viable firm is

forced to operate with a labor force whose size is at least approximately compatible with the requirements of economic efficiency. Technology determines what that efficient size is, and long-run downsizing occurs when technical change requires a reduction in the size of the labor force. In the long run the state of market demand determines the number of firms in a particular market but has a very limited influence on the size of the labor force of a representative firm. Unquestionably, reality is more complex than this. However, stripped down to its most powerful elements, this is at least a plausible depiction of the pertinent relationships.

Chapter 4

Is American Business Really Downsizing? The Facts

I N CHAPTER 2, we provided some promising clues about the reality of American corporate downsizing gleaned from our analysis of a newspaper sample of firms reported to have downsized. In chapter 3, we sketched out the theoretical underpinnings of downsizing. In this chapter, we turn to a comprehensive examination of the actual *facts* of downsizing. Even the *definition* of downsizing is somewhat elusive. So we begin the chapter with a discussion of some definitional and data source issues, noting several respects in which a definition of downsizing that is entirely defensible must give way to compromises dictated by what the available data allow us to measure. Once that is done, the bulk of the chapter is devoted to tabulating and comparing the downsizing experiences of seven major sectors of the U.S. economy for which reasonably good data are available: manufacturing, retail trade, wholesale trade, services, construction, mining, and the combination of transportation, communications, and utilities (TCU). Previous investigations of downsizing have been almost entirely limited to manufacturing. As we will show, this limitation substantially distorts the economy-wide picture. Manufacturing is simply not representative.

This chapter offers numerous details and enters many qualifications, but two basic story lines emerge from our comprehensive look at the data. First, downsizing has been more or less restricted to manufacturing; no other major sector of the economy displays consistent downsizing. Indeed, *increasing,* not decreasing, firm size is closer to the norm in the service and trade sectors, both of which employ many more workers—and have many more firms—than does manufacturing. Second, downsizing in American manufacturing is not something new: it has long been a fact of life, though it appears to have strengthened somewhat during the prime downsizing period, 1987 to 1992.

These two main findings raise an obvious question: What accounts for the stark difference between the patterns in manufacturing and those of other economic sectors? Later in the chapter, we will find that we can travel some way toward an answer with a hypothesis that is almost embarrassingly simple: shrinking industries tend to downsize while growing industries tend to "upsize." That is hardly a subtle thought. But since total employment in the U.S. manufacturing sector has been shrinking for decades while both retail- and service-sector employment have been growing exponentially, the hypothesis suggests that most downsizing should have been found in manufacturing. This is not the entire story, of course, but further explanations must await subsequent chapters. When we get there, we will find that more rigorous and detailed analyses do not undermine the importance of this very simple idea.

Some Definitional and Data Source Matters

"Downsizing," a term coined by journalists, seems to have no agreed-upon definition. It is clear, however, that the most salient feature of the phenomenon, as we saw in chapter 2's look at accounts of it in the popular press, is shrinkage in employment. So it seems natural to say that a *firm* downsizes when it trims its workforce—even if the reduced workforce, perhaps supplemented by more capital, produces just as much (or even more) output as it did before. Thus, the definition of "downsizing" can include changes in the input proportions of different factors of production—say, toward more machinery and less labor (in the technical jargon, movements along an isoquant).

Of course, individual firms expand and contract all the time in any dynamic industry—and for a wide variety of reasons. The downsizing phenomenon is of general interest, it would seem, only if and when many firms downsize at the same time. So we will say that an *industry* downsizes when a typical firm in the industry grows smaller, as measured by employment. This chapter and, indeed, this book concentrate on downsizing at the industry level.

But what precisely do we mean when we say that "firms grow smaller"? The available data permit us to work with two distinct meanings:

Definition 1: The average firm size in the industry falls.

Definition 2: The size distribution of firms in the industry shifts to the left—that is, small firms become more prevalent and large firms become less prevalent. In technical statistical parlance, we would say that the old size distribution *stochastically dominates* the new size distribution.

Clearly definition 2 implies definition 1. If the new distribution is stochastically dominated, it must have a smaller average. But the converse does not hold. Average firm size can and does fall even in some cases where the old distribution does not stochastically dominate the new one. Stochastic dominance is thus the sterner test by far. The analysis in this chapter uses both definitions. As we will see, the results using the two generally agree, although the stochastic dominance criterion leaves many ambiguous cases. The consistency of those findings will give us some confidence when, in later chapters, we concentrate on the simpler definition of downsizing based on average firm size.

So far we have spoken of business *firms* rather than of business *establishments*—the individual factories, stores, or offices owned by a firm—because the firm seems to us (but not to everyone) to be the more natural unit of analysis. For example, if a department store chain restructures itself so that 5 stores with 200 employees each (1,000 employees in total) are replaced by 10 stores with 150 employees each (1,500 employees), we would not want to say the firm downsized even though average establishment size fell markedly. Similarly, if that same firm were to reorganize itself into three larger stores with 250 employees each (750 employees), we *would* want to say it downsized—even though its average establishment size actually increased.

Some economists would argue that an analogous problem bedevils any analysis based on firms. Suppose two firms merge into one, but no workers are hired or fired. The industry is then recorded as "upsizing" (average firm size increases), and the new size distribution stochastically dominates the old (the number of larger firms rises). Similarly, if firms break up, we observe "downsizing" even if no jobs are lost. Such instances do indeed occur, but we are not convinced that they constitute an abuse of the downsizing-upsizing terminology. After all, mergers *do* lead to enlargement of firms (though perhaps not of establishments), and breakups to shrinkage. As long as we remember that shifts in the size distribution of firms may or may not correspond to job loss or gains, it does not seem troubling to us to call a merger wave "upsizing" and a wave of breakups "downsizing." In fact, it seems natural.

Although there is no perfect solution to this definitional issue, it seems to us that, on balance, the firm is conceptually the preferable unit of analysis. Unfortunately, the most commonly used data source, the U.S. Economic Censuses that appear every five years, offer more data on employment by establishment than by firm. The Census of Manufacturing, in particular, offers data *only* on an establishment basis, and as just noted, interest in downsizing centers on manufacturing. The Census of Retail Trade and the Census of Service Industries, which also appear every fifth year, offer some help in this regard because they include *both* firm-based and establishment-based data. So we will use them to make educated guesses as to whether findings on manufacturing *establishments* are likely to be indicative of what is going on in manufacturing *firms*. As it turns out, where both are available, the establishment-based and firm-based data rarely give conflicting answers on whether downsizing has occurred. However, their *quantitative* estimates of downsizing (or upsizing) do differ noticeably.

There is a further definitional issue of some importance, and it is one that is almost always ignored. As everyone knows, large companies often do business in several industries. For example, General Electric is best known as a major electronics company, but it is also a huge financial company, a manufacturer of jet engines, and many other things. General Motors not only is an automobile manufacturer but through its Hughes Electronics subsidiary provides, for example, satellite television services. Standard data from the Economic Censuses deal with these conglomerate companies by breaking them into mythical "firms" that operate in specific industries. So, for example, if XYZ Corporation employs two thousand workers in widget manufacturing, six hundred workers in a chain of retail widget stores, and four hundred workers in a widget repair business, the Economic Censuses would record XYZ as three different firms: a two-thousand-employee manufacturing firm in the Census of Manufacturing, a six-hundred-employee retailing firm in the Census of Retail Trade, and a four-hundred-employee service firm in the Census of Service Industries. But in fact, there is only one XYZ Corporation.

This data problem seems to distort the underlying reality, especially if one is interested in *firm* size. Fortunately, there is a way out. The Census Bureau also publishes a little-known and rarely used data source called the Enterprise Statistics, which puts the mythical pieces back together again. Thus, for example, the Enterprise Statistics would record XYZ as a single manufacturing company (its major line of business) with three thousand employees. For this reason alone, the Enterprise Statistics would seem to be a better source of data than the standard Economic Censuses.[1] The Enterprise Statistics employ their own industrial classification system, called the Enterprise Industrial Classification (EIC). But it differs only slightly from the codes of the familiar U.S. Standard Industrial Classification (SIC) system (now the NAICS, or North American Industrial Classification System).

For a study of downsizing, top-coding in the data presents a nastier, but unavoidable, problem. If the largest recorded firm-size category is, say, "more than one thousand employees," then a merger of two five-thousand-employee firms into one ten-thousand-employee firm raises average firm size—implying that upsizing has occurred. But the size distribution of firms recorded in the data actually shifts to the left, indicating downsizing, because there are now *fewer* firms in the category of more than one thousand employees. Here again the Enterprise Statistics have a distinct advantage because the top-coding problem is substantially smaller than it is in the more familiar Economic Censuses.

This is not a trivial issue, as the following example shows. The largest size category in the 1992 Census of Retail Trade was over one thousand employees for *firms* and over one hundred employees for *establishments.* By contrast, the largest category for retail *firms* in the Enterprise Statistics was over ten thousand. Thus, we are dealing with a much smaller upper tail when we use the Enterprise Statistics. For example, the Enterprise Statistics included 952 firms that employed one thousand or more workers in 1992,[2] but there were only 143 firms that employed ten thousand or more. Thus, the top-coded upper tail is only 15 percent as large as it would be if we stopped at firms with one thousand employees. If we had used the census data on *establishments* instead, the highest size category (one hundred or more employees) would have included 21,371 establishments.

For both of these reasons, we emphasize findings from the Enterprise Statistics in most of this chapter and make only sporadic references to the standard Economic Censuses.[3] Still, even the Enterprise Statistics miss changes that occur in the extreme upper tail of the size distribution, for example, among retailers with more than ten thousand employees. This is why we paid so much attention to the newspaper sample of (mostly giant) companies in chapter 2.

We need to mention one other critical data choice. With a few minor exceptions, we have chosen in this book to focus on what can be described as the *size of a typical firm,* not on the *size of the firm that employs the typical worker.* The two measures differ substantially because the U.S. economy is populated by millions of tiny firms, each of which has negligible employment. Our interest in this study is on whether *firms* have grown smaller (downsizing) or larger (upsizing), not on the experience of the typical worker. That said, we do not believe that the two questions have dramatically different answers.

To cite just one important example, we will find in this chapter that upsizing, not downsizing, has been the dominant pattern in retailing in most industries during most time periods, although there are plenty of exceptions. But does that also mean that over time the typical *worker* found herself working for larger and larger firms? Fortunately, the answer is yes, as table 4.1 shows. For example, at the high end, only about 16 percent of retail employees worked in firms with more than ten thousand employees in 1958. But this share rose steadily to over 30 percent by 1992. At the low end, the share of retail workers in firms with fewer than twenty employees dropped from 46.6 percent in 1958 to just 23 percent in 1992. Each distribution shown in table 4.1 stochastically dominates the previous distribution. In retailing, upsizing clearly occurred.

Table 4.1, incidentally, should go a long way toward dispelling (at least for the giant retail sector) the myth that while most firms are very small, most people work in very large firms. In 1992, for example, more people worked in firms with fewer than one hundred employees (44 percent) than worked in firms with more than ten thousand employees (30 percent).

Finally, an issue of interpretation bears mentioning. Cyclical conditions were rather different in the years of the nine quinquennial censuses that form the backbone of our analysis—1958, 1963, 1967, 1972, 1977, 1982, 1987, and 1992.[4] Specifically, 1958 was a recession year, with the national unemployment rate averaging 6.8 percent. The year 1963 was midcycle (5.7 percent unemployment), hence there is some cyclical bounce as we move from 1958 to 1963. Similarly, 1967 and 1972 were years of essentially full employment, although the unemployment rates were quite different (3.8 percent and 5.6 percent, respectively). But five years later, in 1977, with unemployment at 7.1 percent, the economy was still recovering from the severe recession of 1973 to 1975. In 1982, a deep recession year, unemployment averaged 9.7 percent—the worst annual figure since the Great Depression. But by 1987 unemployment was down to 6.2 percent, which was believed to be close to full employment at the time. Unemployment was a relatively high 7.5 percent in 1992 as the economy slowly recovered from the recession of 1990 to 1991. But 1997 was a boom year, with an average unemployment rate of 4.9 percent.

We know, of course, that both firms and industries generally shrink during recessions and expand during booms; they always have. If downsizing is a new phenomenon, it must be something more than the straightforward fact that many industries shed labor during recessions. It will be important to keep this simple point in mind as we analyze the data. For example, the deep business cycle trough in 1982 should lead us to expect much more downsizing between 1977 and 1982, say, than between 1982 and 1987.

Table 4.1 The Size Distribution of Retail Firms, 1958 to 1992

Number of Employees	1958	1963	1967	1972	1977	1982	1987	1992
1 to 19[a]	46.6%	43.8%	39.3%	34.7%	31.6%	28.9%	23.6%	23.0%
20 to 99[a]	18.8	19.1	20.1	22.3	22.4	23.1	21.7	21.1
100 to 249	4.5	4.3	5.0	5.0	5.6	6.3	7.2	6.9
250 to 499	2.6	2.3	2.6	2.4	2.8	3.4	3.9	3.9
500 to 999	2.3	2.4	2.0	2.3	2.5	2.8	3.2	3.2
1,000 to 2,499	3.4	3.1	2.8	3.4	3.3	3.5	3.8	4.2
2,500 to 4,999	2.9	2.7	2.6	3.1	3.4	3.1	3.2	3.3
5,000 to 9,999	3.0	4.2	2.4	3.3	3.1	3.6	3.9	4.1
10,000 or more	15.9	18.2	23.2	23.5	25.4	25.4	29.3	30.3

Source: Authors' calculations from U.S. Bureau of the Census, Enterprise Statistics (1958 to 1992).
[a]Finer breakdowns for these categories are available for 1967 to 1992 but are not used in order to maintain comparability with 1958 to 1963.

Analysis of the Manufacturing Data

Most downsizing stories in the popular press come out of the manufacturing sector. For example, our electronic search of the *New York Times* and the *Wall Street Journal* for articles about downsizing during the five-year period 1993 to 1997 turned up stories on almost three hundred companies, more than 60 percent of which were engaged in manufacturing. While nothing is proven by the incidence of newspaper articles selected by a highly nonrandom process, the systematic data do support the notion that American manufacturing industries have downsized of late.

Average Firm Size

If we were to look only at the standard data from the Census of Manufacturing (column 3 of table 4.2), we would come away with the clear impression that average establishment size fell steadily until the boom of 1992 to 1997. And the same pattern holds in both the durable and nondurable subsectors (although they are not shown separately). Downsizing in manufacturing thus would look like a continuation of an old pattern. But the Enterprise Statistics on *establishments,* summarized in column 2, paint a more nuanced and equivocal picture. There apparently was mostly downsizing from 1972 until 1992, although the period 1982 to 1987 was an exception. Furthermore, it appears that upsizing was the norm before either 1967 or 1972.[5] More important, the firm-level data in column 1 tell us that manufacturing *firms* were actually *upsizing* most of the time from 1958 to 1967, and downsizing thereafter. Interestingly, the year 1967—which appears to be when the dominant tendency switched from upsizing to downsizing—was precisely when the Census of Manufacturing (column 3) turned the lights on. Without access to the Enterprise Statistics, it would have been natural to assume from looking only at the census data that downsizing had always been the norm. But it was not.

Hence, it appears that downsizing of both firms and establishments in manufacturing has been the rule since about 1967, but not before. Given the extraordinary growth that U.S. manufacturing enjoyed over the period 1992 to 1997, it may be premature to declare that this trend is over. But the Census of Manufacturing data suggest that it has at least been interrupted.

Moving from total manufacturing down to the more detailed two-digit industry level, the data reveal considerable diversity. There are twenty two-digit manufacturing industries: ten in durables and ten in nondurables. While we know from table 4.2 that average firm size in the whole manufacturing sector fell in every five-year period after

Table 4.2   Average Employment per Firm and per Establishment—Manufacturing, 1958 to 1997

Year	(1) Firms (Enterprise Statistics)	(2) Establishments (Enterprise Statistics)	(3) Establishments (Census of Manufacturing)
1958	65.5	46.2	NA
1963	72.6	48.4	NA
1967	92.6	NA	60.5
1972	86.4	49.5	57.7
1977	83.5	48.6	52.8
1982	79.1	45.8	51.1
1987	74.0	47.0	49.4
1992	65.8	43.5	45.7
1997	NA	NA	46.7

Source: Authors' calculations from U.S. Bureau of the Census (various years).
Note: NA = Not available.

1967, table 4.3 shows us that there were always some upsizing industries. The diversity of performance is enormous.

It is not easy to summarize such diverse patterns. With eight time periods and twenty industries, we have 140 observations on *changes* in firm size in table 4.3. Of these, seventy-five observations exhibit upsizing and sixty-five exhibit downsizing—a slender majority for upsizing. But note that downsizing became the rule in the period 1987 to 1992: average firm size fell in seventeen of the twenty industries. If we use establishment data (not shown tabularly) instead, downsizing appears to be more common than upsizing. And as table 4.2 leads us to expect, downsizing is even more common in data from the Census of Manufacturing (which begin only in 1967).

Table 4.4 is a capsule summary of the data in and underlying tables 4.2 and 4.3. The first column is derived from table 4.2: it shows the percentage change in average firm or establishment size for the entire manufacturing sector. Columns 2 and 3 tabulate the number of upsizing and downsizing industries (out of twenty) in each time period, based on the data in table 4.3 for firms (and additional unreported tabulations for establishments.) Both the firm-level and establishment-level data generally show average size shrinking (rising) during times when more industries were downsizing (upsizing). But there are some exceptions. For example, average firm size fell between 1967 and 1972 even though thirteen of the twenty sectors were upsizing.

In general, this table points to more upsizing in the years prior to 1972 and more downsizing since then (again, with some exceptions). The period from 1987 to 1992 appears to exhibit the strongest down-

Table 4.3 Average Employment per Firm, by Manufacturing Industry, 1958 to 1992

EIC	Industry	1958	1963	1967	1972	1977	1982	1987	1992
20	Food and kindred products	55.1	63.2	74.4	102.2	117.6	150.7	126.3	125.5
21	Tobacco products	308.8	433.5	606.6	792.5	899.4	1969.3	2311.2	2150.5
22	Textile mill products	147.2	155.9	179.3	186.7	178.3	159.9	165.6	149.6
23	Apparel and textiles	31.9	51.3	58.2	63.9	58.3	55.3	53.9	49.0
24	Lumber and wood products	16.2	16.8	15.8	22.8	23.0	18.1	21.9	18.7
25	Furniture and fixtures	32.3	39.6	47.7	54.6	53.3	52.3	57.4	50.5
26	Paper and allied products	149.7	167.3	197.4	221.5	212.8	184.1	199.1	208.6
27	Printing and publishing	26.5	28.0	32.9	31.2	31.1	32.5	32.9	30.1
28	Chemicals and allied products	109.6	130.9	150.0	180.2	180.8	176.8	163.2	180.1
29	Petroleum and coal products	544.9	534.9	594.6	502.7	499.3	721.4	446.1	404.1
30	Rubber and plastics	101.8	95.5	113.7	98.4	89.9	65.6	73.3	73.6
31	Leather and leather products	90.2	105.1	129.1	148.3	162.7	95.6	55.2	48.4
32	Stone, glass, clay products	49.0	48.6	50.1	59.4	56.1	57.1	54.0	49.0
33	Primary metal industries	131.0	263.1	292.8	298.2	275.8	220.1	169.2	165.7
34	Fabricated metal industries	46.6	47.2	53.7	55.0	51.6	46.9	45.4	43.3
35	Industrial machinery	53.5	57.5	60.7	56.3	58.9	57.1	46.7	40.7
36	Electronics and related products	207.0	246.7	311.8	238.7	121.5	202.4	133.7	106.3
37	Transportation equipment	353.3	383.5	471.7	481.5	357.3	315.5	378.7	196.0
38	Instruments and related products	82.2	102.5	134.2	111.6	119.9	96.3	175.1	106.9
39	Miscellaneous manufacturing	31.7	33.6	45.8	33.2	30.8	28.3	24.8	24.0
	All manufacturing industries	65.5	72.6	92.6	86.4	83.5	79.1	74.0	65.8

Source: Authors' compilation.

Table 4.4   Changes in Firm and Establishment Size, by Census Period, 1958 to 1992

Period	Change in Average Size	Number Downsizing	Number Upsizing
A. Manufacturing Firms			
1958–1963	10.8%	3	17
1963–1967	27.6	1	19
1967–1972	−6.7	7	13
1972–1977	−3.3	13	7
1977–1982	−5.3	14	6
1982–1987	−6.5	10	10
1987–1992	−11.0	17	3
Total	+0.5	65	75
B. Manufacturing Establishments			
1958–1963	4.6	6	14
1963–1972	2.3	10	10
1972–1977	−1.9	14	6
1977–1982	−5.6	14	6
1982–1987	2.6	9	11
1987–1992	−7.5	15	5
Total	−5.9	68	52

Source: Authors' calculations from U.S. Bureau of the Census, Enterprise Statistics (1958 to 1992).

sizing tendencies; that conclusion is in line with press accounts. Amazingly, average *firm* size winds up almost exactly the same in 1992 as it was in 1958. (Average *establishment* size shrinks by about 6 percent.)

Stochastic Dominance

The stochastic dominance criterion is a sterner test and produces a great many ambiguous cases in which we cannot say whether the industry downsized or upsized. It is also a far more complicated criterion, and we must say a little more about its application to this data set.

The general definition holds that random variable B stochastically dominates random variable A if the cumulative distribution function of B lies entirely to the right of that of A (see figure 4.1).[6] To indicate what that means in less technical terms, we can use a simplified and analogous example. Suppose we are testing whether one group of women, group A, is generally taller than another, group B. Then we say that the height of group A women *stochastically dominates* that of group B women if the average height of the shortest 10 percent of women in A is greater than that in B, the average height of the short-

Figure 4.1   Illustration of Stochastic Dominance

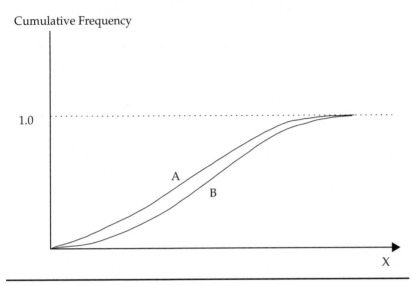

Source: Authors' configuration.

est 20 percent of women in A is greater than that in B, and so on. We end up with the average height calculation for 100 percent of the women in each of the groups.

Looking at the data in table 4.5, we see that the stochastic dominance criterion tells a story that is somewhat similar to the average-size criterion—albeit with many ambiguous cases. Over the years 1958 to 1972, instances of upsizing (twenty-seven) were decidedly more common than instances of downsizing (five) within the manufacturing sector. But this pattern seemed to reverse subsequently, with downsizing (seventeen industries) notably more common than upsizing (eight) over the years 1972 to 1992. The one exception was the boom period of 1982 to 1987, when upsizing was again the prevailing pattern.[7] The only big downsizing periods, according to table 4.5, were 1972 to 1977 and 1987 to 1992. This assessment roughly agrees with table 4.4's results using average firm size.

What about establishment-level data? Table 4.6 displays identical tabulations of stochastic dominance relations for establishments. Looking at the data very roughly, the overall margin of upsizing over downsizing is similar, and we find once again that more upsizing occurred in earlier periods and more downsizing later. The periods 1972 to 1977 and 1987 to 1992 again stand out as times during which

Table 4.5   Upsizing or Downsizing? Manufacturing Firms, by Stochastic Dominance Criterion, 1958 to 1992

Period	Upsizing Industries	Downsizing Industries	Ambiguous
1958–1963	9	2	9
1963–1967	12	1	7
1967–1972	6	2	12
1972–1977	0	7	13
1977–1982	1	1	18
1982–1987	7	1	12
1987–1992	0	8	12
Total	35	22	83

Source: Authors' compilation.

downsizing was unusually prevalent—just as they did with firm-level data. However, the boom period 1982 to 1987 now shows up as a *downsizing* period, which was not true of the firm data in table 4.5. We suspect that this discrepancy once again reinforces the advisability of concentrating on firm-level data.

Analysis of Retail-Sector Data

Manufacturing garners more than its share of the headlines, and it certainly commands more than its share of the government's statistical efforts. But we must remember that only about one American employee in seven works for a manufacturing company. In 1992 service firms employed 29.1 million workers and retailers employed 19.4 mil-

Table 4.6   Upsizing or Downsizing? Manufacturing Establishments, by Stochastic Dominance Criterion, 1958 to 1992

Period	Upsizing Industries	Downsizing Industries	Ambiguous
1958–1963	12	2	6
1963–1972	19	0	1
1972–1977	4	8	8
1977–1982	7	2	11
1982–1987	3	10	7
1987–1992	0	11	9
Total	45	33	42

Source: Authors' compilation.

ure 4.2   Gross Employment, by Industry

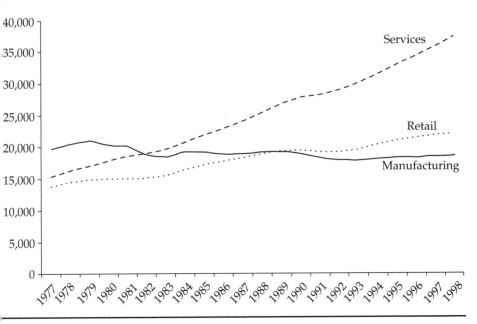

rce: U.S. Department of Labor, Bureau of Labor Statistics.

lion. Thus, each of these sectors was already larger than manufacturing, which employed just 18.1 million. And the gaps have widened
dramatically since then. According to the U.S. Bureau of Labor Statistics data on nonagricultural payrolls, manufacturing employment
grew just 1.8 percent between 1992 and 2000, despite the unprecedented boom. In contrast, retail employment expanded 19.5 percent
and service-sector employment soared 39 percent (see figure 4.2).

It may therefore prove to be a serious mistake to draw general
conclusions from data on the manufacturing sector alone. As we will
see now, data from the retail sector tell a very different story: the
overwhelmingly predominant pattern in both retailing and services is
upsizing rather than downsizing.

In sharp contrast to the data from the service sector, which we will
study in the next section, the definitions of the eight main retail industries used in the Enterprise Statistics have been almost unchanged
since 1958. With seven time periods in our data set once again, we
have fifty-six observations in all. Were retailers downsizing or upsizing?

Table 4.7   Average Employment per Retail Firm and Establishment, 1958 to 1992

Year	By Firm	By Establishment
1958	7.8	6.8
1963	8.0	6.9
1967	10.1	NA
1972	12.1	9.6
1977	13.6	10.6
1982	15.7	11.5
1987	19.4	13.6
1992	19.9	13.6

Source: Authors' calculations from U.S. Bureau of the Census, Enterprise Statistics (1958 to 1992).

Firm-Based Data

Table 4.7 shows that average firm size in retailing rose steadily and without interruption between the 1958 and 1992 censuses—increasing 155 percent in total. Average establishment size also rose (approximately) in each census period, although by less (just 100 percent). Thus, the number of establishments per firm was generally rising.

When we look at the two-digit industry level, table 4.8 shows that average firm size rose in all eight retail industries in four census periods: 1963 to 1967, 1967 to 1972, 1977 to 1982, and 1982 to 1987. From 1987 to 1992, average firm size increased in six of eight sectors and decreased in two, as was the case from 1972 to 1977. In only one period, 1958 to 1963, was downsizing the predominant pattern (five out of eight industries). Overall, when downsizing is appraised by average firm size, we see evidence of downsizing in only nine of fifty-six cases, and upsizing in forty-seven. The recent picture—25 percent of retail industries downsizing from 1987 to 1992—is not much different from the historically average pattern.

Once we set aside the ambiguous cases (twenty-three out of fifty-six), the more complicated stochastic dominance criterion tells an even cleaner story (see table 4.9). In five of the seven time periods, not a single retail industry unambiguously downsized; in the other two time periods, only one did. Overall, the table shows thirty-one cases in which the stochastic dominance relationship declares upsizing, only two cases of downsizing, and twenty-three instances in which the cumulative distribution functions crossed. Unfortunately, we cannot say much about the most recent period (1987 to 1992) because seven of the eight industries give ambiguous readings.

Table 4.8 Average Employment per Firm, by Retail Industry, 1958 to 1992

SIC	Industry	1958	1963	1967	1972	1977	1982	1987	1992
52	Building materials and garden supply	6.3	6.0	6.9	8.0	8.7	9.5	15.8	13.2
53	General merchandise stores	30.9	40.6	52.8	114.5	155.8	176.2	226.5	254.3
54	Food stores	8.1	9.5	12.7	16.7	18.6	23.2	26.3	28.5
55	Automotive dealers	5.7	5.5	6.8	7.5	8.4	9.7	13.3	14.1
56	Apparel and accessory stores	8.6	8.2	9.7	10.4	11.5	12.3	16.6	21.9
57	Furniture and home furnishings	6.2	5.6	7.2	7.5	7.0	7.8	9.7	10.2
58	Eating and drinking places	6.2	6.7	8.9	11.1	14.9	19.0	24.3	23.4
59	Miscellaneous retail stores	5.4	5.1	6.4	7.8	7.7	8.3	9.6	9.9

Source: Authors' calculations from U.S. Bureau of the Census, Enterprise Statistics (1958 to 1992).

Table 4.9   Upsizing or Downsizing? Retail Firms, by Stochastic
             Dominance Criterion, 1958 to 1992

Period	Upsizing Industries	Downsizing Industries	Ambiguous
1958–1963	2	1	5
1963–1967	7	0	1
1967–1972	6	0	2
1972–1977	3	1	4
1977–1982	6	0	2
1982–1987	6	0	2
1987–1992	1	0	7
Total	31	2	23

Source: Authors' compilation.

Establishment-Level Data

We know from table 4.7 that the typical firm grew faster from 1958 to 1992 than the typical establishment. Together, these facts suggest that firms "upsized" partly by adding more establishments. If so, we could conclude that there has been a stronger upsizing trend at the firm level than at the establishment level. This conclusion can be false only if many large firms broke up into smaller ones even as establishments grew larger. The data support the inference that there has been somewhat less upsizing of establishments than of firms.

As table 4.10 shows, average establishment size generally increased in retailing, except for the period 1958 to 1963, when five of the eight retail industries downsized. Over two time periods, 1963 to 1972 and 1982 to 1987, all eight sectors increased their average establishment size. And in the other three periods, six out of eight did so. Thus, in total, thirty-seven of the forty-eight cases exhibited upsizing and eight exhibited downsizing.

It is ironic that, despite a substantial number of cases of crossing distribution functions (seventeen out of forty-eight), the stochastic dominance criterion once again tells an even clearer tale of upsizing than the average-size criterion (see table 4.11). There is not a single case of downsizing among the thirty-one unambiguous cases; every one displays upsizing. The prevalence of downsizing in the latest period (1987 to 1992) once again looks rather similar to that of earlier periods.

Analysis of Service-Sector Data

The analysis is, regrettably, more complicated in the service sector because industrial definitions have changed more over time than in

Table 4.10 Average Employment per Establishment, by Retail Industry, 1958 to 1992

EIC	Industry	1958	1963	1972	1977	1982	1987	1992
52	Building materials and garden supply	5.6	5.3	6.7	7.3	7.9	12.5	10.3
53	General merchandise stores	22.1	25.2	39.5	44.8	41.5	48.7	52.8
54	Food stores	6.8	7.7	11.5	12.6	14.7	17.2	18.8
55	Automotive dealers	5.3	5.1	6.8	7.3	8.1	10.5	10.6
56	Apparel and accessory stores	6.6	6.2	7.2	7.7	7.3	8.4	9.2
57	Furniture and home furnishings	5.4	4.9	6.1	5.7	6.0	7.16	7.19
58	Eating and drinking places	5.7	6.2	9.7	12.4	15.1	17.8	17.1
59	Miscellaneous retail stores	4.8	4.4	6.21	6.17	6.5	7.3	7.4

Source: Authors' calculations from U.S. Bureau of the Census, Enterprise Statistics.

retailing. Our basic procedure was to use as a data point any industry whose definition remained essentially unchanged between any two consecutive censuses (say, 1982 and 1987), rather than insisting on full comparability across all eight censuses, which would have limited us to just seven industries. This decision left us with a different number

Table 4.11 Upsizing or Downsizing? Retail Establishments, by Stochastic Dominance Criterion, 1958 to 1992

Period	Upsizing Industries	Downsizing Industries	Ambiguous
1958–1963	4	0	4
1963–1972	6	0	2
1972–1977	5	0	3
1977–1982	8	0	0
1982–1987	4	0	4
1987–1992	4	0	4
Total	31	0	17

Source: Authors' compilation.

Table 4.12   Upsizing or Downsizing? Service Firms, by Average Firm Size, 1958 to 1992

Period	Upsizing Industries	Downsizing Industries
1958–1963	7	0
1963–1967	7	0
1967–1972	5	5
1972–1977	8	2
1977–1982	8	1
1982–1987	11	1
1987–1992	9	3
Total	55	12

Source: Authors' compilation.

of comparable industries in each time period: seven from 1958 to 1967,[8] ten for 1967 to 1977,[9] only nine from 1977 to 1982, and twelve for 1982 to 1992.[10] For this reason, disaggregated tables comparable to tables 4.3 and 4.8 are not presented for the service sector.

Firm-Based Data

The basic story here is similar to that of retailing, although a bit more equivocal: upsizing is, once again, the predominant pattern. Specifically, the number of service industries that increased or decreased their average firm size is as shown in table 4.12. In sum, we find that average firm size increased in fifty-five of the sixty-seven usable cases, with barely any tendency for the trend toward bigger firms to weaken in the most recent period.

Using the more complicated stochastic dominance criterion (table 4.13), the pattern is similar except that we now encounter a large number of ambiguous cases where distribution functions cross. Of the thirty-four unambiguous cases, thirty-two exhibit upsizing and only two (both in the 1987 to 1992 period) exhibit downsizing. The rest are ambiguous.

Establishment-Level Data

Just as in retailing, upsizing remains the clearly predominant pattern when we move from firm-level data to establishment-level data. Using average establishment size as the criterion, the results are even more lopsided than they were using firm-level data (see table 4.14). Under the stochastic dominance criterion, which again leaves many cases

Table 4.13   Upsizing or Downsizing? Service Firms, by Stochastic
Dominance Criterion, 1958 to 1992

Period	Upsizing Industries	Downsizing Industries	Ambiguous
1958–1963	4	0	3
1963–1967	5	0	2
1967–1972	4	0	6
1972–1977	4	0	6
1977–1982	5	0	4
1982–1987	6	2	4
1987–1992	4	0	8
Total	32	2	33

Source: Authors' compilation.

ambiguous, we get the breakdown detailed in table 4.15. Here, just as
in retailing, upsizing is by far the predominant pattern in the unambiguous cases.

Other Sectors

We also have data, though much spottier, from the Enterprise Statistics for industries in four other major sectors: wholesale trade (two industries), mining (four industries), construction (four industries, but starting only in 1972), and the transportation, communications, and utilities (TCU) aggregate (very spotty coverage), in which the data pertain mostly to transportation.[11] What do we learn from data on these sectors?

Table 4.14   Upsizing or Downsizing? Service Establishments, by Average
Establishment Size, 1958 to 1992

Period	Upsizing Industries	Downsizing Industries
1958–1963	6	1
1963–1972	7	0
1972–1977	8	2
1977–1982	9	0
1982–1987	8	1
1987–1992	9	2
Total	47	6

Source: Authors' compilation.

**Table 4.15   Upsizing or Downsizing? Service Establishments, by
Stochastic Dominance Criterion, 1958 to 1992**

Period	Upsizing Industries	Downsizing Industries	Ambiguous
1958–1963	5	0	2
1963–1972	5	3	2
1972–1977	5	0	5
1977–1982	5	0	4
1982–1987	6	1	5
1987–1992	5	0	6
Total	31	4	24

Source: Authors' compilation.

Merchant Wholesalers

Within the merchant wholesaling sector, we can obtain data on one industry (durable goods) continuously for every census period since 1958, and for one other industry (nondurable goods) since 1972. This gives us eleven observations in all on *changes* in the firm-level data, and ten in the establishment-level data. Table 4.16 summarizes the results very succinctly, ignoring the period-by-period breakdowns that we investigated for the larger sectors.

The average size of both firms and establishments in wholesale trade rose between 1958 and 1992, but not monotonically. Both declined from 1958 to 1963 and from 1987 to 1992. (Firm size also declined slightly from 1967 to 1972.) Thus, upsizing is the norm but not the rule, and there are many ambiguous cases. That, more or less, is also the message we obtain from the stochastic dominance criterion.

Table 4.16   Upsizing or Downsizing in Merchant Wholesaling

Data Type	Criterion	Upsizing Industries	Downsizing Industries	Ambiguous
Firms	Average size	8	3	0
Firms	Stochastic dominance	4	2	5
Establishments	Average size	8	2	0
Establishments	Stochastic dominance	3	0	7

Source: Authors' compilation.

Table 4.17   Upsizing or Downsizing in Construction

Data Type	Criterion	Upsizing Industries	Downsizing Industries	Ambiguous
Firms	Average size	8	7	0
Firms	Stochastic dominance	1	3	11
Establishments	Average size	6	6	0
Establishments	Stochastic dominance	0	4	8

Source: Authors' compilation.

Construction

Within construction, we can track three industries (general building contractors, heavy construction, and special trade contractors) over each of the five censuses since 1967—a total of fifteen observations on changes.[12] Average firm and establishment size bounce up and down in this sector, but both are lower at the end than at the beginning. Thus, at least in this weak sense, construction was downsizing—although, strikingly, not during the critical 1987 to 1992 period. Table 4.17 summarizes the industry-by-industry evidence in the same abbreviated form as in table 4.16. Although mostly ambiguous because of crossing distribution functions, the stochastic dominance criterion points toward downsizing rather than upsizing. The average-size criterion detects about equal numbers of cases of upsizing and downsizing.

Mining

For the mining sector, there exist surprising amounts of detailed data, even though the sector constitutes a tiny share of the overall U.S. economy. We can track four different mining industries (metal, coal, oil and gas, and nonmetallic minerals) from 1958 right up to 1992. For the sector as a whole, average firm and establishment size fell from 1958 to 1963, and then started to rise, peaking in 1977. The recession that occurred in the 1977 to 1982 period sharply reduced the average size of both firms and establishments, but they subsequently began to rise again. On balance, mining *firms* are much larger and mining *establishments* are slightly larger in 1992 than in 1958.

Should we then consider mining an upsizing sector? Perhaps not. Table 4.18 offers the same overview of the industry-by-industry data as in the previous two tables. It shows that mining industries upsized and downsized roughly 50 percent of the time.

Table 4.18   Upsizing or Downsizing in Mining

Data Type	Criterion	Upsizing Industries	Downsizing Industries	Ambiguous
Firms	Average size	15	13	0
Firms	Stochastic dominance	5	3	20
Establishments	Average size	12	12	0
Establishments	Stochastic dominance	5	3	16

Source: Authors' compilation.

Transportation, Communications, and Utilities

The final sector, an amalgam of transportation, communications, and utilities, offers only very spotty data—mostly from transportation industries. For completeness, we display the usual tabulations in table 4.19. There is no clear pattern of either downsizing or upsizing.

In sum, the general pattern of downsizing (with some exceptions) since 1972 that we encountered in manufacturing seems not to be replicated in any other sector of the U.S. economy. Upsizing is overwhelmingly the pattern in retail trade, wholesale trade, and services, and the other sectors are quite mixed.

The View from the Compustat Data

We turn next to a rather different source of firm-level data, Standard & Poor's Compustat file. Compustat data differ from the census data in a number of ways. Most fundamentally, Compustat is a sample; it is not a complete census of all the firms in an industry at a point in

Table 4.19   Upsizing or Downsizing in TCU

Data Type	Criterion	Upsizing Industries	Downsizing Industries	Ambiguous
Firms	Average size	4	3	0
Firms	Stochastic dominance	2	0	5
Establishments	Average size	2	3	0
Establishments	Stochastic dominance	0	0	5

Source: Authors' compilation.

time. More important for our purposes, this sample is far from representative; it consists primarily of the largest firms in each industry.
The Compustat file is also a quasi-panel, which follows the same
firms over time but sometimes adds new firms and omits old ones.
For example, when firms merge (or join through acquisition), or when
a firm splits up, the sample will include the new entities formed in
place of the previous organization. In the tabulations that follow, we
do not correct for such mergers or breakups.

Despite these disadvantages, the Compustat data permit us to look
at a wide variety of industries and to see what happened after 1992.
Table 4.20 shows the two-digit industries we selected for analysis. The
selection was based mainly on the number of firms that Compustat
included in the sample. Specifically, we tabulated data only for industries with an average of at least fifteen firms over the period of analysis, 1978 to 1997. The number fifteen was an arbitrary choice: it is
low enough so that we did not exclude too many industries, but high
enough so that we could hope to get reasonable estimates of the average number of employees and the size distribution of firms over time.

Although the Compustat database in principle covers the entire
economy, the actual sample of firms is heavily weighted toward manufacturing, trade, and finance and insurance.[13] However, a few industries are also available in the mining, construction, transportation,
communications, utilities, and service sectors. In the table, we have
somewhat arbitrarily divided the industries into four sectors: manufacturing; trade; finance, insurance, and services; and miscellaneous.

Although Compustat offers annual data, we selected just five years—
1978,[14] 1982, 1987, 1992, and 1997—to correspond to the years of the
industrial censuses. Despite these limitations, the results are illuminating and provide additional details on changes in firm size over
time. We first consider the simpler average firm size criterion (table
4.21).

As in the census data, manufacturing appears to be somewhat
of an outlier in terms of changes in firm size. Downsizing is clearly
the dominant pattern in manufacturing, occurring in more than two-
thirds of the cases, with upsizing occurring in the rest. As with the
Enterprise Statistics on manufacturing, the relative number of downsizers is greater in the periods 1978 to 1982 and 1987 to 1992, although
the differences are not marked.

Among industries in wholesale and retail trade, upsizing is the
predominant trend, though not by as lopsided a margin as in the
census data. (Remember, these are much larger firms, on average.)
And the tendency to upsize seems to become stronger over time, particularly in the most recent period, 1992 to 1997. For industries in

Table 4.20   Average Firm Size by Industry, Compustat Data, 1978 to 1997

SIC	Industry	Average Employment per Firm					Average Number of Firms[a]
		1978	1982	1987	1992	1997	
Manufacturing industries							
20	Food and kindred products	20.8	32.6	36.9	34.0	24.2	46.6
22	Textile mill products	7.4	6.1	6.5	6.3	7.3	24.2
23	Apparel and other textile products	7.4	6.7	7.6	6.3	6.2	21.2
25	Furniture and fixtures	8.9	9.2	9.6	7.3	12.9	15.6
26	Paper and allied products	15.7	13.6	13.6	13.8	12.9	35.4
27	Printing and publishing	6.6	7.5	9.0	9.0	10.8	37.8
28	Chemicals and allied products	21.9	19.3	14.6	12.5	12.3	106.6
29	Petroleum and coal products	42.4	47.3	35.4	27.4	22.9	31.6
30	Rubber and plastics	12.6	10.0	8.3	6.9	6.6	24.8
32	Stone, glass, clay products	15.0	11.7	8.9	8.2	6.7	18.0
33	Primary metal industries	24.2	14.7	12.3	10.2	7.8	44.8
34	Fabricated metal products	7.6	7.2	7.0	5.5	6.5	41.6
35	Industrial machinery and equipment	15.1	13.7	12.1	12.8	11.6	109.0
36	Electrical and electronic equipment	24.4	22.2	20.3	17.8	16.7	103.6
37	Transportation equipment	87.6	70.7	75.1	64.7	49.6	55.8
38	Instruments and related products	18.1	16.4	14.2	10.7	11.3	57.4
39	Miscellaneous manufacturing	2.9	3.1	2.7	3.0	3.1	19.2
Wholesale and retail trade							
50	Wholesale trade— durables	5.8	4.5	4.1	3.6	5.2	37.6
51	Wholesale trade— nondurables	8.5	7.1	7.2	7.0	9.2	24.6
53	General merchandise stores	87.2	91.6	95.7	88.4	98.8	19.0

Table 4.20 *Continued*

SIC	Industry	Average Employment per Firm					Average Number of Firms[a]
		1978	1982	1987	1992	1997	
54	Food stores	33.6	37.5	43.4	50.3	60.1	17.2
56	Apparel and accessory stores	35.8	23.7	25.0	28.5	29.6	11.8
58	Eating and drinking places	17.2	17.2	18.1	18.6	42.0	21.0
59	Miscellaneous retail	9.5	12.5	11.6	13.1	14.3	25.2
Finance, insurance, and services							
60	Depository institutions	5.7	8.2	9.4	9.9	14.3	93.8
61	Nondepository credit institutions	13.2	18.6	12.6	9.6	6.6	13.4
62	Security, commodity brokers, and services	5.9	6.4	4.0	4.6	8.6	22.6
63	Insurance carriers	14.2	12.6	9.2	7.2	5.2	77.0
65	Real estate	1.3	0.8	0.7	1.0	1.6	17.2
67	Holding and other investment offices	1.5	0.6	0.4	0.1	2.7	29.6
73	Business services	11.7	10.1	12.2	11.9	10.1	67.0
79	Amusement and recreational services	0.8	1.5	2.2	4.3	7.9	16.4
80	Health services	6.0	19.0	13.3	11.2	23.3	20.8
87	Engineering and management services	7.6	8.1	5.7	4.7	5.7	18.6
Miscellaneous industries							
13	Oil and gas extraction	8.4	8.4	4.4	3.1	3.2	59.0
15	General building contractors	3.3	2.2	1.8	1.1	1.5	21.0
45	Transportation by air	16.4	18.0	31.8	41.4	28.5	15.2
48	Communications	82.2	70.8	48.4	35.5	24.0	39.0
49	Electric, gas, and sanitary services	4.2	4.7	5.3	5.4	4.5	188.0

Source: Authors' calculations from Compustat files (1978, 1982, 1987, 1992, and 1997).
[a]Average number of firms in the industry over the five years.

Table 4.21   Upsizing or Downsizing? Compustat Firms, by Average Firm Size, 1978 to 1997

Period	Upsizing Industries	Downsizing Industries
Manufacturing		
1978–1982	5	12
1982–1987	6	10
1987–1992	4	13
1992–1997	6	11
Total	21	46
Wholesale and retail trade		
1978–1982	3	4
1982–1987	5	2
1987–1992	4	3
1992–1997	7	0
Total	19	9
Finance, insurance, and services		
1978–1982	6	4
1982–1987	3	7
1987–1992	4	6
1992–1997	7	3
Total	20	20
Miscellaneous industries		
1978–1982	2	2
1982–1987	2	3
1987–1992	2	3
1992–1997	2	3
Total	8	11

Source: Authors' calculations from Compustat files (1978, 1982, 1987, 1992, and 1997).
Note: Industries in which average firm size changes by less than 0.1 percent are excluded from the tabulation.

finance, insurance, and services, the upsizers and downsizers are evenly split, and there is no clear trend over time. Among the other industries—spanning mining, construction, transportation, communications, and utilities—downsizing has a slight edge over upsizing.

When the stochastic dominance criterion is employed to measure downsizing or upsizing, the results are quite similar, although with the usual greater number of ambiguous cases, as before (see table 4.22). The downsizers greatly outnumber the upsizers in both manufacturing and among miscellaneous industries. But both wholesale and retail trade and finance, insurance, and services are pretty evenly

Table 4.22   Upsizing or Downsizing? Compustat Firms, by Stochastic
Dominance Criterion, 1978 to 1997

Period	Upsizing Industries	Downsizing Industries	Ambiguous
Manufacturing			
1978–1982	0	6	11
1982–1987	0	2	15
1987–1992	0	1	16
1992–1997	2	1	14
Total	2	10	56
Wholesale and retail trade			
1978–1982	1	1	5
1982–1987	0	1	6
1987–1992	1	1	5
1992–1997	2	0	5
Total	4	3	21
Finance, insurance, and services			
1978–1982	1	3	6
1982–1987	1	2	7
1987–1992	2	1	7
1992–1997	1	0	9
Total	5	6	29
Miscellaneous industries			
1978–1982	1	1	3
1982–1987	0	1	4
1987–1992	0	4	1
1992–1997	0	2	3
Total	1	8	11

Source: Authors' compilation.

split between upsizers and downsizers. In sum, the stories that
emerge from the two data sources are quite consistent.

A Truly Naive Interpretation

At the risk of doing some injustice to the richer detail already provided, we can summarize the findings in three simple statements:

1. Downsizing is not a new phenomenon in American manufactur-
    ing. It appears to have been going on since about 1967, although
    it did seem to intensify a bit in the period 1987 to 1992.

2. Manufacturing is not typical of the U.S. economy. In the trade and service sectors, the predominant tendency over the last thirty to forty years has been toward upsizing rather than downsizing. However, this trend may have weakened a bit in the prime downsizing period, 1987 to 1992.

3. In other major sectors of the economy (construction, mining, transportation), there is no systematic trend toward either upsizing or downsizing.

Thus, we seem to have something of a puzzle. Why should the behavior of manufacturing industries be so radically different from that of the other sectors? In particular, what economic forces could have induced the typical manufacturing industry to downsize while the typical retail or service industry was upsizing?

One possible explanation may lie in the technological changes that we discussed in chapter 3. If technical change shifts the minimum point of the average cost curve leftward for manufacturers but rightward for retailers and service businesses, then manufacturing industries would downsize while the others upsized. But why should this be so? One possibility is computerization, which has had profound influences throughout the economy.

A plausible story is the suggestion that new computer technology may have induced manufacturing establishments to shrink and retail and service establishments to grow. The story starts by noting that the typical establishment is far larger in manufacturing than in either retailing or services. Computerization may enable old-line manufacturers to customize their outputs more than has been possible historically with mass-production assembly lines. In the process of adjusting to the new technology, the typical manufacturing establishment may therefore tend to grow smaller. On the other hand, very small retail and service establishments may have to become larger in order to avail themselves of the benefits of computer technology. The implication is that we should observe regression toward the mean: large firms should grow smaller while small firms should grow larger (see figure 4.3).

Is it true? As we will see in chapter 5, there is evidence for regression toward the mean in many manufacturing industries: both the upper and lower tails seem to have shrunk relative to the middle of the size distribution, as shown in figure 4.3. But in retailing and services, the evidence rejects regression toward the mean in favor of straight upsizing—the density function often appears to shift to the right, as in figure 4.4. So we will not consider this idea further in this

Figure 4.3   Regression Toward the Mean

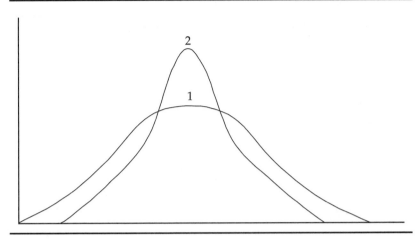

Source: Authors' configuration.

chapter. (We return to it in discussing manufacturing in chapter 5.) Instead, let us first explore an embarrassingly simple explanation for the difference in behavior patterns between manufacturing and retailing and services. One obvious difference is that manufacturing has been shrinking (in terms of employment) since about 1967—not just relatively, but in most years absolutely—while retailing and services

Figure 4.4   Upsizing

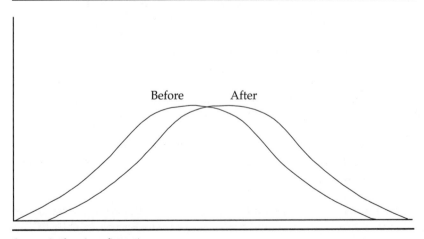

Source: Authors' configuration.

Table 4.23   Growth of U.S. Payroll Employment in Three Major Sectors, 1958 to 1992

Period	Manufacturing	Retail	Services
1958–1963	6.6%	9.8%	22.4%
1963–1967	15.4	18.5	25.9
1967–1972	−1.5	19.3	22.2
1972–1977	2.8	16.7	24.7
1977–1982	−4.6	9.9	24.3
1982–1987	1.1	21.5	26.7
1987–1992	−4.7	5.1	20.5
1992–1997	3.1	13.5	24.1
1958–1997	17.1	183.1	432.7
1967–1992	−6.9	95.4	189.2

Source: U.S. Department of Labor, Bureau of Labor Statistics (1958 to 1997).

have been expanding rapidly. For example, the upper parts of table 4.23 shows the Bureau of Labor Statistics five-year (not annualized) growth rates of payroll employment in the three major sectors.

On balance, manufacturing employment fell slightly over the twenty-five-year period 1967 to 1992, while employment in retailing and services surged. These long-run trends are driven by both shifting demand patterns (especially toward services) and differential productivity growth (higher in manufacturing). These numbers also remind us that the business cycle is quite pronounced in manufacturing and retailing, but modest in services. (The cycle is apparent if you think of 1982 and 1992 as trough years and 1967, 1987, and 1997 as peaks.) Both facts bear on the distinctiveness of manufacturing.

It is true by definition that $E \equiv S \times N$, where E is total employment in an industry, S is average firm (or establishment) size, and N is the number of firms (or establishments). When an industry is expanding, whether secularly or cyclically, it must be adding new business units (firms or establishments) and/or increasing average firm or establishment size. Normally, it can be expected to do both. To the extent that S rises, we conclude the industry is upsizing. But when total employment falls, whether because of secular shrinkage or a cyclical downturn, we can expect both N and S to fall. In a cyclical downturn, the industry would be labeled a downsizer. Hence our embarrassingly simple hypothesis is:

Shrinking industries (as measured by total employment) downsize (as measured by average firm or establishment size), while expanding industries upsize.

For this reason alone, we would expect to find much more downsizing in manufacturing than elsewhere.

Is the hypothesis true? Figure 4.5, which offers a bird's-eye view of the firm-level data, suggests an affirmative answer. Each point in the six scatter diagrams represents *changes* in a particular manufacturing, retail, or service industry between one census year and the next. Thus, a typical point records, for example, the changes in the transportation equipment industry from 1977 to 1982.

The uppermost panel of each page displays the simple correlations between e = the change in (the log of) employment and either s = the change in (the log of) average firm size (left-hand panel) or n = the change in the (log of the) number of firms (right-hand panel) over all 140 observations that we have for manufacturing industries (twenty industries, seven time periods). The two center panels do the same for retailing (fifty-six observations), and the two lower panels repeat the same information for the service industries for which we have data (sixty-seven observations). What do these scatters show us?

In general, the three panels on page 124 demonstrate that changes in the log of firm size (s) correlate rather well with changes in the log of total employment (e). The simple correlations are 0.85 in manufacturing, 0.59 in retailing, and 0.70 in services. The three panels on page 125 offer the same scatter plots for changes in the log of the number of firms (n) versus changes in the log of total industry employment (e). Although the correlations are all clearly positive, they are substantially smaller in manufacturing (just 0.24) and retailing (0.32) and trivially smaller in services (0.66). It can hardly be surprising that all six correlations are positive. Growing industries tend to upsize and to add new firms, while shrinking industries tend to do the reverse. But the raw correlations suggest that the change in average firm size, s, is more closely attuned to log changes in total employment, e, than is the number of firms, n, especially in manufacturing and in retail industries.[15] In plain English, when industries grow (or shrink), they tend to grow (or shrink) more by increasing (or decreasing) firm size than by adding (or subtracting) firms.

How is employment growth (e) typically apportioned between increasing firm size (s) and increasing firm population (n)? In answering this question, we also used data from the four smaller sectors not shown in figure 4.5: construction, mining, wholesale trade, and TCU. For each of the seven major sectors, we estimated a pair of regressions of the form:

$$s_{it} = a + be_{it} + u_{it} \qquad (4.1)$$

$$n_{it} = c + de_{it} - u_{it} \qquad (4.2)$$

One of these two regressions is, of course, redundant because the identity $e_{it} = s_{it} + n_{it}$ holds for all i and t—which implies that a +

Figure 4.5   Correlations Between Changes in Industry Employment (e) and Either Average Firm Size (s) or Number of Firms (n)

Manufacturing Firms: e Versus s

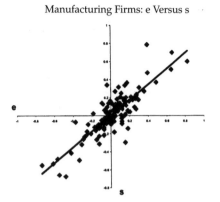

Retail Firms: e Versus s

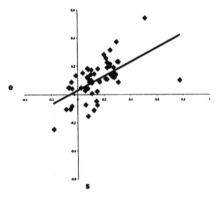

Service Firms: e Versus s

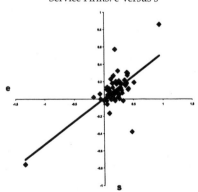

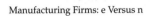

Manufacturing Firms: e Versus n

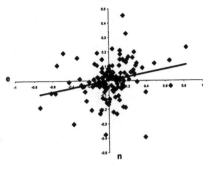

Retail Firms: e Versus n

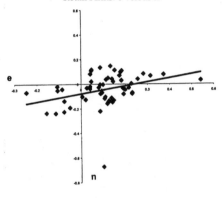

Service Firms: e Versus n

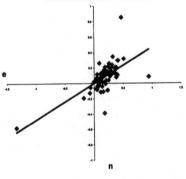

Source: Authors' configurations.

Table 4.24   Logarithmic Average Firm Size (s) and Number of Firms (n) on Industry Employment (e)

Sector	s =	n =	Number of Observations
Manufacturing	$-.002 + .87$ e	$.002 + .13$ e	140
	(.010) (.05)	(.010) (.05)	
	$R^2 = 0.72$	$R^2 = 0.06$	
Retail, wholesale, and mining	$.076 + .58$ e	$-.076 + .42$ e	95
	(.019) (.08)	(.019) (.08)	
	$R^2 = 0.38$	$R^2 = 0.24$	
Service and TCUC	$-.012 + .55$ e	$.012 + .45$ e	89
	(.017) (.06)	(.017) (.06)	
	$R^2 = 0.49$	$R^2 = 0.40$	

Source: Authors' compilation.

$c = 0$ and $b + d = 1$. In what follows, we report both regressions only to display the respective R^2s.

In an effort both to increase the number of observations and to summarize the results more succinctly, we first performed a series of Chow tests to see whether the same statistical model could describe the data from different sectors. Our procedure for aggregating sectors was opportunistic and data-based rather than theoretically based—a consequence of the paucity of data. In the end, we concluded that we could boil it all down to manufacturing and two composite sectors.

To start, we observed that fitting equation 4.1 to the data from construction and TCU produced very nearly the same regression. Since each sector offered precious few observations, we simply pooled them into a new composite sector (henceforth, TCUC). But the service-sector regression also looked strikingly similar, and a Chow test did not come close to rejecting the hypothesis that the same model applied to the service industries as to TCUC (F = 1.0, p-value = 0.36). Similarly, when equation 4.1 was run separately over mining (twenty-eight observations) and wholesale trade (eleven observations), the coefficients were very similar. So we next pooled these two sectors.[16] Finally, we noticed that the retail-sector regression looked much like the regression for wholesale trade and mining combined; the pooling hypothesis easily passed a Chow test (F = 0.5, p = .58). That left us with only two composite sectors: one was TCUC plus services, the other was trade (retail and wholesale) plus mining. Chow tests resoundingly rejected the hypothesis of pooling these two composites (F = 7.1) or of pooling either composite with manufacturing (Fs = 11.4 and 12.1). Table 4.24 reports the remaining three models.[17]

Table 4.25   Correlations Between Industry Employment (e) and Either Average Firm Size (s) or Number of Firms (n), by Industry

Sector	Corr (e, s)	Corr (e, n)	Number of Observations
Manufacturing	.85	.24	140
Retail trade	.59	.32	56
Services	.70	.66	67
Wholesale trade	.44	.92	11
Mining	.62	.76	28
TCUC	.64	.55	22

Source: Authors' compilation.

In manufacturing, the overwhelming majority (about 87 percent) of typical employment changes apparently are accomplished by increasing or decreasing firm size. (And remember, this pertains to a five-year adjustment period.) The near-zero constant in the regression tells us that there is no secular trend toward either upsizing (and fewer firms) or downsizing (and more firms). In other words, the shrinkage in average firm size is entirely attributed to the shrinkage in industrywide employment, not to any exogenous trend toward smaller firms.

In the rest of the economy, changing firm size apparently absorbs only 55 to 58 percent of employment fluctuations—still a majority, but less so. Secularly, the constants point to a strong (and statistically significant) secular trend toward upsizing in retailing, wholesaling, and mining, and a weak (and insignificant) trend toward downsizing in services, construction, and TCU.[18]

Although the precise numerical correlations are not robust, the central message—that growing industries tend to upsize while shrinking industries downsize—is reasonably robust. If we separate the observations by major sector, we see the correlations cited in table 4.25. The tighter correlation between e and s (as opposed to that between e and n) disappears when we look only at wholesale trade or at mining, and the margin is trivial in the service sector.

If, instead, we disaggregate the data by time periods, but merge all the sectors, the dominance of s (firm size) over n (firm population) is seen to apply to all periods except 1967 to 1972 (see table 4.26).

Finally, using manufacturing and the two composite sectors explained earlier, we can disaggregate both by sector and time period simultaneously to get the correlations reported in table 4.27.

Within manufacturing, there is a reasonably robust and fairly tight statistical relationship between changes in employment and changes

Table 4.26   Correlations Between Industry Employment (e) and Either
Average Firm Size (s) or Number of Firms (n), by Period

Period	Corr (e, s)	Corr (e, n)	Number of Observations
1958–1963	.75	.56	41
1963–1967	.75	.30	41
1967–1972	.47	.48	48
1972–1977	.67	.44	47
1977–1982	.70	.41	46
1982–1987	.82	.69	49
1987–1992	.84	.32	52

Source: Authors' compilation.

in average firm or establishment size, but a much less robust (and generally weaker) relationship between changes in employment and changes in the number of firms or establishments. The "margins of victory," however, are much less pronounced in the two composite sectors.

So our embarrassingly simple hypothesis seems to be reasonably well confirmed by the data, especially in manufacturing. More precisely, the hypothesis is confirmed *cyclically:* the chief mode of adjustment during business expansions and contractions appears to be the size of the average firm rather than the number of firms. Thus, the upsurge in downsizing in the manufacturing sector from 1987 to 1992 may have mainly reflected weak macroeconomic conditions. Secularly, the observed trend toward downsizing in manufacturing is essentially attributable to the sector's shrinkage.

Conclusions

The major findings of this chapter are easy to summarize. First, we find that media reports of widespread downsizing in manufacturing in the late 1980s and early 1990s were not necessarily misleading. There is much evidence of downsizing in many manufacturing industries in the 1987 to 1992 period, regardless of whether we measure average firm size or look for stochastic dominance relations over time. But the phenomenon is not new: American manufacturing industries have been downsizing for more than twenty years. And the evidence is not uniform: some manufacturing industries have upsized.

Second, this downsizing trend is more or less restricted to manufacturing; few retail, service, or other industries exhibit downsizing. In fact, the overwhelmingly predominant pattern in the major retail

Table 4.27   Correlations Between Industry Employment (e) and Either
Average Firm Size (s) or Number of Firms (n), by Industry
and Period

Sector and Period	Corr (e, s)	Corr (e, n)	Number of Observations
Manufacturing			
1958–1963	.78	.29	20
1963–1967	.69	.52	20
1967–1972	.62	.08	20
1972–1977	.65	.26	20
1977–1982	.90	.12	20
1982–1987	.99	.88	20
1987–1992	.83	.26	20
Retail, et cetera			
1958–1963	.62	.77	13
1963–1967	.88	.17	13
1967–1972	.63	.31	13
1972–1977	.51	.65	14
1977–1982	.45	.50	14
1982–1987	.77	.81	14
1987–1992	.75	.61	14
Services, et cetera			
1958–1963	.72	.89	8
1963–1967	.46	.71	8
1967–1972	.15	.84	15
1972–1977	.62	.59	13
1977–1982	.62	.88	12
1982–1987	.79	.72	15
1987–1992	.86	.12	18

Source: Authors' compilation.

and service sectors—which account for many more jobs than does manufacturing—has been upsizing. The typical American retail or service firm (or establishment) has been growing larger over time, not smaller. However, this trend may have weakened a bit during the most recent downsizing period (1987 to 1992).

Third, some of these disparate sectoral patterns of downsizing and upsizing can be explained by overall employment changes. Growing industries (as measured by total employment), which are mainly found *outside* manufacturing, tend to upsize, while shrinking industries (which are mainly found *inside* manufacturing) tend to downsize. Changes in average firm size account for the majority share of total employment change, especially in manufacturing. Increases or decreases in the number of firms account for less.

In other words, the simple hypothesis that growing industries up-size while shrinking industries downsize takes us a reasonable distance, though not all the way, toward an explanation of why the manufacturing sector looks so different.

Chapter 5

Downsizing in U.S. Manufacturing: An Empirical Analysis of Causes

W E HAVE now seen that the downsizing phenomenon in reality is very different from what its name may suggest. In some sectors of the economy, it is upsizing and not downsizing that predominates, while in manufacturing, large firms have tended to become smaller (or to be replaced by smaller firms) and small firms have tended to expand; the overall tendency in this sector has been movement toward the middle. At the end of chapter 4, we broached a rather disconcertingly uncomplicated hypothesis describing these developments—growing industries upsize, shrinking industries downsize. The obvious next step is to fill in the picture. This chapter focuses on manufacturing and explores empirically some of the influences that may account for changes in average firm or establishment size within this sector. In chapter 6, we do the same for the retail and service industries.

We proposed six possible explanations for downsizing in chapter 1. These six hypotheses are:

1. Downsizing occurs because technological change favors smaller business units (firms or establishments).

2. Faster innovation leads to more labor market churning.

3. Foreign competition compels domestic industry to downsize by trimming "fat."

4. Downsizing occurs when capital is substituted for labor.

5. Downsizing is a consequence of the breakdown of the social contract between labor and capital.

131

6. Downsizing amounts to the "blue-collarization" of white-collar labor.

Operating in reverse, most of these hypotheses should presumably also be able to account for upsizing or for regression toward the mean.

This list suggests, in turn, a number of empirical variables that may represent the proximate causes of changes in the size distribution of enterprises within manufacturing, including:

1. *Technical progress:* Is there any evidence that industries undergoing more rapid technological change have downsized more? Are industries that are more research and development (R&D)–intensive more apt to reduce their enterprise size? Is there any evidence that skill-biased technical change has played a role? (hypotheses 1 and 2)

2. *Degree of computerization:* Has the rapid increase of computerization over the last two decades reduced economies of scale and made smaller units relatively more productive? Or has computerization moved the efficient size toward the middle, leading to a decline in the variation of enterprise size within industry? (hypotheses 1 and 2)

3. *International trade:* Are industries with growing international competitive pressures more likely to downsize? Does this influence show up primarily in import competition or export competition? (hypothesis 3)

4. *Capital substitution:* Have firms really replaced labor with capital? Does rising capital intensity lead to more downsizing among firms within an industry? (hypothesis 4)

5. *The weakening of organized labor:* Does downsizing reflect a decline in the power of the unions and suggest that they cannot protect their workers to the degree that they did before? Can organized labor, which is such a small percentage of all labor in the United States, be that important? (hypothesis 5)

6. *Declining profitability:* Has a decline in profitability—perhaps itself a reflection of increased foreign competition—led to greater pressure to reach the most efficient size? Does this increased pressure show up as downsizing or as regression to the mean? (hypothesis 3)

7. *Change in industry employment:* Finally, we will test chapter 4's additional, and remarkably simple, hypothesis: changes in the size

of the average business unit are directly associated with changes in overall industry employment—that is, when industry employment falls, average size also declines, and conversely.

The econometric results on the determinants of downsizing in manufacturing that are reported in this chapter provide considerable support for the idea that expanding industries tend to upsize while contracting industries downsize; for the notion that technology has favored smaller business units (at least since 1967); and for the hypothesis that falling profits put pressure on firms to downsize. We also find support for the idea that foreign competition, at least in terms of export markets, pushes firms to downsize. However, our findings are not consistent with the notions that unions are an effective impediment to downsizing and that faster capital (or information-technology capital) formation leads to downsizing by substituting capital for labor. Indeed, the evidence indicates, if anything, that unionized industries are *more* apt to downsize—perhaps to get rid of more expensive union labor. Moreover, the growth in information-technology capital does appear to have a significant negative effect on changes in the overall dispersion of employment among different-size classes.

Changes in the Size Distribution of Firms and Establishments in Manufacturing

Chapter 4 documented the pattern of downsizing in manufacturing. We have reproduced some of the results in tables 5.1 and 5.2. Here we explore the subject further, using four different data sources: the U.S. Census Bureau's Census of Manufacturing data on establishments over the period 1967 to 1997; the Census Bureau's Enterprise Statistics on firms over the period 1958 to 1992; Enterprise Statistics on establishments over the period 1958 to 1992; and Standard & Poor's Compustat data on firms over the period 1978 to 1997. As discussed in chapter 4, each of these sources has its distinct advantages and disadvantages. The Census of Manufacturing data begin in 1967 and are complete through 1992. Some additional data are available for 1997 on average establishment size by two-digit industry.[1] This source includes data on single-establishment and multi-establishment firms. The Enterprise Statistics go back all the way to 1958 but are not available for 1997. They include comprehensive information on both firms and establishments and also cover both single- and multi-establishment firms.

As we saw earlier, the difference between the two sources is somewhat subtle. In the Census of Manufacturing, each establishment is classified into a particular industry on the basis of its main product.

Table 5.1 Average Number of Employees per Establishment or Firm for Two-Digit SIC Manufacturing Industries, 1958 to 1997

		Census of Manufacturing					Enterprise Statistics		
					Percentage Change				Percentage Change
SIC	Industry	1967	1992	1997	1967–1992	1967–1997	1958	1992	1958–1992
20	Food and kindred products	50.7	72.3	74.8	42.4	47.4	35.7	56.9	59.4
21	Tobacco products	228.3	333.3	NA	46.0	NA	129.2	138.0	6.8
22	Textile mill products	131.2	104.7	91.3	−20.2	−30.4	102.1	86.3	−15.5
23	Apparel and other textile products	51.4	42.7	35.4	−17.0	−31.1	29.1	38.2	31.3
24	Lumber and wood products	15.1	18.3	20.6	21.6	36.9	15.3	17.2	12.1
25	Furniture and fixtures	42.5	40.4	43.3	−4.9	1.9	29.4	38.7	31.9
26	Paper and allied products	108.5	97.6	NA	−10.0	NA	87.9	83.9	−4.5
27	Printing and publishing	27.1	22.8	24.6	−15.9	−9.3	24.6	24.9	1.3
28	Chemicals and allied products	71.3	70.7	66.3	−0.9	−7.0	55.7	61.8	10.9
29	Petroleum and coal products	75.3	53.9	49.4	−28.5	−34.4	19.8	28.3	42.9
30	Rubber and miscellaneous plastics products	80.0	57.2	61.4	−28.5	−23.3	52.4	42.6	−18.7
31	Leather and leather products	89.2	49.6	NA	−44.4	NA	55.8	29.6	−47.0
32	Stone, clay, and glass	37.9	28.8	30.8	−23.8	−18.6	36.1	28.2	−21.9
33	Primary metal industries	187.4	101.8	110.3	−45.6	−41.1	68.3	66.6	−2.5
34	Fabricated metal products	48.9	37.4	40.8	−23.6	−16.6	39.3	34.1	−13.1
35	Industrial machinery and equipment	49.2	32.2	35.1	−34.5	−28.7	41.3	32.8	−20.7
36	Electronic and electrical equipment	175.1	85.0	92.5	−51.4	−47.2	101.1	59.4	−41.3
37	Transportation equipment	245.1	145.9	126.1	−40.5	−48.6	224.2	68.4	−69.5
38	Instruments and related products	88.5	79.9	NA	−9.8	NA	46.5	69.2	48.8
39	Miscellaneous industries	30.1	21.5	21.8	−28.6	−27.4	28.9	21.5	−25.5
	Nondurables	56.0	47.0	NA	−16.0	NA	38.6	43.4	12.6
	Durables	61.8	44.7	NA	−27.6	NA	48.9	39.7	−18.7
	All manufacturing industries	60.5	45.7	46.5	−24.5	−23.2	46.2	43.5	−5.9

Table 5.2 Average Number of Employees per Firm in Two-Digit SIC Manufacturing Industries, 1958 to 1997

SIC	Industry	Enterprise Statistics			Compustat (Thousands)		
		1958	1992	Percentage Change 1958–1992	1978	1997	Percentage Change 1978–1997
20	Food and kindred products	55.1	125.5	127.8	20.8	24.2	16.3
21	Tobacco products	308.8	2150.5	596.4	40.8	25.0	−38.8
22	Textile mill products	147.2	149.6	1.7	7.4	7.3	−1.6
23	Apparel and other textile products	31.9	49.0	53.5	7.4	6.2	−16.5
24	Lumber and wood products	16.2	18.7	15.6	14.2	8.6	−39.8
25	Furniture and fixtures	32.3	50.5	56.2	8.9	12.9	44.1
26	Paper and allied products	149.7	208.6	39.4	15.7	12.9	−17.4
27	Printing and publishing	26.5	30.1	13.6	6.6	10.8	64.6
28	Chemicals and allied products	109.6	180.1	64.4	21.9	12.3	−43.7
29	Petroleum and coal products	544.9	404.1	−25.8	42.2	22.9	−45.8
30	Rubber and miscellaneous plastics products	101.8	73.6	−27.6	12.6	6.6	−47.7
31	Leather and leather products	90.2	48.4	−46.3	4.8	4.0	−16.8
32	Stone, clay, and glass	49.0	49.0	0.0	15.0	6.7	−55.1
33	Primary metal industries	131.0	165.7	26.5	24.2	7.8	−68.0
34	Fabricated metal products	46.6	43.3	−7.1	7.6	6.5	−15.4
35	Industrial machinery and equipment	53.5	40.7	−23.9	15.1	11.6	−23.1
36	Electronic and electrical equipment	207.0	106.3	−48.6	24.4	16.7	−31.6
37	Transportation equipment	353.3	196.0	−44.5	87.6	49.6	−43.4
38	Instruments and related products	82.2	106.9	29.9	18.1	11.3	−37.6
39	Miscellaneous industries	31.7	24.0	−24.2	2.9	3.1	10.0
	Nondurables	28.9	22.2	−23.0	18.5	13.5	−26.9
	Durables	43.5	47.0	8.1	26.5	15.3	−42.3
	All manufacturing industries	65.5	65.8	0.5	23.2	14.6	−37.3

Source: Authors' computations from U.S. Bureau of the Census, Enterprise Statistics (1958 to 1992) and Standard & Poor's Compustat data (1978 to 1997).

In the Enterprise Statistics, each *firm* is classified into an industry on the basis of its main product, with all *establishments* belonging to that firm also classified into that industry (whether or not the establishment produces the same or a different product). Thus, the Enterprise Statistics can include as part of the manufacturing sector establishments that do not necessarily produce manufacturing output. For example, GE Capital and GMAC (General Motors Acceptance Corporation), which are financial entities owned by General Electric and General Motors, respectively, are classified as manufacturing establishments in the Enterprise Statistics, because the main activities of GE and GM are in manufacturing. On the other side, the Enterprise Statistics *exclude* from manufacturing those establishments that do produce manufacturing output but belong to firms whose major product is *non*manufacturing. Possible examples include the manufacturing units that are part of the McDonald's chain of restaurants, or part of the retail giant Wal-Mart.

The Compustat data are available from 1978 to 1997. As we noted in chapter 4, these data do not provide a complete census of firms in an industry at each point in time but rather provide a sample that consists primarily of the *largest* firms in each industry. The sample is a quasi-panel: it tends to follow the same firms over time but sometimes adds new firms and omits previous members of the group. When firms merge (or are acquired) or split up, the Compustat sample includes the new entities formed in place of the previous ones. As in chapter 4, we do not correct for such mergers or breakups because our interest here is in firm size. Despite these limitations, the Compustat results are illuminating and provide at least some information on changes in firm size over time. As in chapter 4, we select five years of data—1978,[2] 1982, 1987, 1992, and 1997—to correspond to the industrial census years.

According to the Census of Manufacturing data, the average establishment size in total manufacturing has fallen rather sharply over time, from 60.5 employees in 1967 to 45.7 employees in 1992, followed by a slight increase to 46.5 employees in the boom year 1997 (see table 5.1). The change has been fairly continuous over time, though it accelerated a bit in the downsizing period between 1987 and 1992. (Over the entire period of 1967 to 1992, average establishment size fell at an average annual rate of 1.12 percent; between 1987 and 1992, it fell at an annual rate of 1.54 percent.)

Table 5.1 also shows changes in average establishment size by two-digit SIC manufacturing industries over the same period. Of the twenty industries, seventeen experienced reductions in average establishment size from 1967 to 1992; the other three experienced increases. Of the sixteen industries with data available through 1997, thirteen show a decline in average establishment size and three an increase. Within the group showing declines, the most notable are electronics and other electrical equipment, primary metals, and leather and leather products, whose average establishment size fell by about half over the period. On the other hand, food and tobacco products both experienced substantial increases in their average establishment sizes. It is also of interest that durable goods industries experienced greater declines in their average establishment size (26 percent between 1967 and 1992) than did nondurables (16 percent). Finally, the rate of decline of average establishment size accelerated (or the rate of increase declined) in the 1987 to 1992 period compared to 1967 to 1987 in fourteen of the twenty industries, particularly in durable goods.

The Enterprise Statistics on manufacturing show a much smaller decline in average establishment size than the Census of Manufacturing data: only 6 percent over the period 1958 to 1992 compared to 25 percent over 1967 to 1992. The main reason for this striking difference is the time period. As we learned in chapter 4, upsizing rather than downsizing was the dominant pattern from 1958 to 1972; most of the downsizing in manufacturing took place after 1972. The Census of Manufacturing data pick up only the downsizing. Moreover, like the Census of Manufacturing data, the Enterprise Statistics show a fairly substantial drop in average size (19 percent) for industries producing durable goods. In contrast to the Census of Manufacturing results, the Enterprise Statistics show that average size in nondurables industries actually rose by 13 percent. Of the twenty two-digit manufacturing industries in the Enterprise Statistics, eleven record a fall in average size and nine an increase over the period 1958 to 1992.

The Enterprise Statistics also show virtually no overall change in average *firm* size in manufacturing between 1958 and 1992 (see table 5.2). Again, there was more upsizing until 1967 and more downsizing thereafter. As with the establishment data, average firm size declined in durables but increased in nondurables. Of the twenty two-digit industries, only eight record a drop in average firm size.

The Compustat data paint a rather different picture. However, it is important to note that the average firm size in the Compustat data is much larger than average firm size in the Enterprise Statistics (or in the Census of Manufacturing). In fact, there is about a three-hundred-fold difference. (Note that the Compustat statistics are in thousands of employees.) Of the twenty two-digit industries, all but four show reductions in average firm size between 1978 and 1997. Overall, average firm size fell by 37 percent in total manufacturing, 42 percent in durable goods, and 27 percent in nondurable goods.

Table 5.3 (reproduced, in part, from chapter 4) provides a summary of the number of industries downsizing and upsizing by census pe-

Table 5.3   Number of Two-Digit Manufacturing Industries Upsizing and Downsizing, by Census Period, 1958 to 1997

Period	Change in Average Size: Total Manufacturing	Number of Industries Downsizing	Number of Industries Upsizing
A. Manufacturing establishments: Census of Manufacturing			
1967–1972	−4.7%	11	9
1972–1977	−8.5	18	2
1977–1982	−3.1	14	6
1982–1987	−3.5	11	9
1987–1992	−7.4	14	6
1992–1997	1.7	5	11
Total	−23.2	73	43
B. Manufacturing establishments: Enterprise Statistics			
1958–1963	4.6	6	14
1963–1972	2.3	10	10
1972–1977	−1.9	14	6
1977–1982	−5.6	14	6
1982–1987	2.6	9	11
1987–1992	−7.5	15	5
Total	−5.9	68	52
C. Manufacturing firms: Enterprise Statistics			
1958–1963	10.8	3	17
1963–1967	27.6	1	19
1967–1972	−6.7	7	13
1972–1977	−3.3	13	7
1977–1982	−5.3	14	6
1982–1987	−6.5	10	10
1987–1992	−11.0	17	3
Total	0.5	65	75
D. Manufacturing firms: Compustat data			
1978–1982	−9.3	12	5
1982–1987	−7.5	10	6
1987–1992	−14.7	13	4
1992–1997	−12.4	11	6
Total	−37.3	46	21

Table 5.3 *Continued*

Period	Change in Average Size: Total Manufacturing	Number of Industries Downsizing	Number of Industries Upsizing
E. Manufacturing establish-ments: Census of Manufac-turing: coworker mean[a]			
1967–1972	− 17.1	13	7
1972–1977	− 3.0	16	4
1977–1982	− 8.9	19	1
1982–1987	0.4	15	5
1987–1992	− 14.0	15	5
1992–1997	—		
Total[b]	− 36.8	78	22

Source: Standard & Poor's Compustat data (1978 to 1997).
Note: Census of Manufacturing data on average-establishment size are missing for five industries in 1997. Industries in which average size changes by less than 0.1 percent are excluded from the tabulation.
[a]The coworker mean is the employment-weighted average establishment size.
[b]1967 to 1992.

riod. The Census of Manufacturing data on establishments (panel A in table 5.3) shows a clear pattern: average establishment size in total manufacturing fell steadily from 1967 until the boom years of 1992 to 1997. However, even though average establishment size in all manufacturing declined in every five-year period (until the 1992 to 1997 period), there were always *some* upsizing industries. Of the 116 observations in all (five census periods with twenty industries and the last census period with sixteen), downsizing occurred in seventy-three cases while upsizing occurred in the other forty-three. So, while downsizing was the most common occurrence, there were plenty of exceptions.

There are also interesting differences by period in the census data. Manufacturing industries were less likely to downsize during 1967 to 1972 and 1982 to 1987, when the overall decline in manufacturing employment was low, than during 1972 to 1977 and 1987 to 1992, when manufacturing employment fell rapidly. In this respect, the 1977 to 1982 period is a bit of an anomaly, since it ended in a deep recession, but the tendency to downsize was weak. We may speculate that perhaps the cheap dollar of the 1977 to 1980 period helped manufacturing.

The Enterprise Statistics on establishments (panel B of table 5.3) give a more mixed picture. Average establishment size in total manufacturing increased during the early periods 1958 to 1963 and 1963 to 1972.[3] It declined in the later periods 1972 to 1977, 1977 to 1982, and 1987 to 1992—as it also did in the Census of Manufacturing data—

but rose in the 1982 to 1987 period, in contrast to the Census of Manufacturing results. In terms of overall count, the Enterprise Statistics show that downsizing occurred in sixty-eight industries while upsizing occurred in fifty-two. However, the number of downsizers clearly outweighed the number of upsizers after 1972—again with the exception of the period 1982 to 1987, when the split was pretty even. (The numbers were also close in the Census of Manufacturing data.)

The firm-level data tell a similar story. According to the Enterprise Statistics (panel C in table 5.3), average firm size in total manufacturing climbed sharply in the 1958 to 1963 and 1963 to 1967 periods, and the number of upsizing industries clearly outweighed the number of downsizers. After 1967, average firm size declined in each of the census periods, and this trend accelerated over time. Likewise, with the exception of the period 1967 to 1972, the number of downsizers was greater than the number of upsizers, and the difference widened over time (except for the period 1982 to 1987).

In panel D of table 5.3, we summarize the Compustat data. Average firm size computed for the total sample of companies declined in each of the four subperiods. As with the Enterprise Statistics, there is a marked acceleration in the degree of downsizing between the periods 1978 to 1982 and 1987 to 1992. Interestingly, the degree of decline in average firm size was almost as great in the period 1992 to 1997 as in the period 1987 to 1992—a finding that stands in sharp contrast to the findings from the Census of Manufacturing in panel A. The main reason, we presume, is that Compustat concentrates on very large companies.

As was true of the industrial census data, downsizing is the dominant trend in average firm size in the Compustat data: downsizing occurs in 69 percent of the cases, and upsizing in the other 31 percent. (The corresponding figures from the Census of Manufacturing establishment data are 63 and 37 percent, respectively.) As with the Census of Manufacturing data and the Enterprise Statistics, the relative number of Compustat downsizers was greater in the periods 1978 to 1982 and 1987 to 1992 than in the 1982 to 1987 period. There is again evidence here of an acceleration of downsizing in the 1987 to 1992 period. Thus, according to all our three data sources, the period 1987 to 1992 appears to exhibit the strongest downsizing (second strongest in the case of the Census of Manufacturing data)—a finding that is in line with chapter 2's investigation of the popular press version of the downsizing phenomenon.

In table 5.3, we also introduce another measure of establishment size using the Census of Manufacturing data: the so-called coworker mean. The coworker mean is the *weighted* average of average establishment size by size class, with the percentage of total employment in the size class used as the weight.[4] The reason for using the coworker mean is that the size distribution of establishments (and firms) in the United States is, as we have seen, highly skewed: the vast majority of American businesses are very small, but many U.S. employees work in large businesses (and most manufacturing employees work in large businesses). That means that measuring the average establishment size or the average firm size tells us about the average business entity, but not about the size of the average *worker's* place of employment. The coworker mean provides us with a closer reflection of the experience of the average employee in an industry in terms of the size of the business he (or she) is working in.

Panel E of table 5.3 shows our computation of the change in the coworker mean for Census of Manufacturing establishments. It is noteworthy that the coworker mean size of establishment is, as expected, much larger than the average size of establishment. For the year 1967, the coworker mean for total manufacturing is 1,424 employees, compared to an average establishment size of 60.5 employees. This means that the typical manufacturing worker in 1967 was employed in an establishment of about 1,500 workers. However, like the average establishment size, the coworker mean establishment size also shows a significant downward trend between 1967 and 1992.[5] Over this period, the coworker mean fell by 37 percent, compared to a 25 percent decline for average establishment size over the same years. The coworker mean, like average establishment size, fell in every period except 1982 to 1987, when it essentially remained unchanged. The downsizing pattern was much stronger for individual industries according to the implications of the coworker mean as compared to those of the simple mean. Of the one hundred observations in all (five census periods with twenty industries), downsizing occurred in 78 percent of the cases (compared to 63 percent of the cases on the basis of the simple mean).

On the surface at least, there appears to be a close correspondence of the reported changes in establishment or firm size among the four data sources—they appear to follow the same general pattern over the overlapping periods. However, on closer inspection, there are a number of anomalies. For example, while average *establishment* size increased somewhat in paper products and instruments and related products between 1977 and 1992 according to the Census of Manufacturing figures, average *firm* size declined in both cases according to the Compustat data. To delve deeper, we carried out calculations of correlation coefficients in order to measure the correspondence between changes in establishment size and changes in firm size, using the various sources of data at the industry level (see table 5.4). The computation is based on the percentage change in average establishment or firm size for each of the twenty industries in each census period, using the pertinent data. The correlations for each of the

142   Downsizing in America

Table 5.4   Correlation Coefficients Between the Percentage Change in Establishment or Firm Size Among the Four Data Sources, by Period, 1958 to 1997

Source and Period	Enterprise Statistics: Establishments	Enterprise Statistics: Firms	Compustat: Firms	Census of Manufacturing: Establishment Coworker Mean
1958–1963 period Enterprise Statistics: establishments	—	0.959	—	—
1963–1972 period Enterprise Statistics: establishments	—	−0.141	—	—
1967–1972 period Census of Manufacturing: establishments	—	0.766	—	−0.575
1972–1977 period Census of Manufacturing: establishments	0.327	0.692	—	−0.094
Enterprise Statistics: establishments	—	0.622	—	—
1977–1982 period[a] Census of Manufacturing: establishments	0.028	0.754	0.676	0.277
Enterprise Statistics: establishments	—	0.233	0.130	—
Enterprise Statistics: firms	—	—	0.387	—
1982–1987 period Census of Manufacturing: establishments	0.101	0.856	0.086	0.216
Enterprise Statistics: establishments	—	0.368	0.481	—
Enterprise Statistics: firms	—	—	0.200	—

Table 5.4 *Continued*

Source-Period	Enterprise Statistics: Establishments	Enterprise Statistics: Firms	Compustat: Firms	Census of Manufacturing: Establishment Coworker Mean
1987–1992 period				
Census of Manu-facturing: estab-lishments	0.749	0.769	0.176	0.032
Enterprise Statis-tics: establish-ments	—	0.861	0.221	—
Enterprise Statis-tics: firms	—	—	0.274	—
1992–1997 period[b]				
Census of Manu-facturing: estab-lishments	—	—	0.122	—

Source: Authors' compilation.
[a]Compustat data are available only from 1978 to 1982.
[b]Sixteen industries only.

census periods are positive, with only one exception. In many cases they are quite strong. This is particularly so between the Enterprise Statistics' establishment and firm size data (with 1963 to 1972 as the glaring exception). Changes in establishment size calculated from the Census of Manufacturing data are highly correlated with changes in firm size derived from the Enterprise Statistics data (correlations of 0.69 or greater), but surprisingly, they are weakly correlated with changes in establishment size based on the Enterprise Statistics data (with the exception of 1987 to 1992). Changes in firm size determined from the Compustat data are highly correlated with changes in establishment size in the Census of Manufacturing data in the period 1977 to 1982, but weakly correlated in the other periods. Firm size changes computed from Compustat data are also weakly to moderately correlated with both firm size changes and establishment size changes calculated from the Enterprise Statistics. Changes in the coworker mean based on Census of Manufacturing establishment data are actually negatively correlated with changes in average establishment size based on the same source in the earlier two periods but positively correlated with them in the later three periods.

However, when the correlation coefficients are calculated for changes over the entire fifteen-year period of 1977 to 1992 (or 1978 to 1992 in

Table 5.5   Size Distribution of Establishments and Employment, in Total Manufacturing, 1967 to 1992

Size Class by Number of Employees	1967	1972	1977	1982	1987	1992
A. Establishments						
1 to 4	38.4%	35.9%	40.1%	32.5%	32.6%	34.8%
5 to 9	12.9	14.9	13.7	17.2	17.5	17.8
10 to 19	13.6	14.0	13.8	16.4	16.3	15.3
20 to 49	16.0	16.0	14.7	16.1	16.1	15.3
50 to 99	8.2	8.2	7.6	7.9	7.9	7.6
100 to 249	6.5	6.7	6.1	6.1	6.1	5.9
250 to 499	2.5	2.6	2.4	2.3	2.2	2.1
500 to 999	1.1	1.1	1.0	1.0	0.9	0.8
1,000 to 2,499	0.5	0.5	0.4	0.4	0.4	0.3
2,500 or more	0.2	0.2	0.2	0.1	0.1	0.1
All establishments	100.0	100.0	100.0	100.0	100.0	100.0
Memo						
20 or more	35.0	35.2	32.5	33.9	33.7	32.1
1,000 or more	0.8	0.7	0.6	0.5	0.5	0.4
B. Employment						
1 to 4	1.1	1.1	1.2	1.2	1.3	1.3
5 to 9	1.4	1.7	1.7	2.3	2.4	2.6
10 to 19	3.1	3.4	3.6	4.4	4.5	4.6
20 to 49	8.3	8.7	8.7	9.8	10.2	10.4
50 to 99	9.4	9.9	10.1	10.7	11.1	11.6
100 to 249	16.6	17.9	18.0	18.4	19.1	19.8
250 to 499	14.5	15.4	15.6	15.3	15.4	15.9
500 to 999	12.8	13.1	13.5	12.7	12.3	12.5
1,000 to 2,499	13.2	12.5	11.8	11.4	10.7	10.6
2,500 or more	19.6	16.2	15.7	13.7	13.0	10.6
All establishments	100.0	100.0	100.0	100.0	100.0	100.0
Memo						
Under 20	5.6	6.2	6.5	7.9	8.2	8.5
1,000 or more	32.8	28.7	27.5	25.2	23.7	21.2
Average size	60.5	57.7	52.8	51.1	49.4	45.7
Standard deviation	287.3	254.5	240.2	225.3	221.9	197.7
Coefficient of variation	4.75	4.41	4.55	4.40	4.50	4.33
Gini coefficient	0.828	0.815	0.824	0.799	0.794	0.796

Source: Authors' computations from U.S. Bureau of the Census, Census of Manufacturing (1967 to 1992).

the case of the Compustat data), the correlations are positive and fairly strong: 0.52 and 0.66 (results not shown in the table). Moreover, changes in the coworker mean over the 1967 to 1992 period are positively correlated with changes in average establishment size—a correlation coefficient of 0.31 (results not shown in the table). Thus, it appears that changes in establishment size in an industry are not very closely related to changes in firm size over short periods of time, but they are quite strongly correlated over longer stretches of time. This suggests that the factors that affect changes in establishment size may be different from those that cause firm size to change over the short term, but they may be similar over the long term.

Table 5.5 and figures 5.1 and 5.2 show the dramatic changes in the overall size distribution of manufacturing establishments based on Census of Manufacturing data over the period 1967 to 1992. The percentage of establishments in all size classes above 19 employees has declined over time, and particularly so for establishments of 1,000 employees or more, while the percentage of establishments has increased in the 5-to-9-employees and 10-to-19-employees size classes. Interestingly, however, the percentage of establishments in the 5-employees-or-fewer size class has fallen.

Even more dramatic is the change in the size *distribution* of employment. The share of total employment in establishments of 2,500 employees or more has plummeted almost by half, from 19.6 percent in 1967 to 10.6 percent in 1992. The share of total employment in the size class of 1,000 to 2,499 employees has also fallen sharply, from 13.2 percent to 10.6 percent, while the proportion of employment in the size class of 500 to 999 employees has declined somewhat. In contrast, the share of total employment in all the smaller size classes has risen.

The last two lines of table 5.5 show two measures of the overall dispersion of employment by size class within total manufacturing. The first is the coefficient of variation, defined as the standard deviation divided by the mean; the second is the Gini coefficient, which is an index that ranges from zero (all establishments are in a single size class) to one (maximum dispersion of establishments by size class). Both measures show a moderate decline in the degree of dispersion of employment by size class between 1967 and 1992. Moreover, according to both indices, this decline in dispersion was continuous, except for the period from 1972 to 1977. These results support the argument that, along with downsizing in manufacturing, the U.S. economy has shown a tendency toward regression to the mean. In particular, larger establishments have contracted both in terms of number and share of total employment.

Somewhat similar patterns show up in tabulations by firm size class computed from the Enterprise Statistics data.[6] The percentage of firms in the size class with nineteen or fewer employees fell from 71.5 percent in 1958 to 66.6 percent in 1967 and then recovered to 73.2 percent by

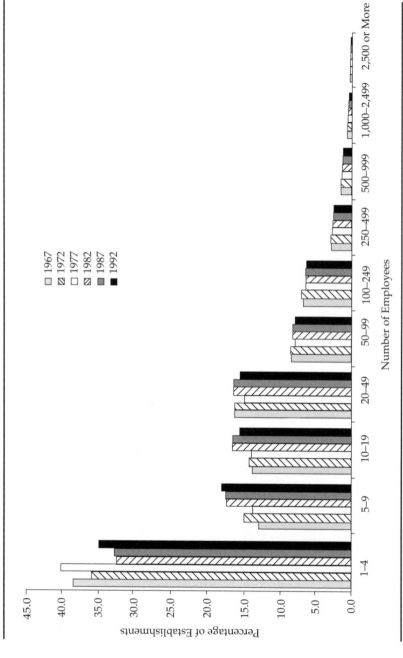

Figure 5.1 Size Distribution of Establishments, by Number of Employees, 1967 to 1992

1967
1972
1977
1982
1987
1992

Percentage of Establishments

45.0
40.0
35.0
30.0
25.0
20.0
15.0
10.0
5.0
0.0

1–4 5–9 10–19 20–49 50–99 100–249 250–499 500–999 1,000–2,499 2,500 or More

Number of Employees

Source: U.S. Bureau of the Census, Census of Manufacturing (1967 to 1992).

Figure 5.2 Size Distribution of Employment, by Size of Establishment in Number of Employees, 1967 to 1992

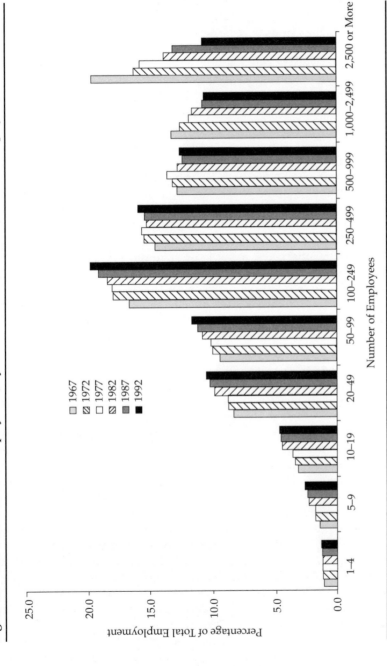

Source: U.S. Bureau of the Census, Census of Manufacturing (1967 to 1992).

1992. In contrast, the proportion of companies in the size classes of 20 to 99 employees, 100 to 249 employees, and 250 to 499 employees show exactly the opposite pattern: this proportion rose between 1958 and 1967 and then declined over the next twenty-five years.

The share of total employment in firms of 10,000 employees or more, after rising from 33 percent in 1958 to 45 percent in 1972, stabilized and then dropped between 1982 and 1992, ending at just 36 percent (see table 5.6 as well as figures 5.3 and 5.4). However, the share of total employment in the size class of 5,000 to 9,999 employees exhibited only minor fluctuations over the period from 1958 to 1992, with little net change. Turning to very small firms, the share of total employment in companies with 19 or fewer employees made a round trip, falling from 6.5 percent of total employment in 1958 to as low as 4.2 percent in 1967, but then recovering to 6.6 percent by 1992. A similar U-shaped pattern is evident for the size class of 20 to 99 employees, and in fact, for all other size classes under 5,000 employees. Thus, these results show a fairly pronounced shift of employment away from smaller manufacturing firms and toward giant firms (10,000 or more employees) between 1958 and 1972, followed by an equally pronounced shift toward smaller firms after 1972 or so as the largest firms contracted in terms of share of total employment. The net result is that the size distribution of employment by firm size in 1992 winds up quite similar to that of 1958.

Movements of the Gini coefficient tend to confirm this result. This measure shows a noticeable increase in the dispersion of employment by size class between 1958 and 1972, followed by a moderate decline from 1972 to 1992. The dispersion in employment by size class, according to this measure, was a bit greater in 1992 than in 1958. In contrast, the coefficient of variation shows little movement over the period 1958 to 1992. (The 1967 observation seems to be anomalous.) However, the standard deviation moves more in accord with the Gini coefficient, showing rising dispersion from 1958 to 1972 and then an almost equal decline from 1972 to 1992. Thus, while the Gini coefficient and the standard deviation give some indication of regression to the mean after 1972, the coefficient of variation measure does not.

Next we turn to dispersion of employment at the more detailed two-digit industry level, calculated from the Census of Manufacturing data on establishments (see table 5.7). It is noteworthy, first, that the degree of dispersion varies considerably among industries. In 1992, for example, the coefficient of variation ranged from a low of 1.86 in paper and allied products to a high of 4.66 in industrial machinery and equipment. In that same year, the Gini coefficient (which, it will be recalled, is bounded between zero and one) ranged from 0.602 in stone, glass, and clay products to 0.863 in transportation equipment.

Between 1967 and 1992, the coefficient of variation fell in sixteen of twenty industries, while the Gini coefficient declined in eighteen of twenty industries. The industry-level data from this source thus provide very strong evidence that regression to the mean was the predominant pattern in terms of the size distribution of employment by employee size class.[7]

Decomposition Analysis of the Data

Changes over time in average establishment or firm size within total manufacturing may be attributable to a combination of three effects: rising or falling establishment (firm) sizes within industries; relative growth in the number of establishments (firms) in industries in which smaller or larger establishments (firms) are typical; and shifts in manufacturing employment toward industries with smaller or larger establishment (firm) sizes. Clearly, these three effects are not independent. We will provide one decomposition based on the first two effects (since it provides the most straightforward algebra) to assess their relative importance.

There are two main results. First, there was a marked shift in the distribution of establishments and employment away from low-tech industries toward medium-tech and high-tech industries. Second, over the entire period of our study, average establishment size in total manufacturing declined by 14.8 employees, a decline that was entirely attributable to decreasing average establishment sizes *within* industries (the within-industry effect). Shifts in the distribution of establishments *among* industries contributed almost nothing.

To demonstrate these results, we use the following notation:

N_t = number of establishments in all manufacturing at time t

N_{jt} = number of establishments in industry j at time t

$s_{jt} = N_{jt}/N_t$ = share of total manufacturing establishments in industry j at time t

E_t = number of employees in all manufacturing at time t

E_{jt} = number of employees in industry j at time t

$e_t = E_t/N_t$ = average number of employees per establishment in all manufacturing at time t

$e_{jt} = E_{jt}/N_{jt}$ = average number of employees per establishment in industry j at time t

With this notation, it is obvious that:

$$e_t = \Sigma \, s_{jt} e_{jt},$$ (5.1)

(Text continues on p. 155.)

Table 5.6 Size Distribution of Firms and Employment in Total Manufacturing, 1958 to 1992

Size Class by Number of Employees	1958	1963	1967	1972	1977	1982	1987	1992
A. Firms								
1 to 19	71.5%	70.4%	—	—	—	—	—	—
1 to 4	—	—	36.3%	36.1%	38.6%	33.0%	33.0%	36.8%
5 to 9	—	—	14.8	17.9	16.7	20.1	20.2	20.2
10 to 19	—	—	15.5	15.9	15.9	18.2	17.9	16.2
20 to 99	21.8	22.7	—	—	—	—	—	—
20 to 49	—	—	17.3	16.3	15.4	15.9	15.9	14.5
50 to 99	—	—	7.9	7.0	6.7	6.4	6.4	6.0
100 to 249	4.0	4.3	5.0	4.2	4.1	3.8	4.0	3.8
250 to 499	1.3	1.4	1.7	1.3	1.3	1.2	1.3	1.2
500 to 999	0.6	0.6	0.7	0.6	0.6	0.6	0.6	0.6
1,000 to 2,499	0.4	0.4	0.4	0.4	0.4	0.4	0.4	0.4
2,500 to 4,999	0.1	0.1	0.2	0.2	0.1	0.1	0.1	0.1
5,000 to 9,999	0.1	0.1	0.1	0.1	0.1	0.1	0.1	0.1
10,000 or more	0.1	0.1	0.1	0.1	0.1	0.1	0.1	0.1
All establishments	100.0	100.0	100.0	100.0	100.0	100.0	100.0	100.0
Memo								
Under 20	71.5	70.4	66.6	69.8	71.2	71.4	71.1	73.2
1,000 or more	0.6	0.7	0.8	0.8	0.7	0.7	0.7	0.6

B. Employment

1 to 19	6.5	5.9	—	—	—	—	—	—
1 to 4	—	—	0.8	0.9	1.0	0.9	1.0	1.1
5 to 9	—	—	1.1	1.4	1.3	1.7	1.8	2.0
10 to 19	—	—	2.4	2.5	2.6	3.1	3.3	3.4
20 to 99	14.1	13.2	—	—	—	—	—	—
20 to 49	—	—	5.9	5.9	5.7	6.2	6.6	6.8
50 to 99	—	—	5.8	5.6	5.5	5.6	6.0	6.3
100 to 249	9.4	8.9	8.0	7.3	7.4	7.3	8.2	8.7
250 to 499	7.1	6.5	6.2	5.3	5.4	5.4	6.0	6.4
500 to 999	6.4	5.9	4.8	5.0	5.3	4.9	5.7	6.0
1,000 to 2,499	8.5	7.9	8.1	6.9	7.1	7.0	7.6	8.6
2,500 to 4,999	6.6	7.2	6.4	6.2	6.2	5.6	6.0	6.9
5,000 to 9,999	7.9	7.8	7.8	7.9	7.2	7.2	7.5	7.7
10,000 or more	33.4	36.7	42.7	45.2	45.1	45.0	40.2	36.0
All establishments	100.0	100.0	100.0	100.0	100.0	100.0	100.0	100.0
Memo								
Under 20	6.5	5.9	4.2	4.8	4.9	5.8	6.2	6.6
1,000 or more	56.5	59.6	65.1	66.1	65.7	64.8	61.3	59.2
Average size	65.5	72.6	92.3	86.4	83.5	79.1	74.0	65.8
Standard deviation	869.4	947.9	1,148.4	1,137.6	1,122.2	1,113.2	1,012.8	881.2
Coefficient of variation	13.3	13.1	12.4	13.2	13.4	14.1	13.7	13.4
Gini coefficient	0.853	0.861	0.897	0.901	0.903	0.894	0.885	0.885

Source: Authors' computations from U.S. Bureau of the Census, Enterprise Statistics (1958 to 1992).

Figure 5.3   Size Distribution of Firms, by Number of Employees, 1958 to 1992

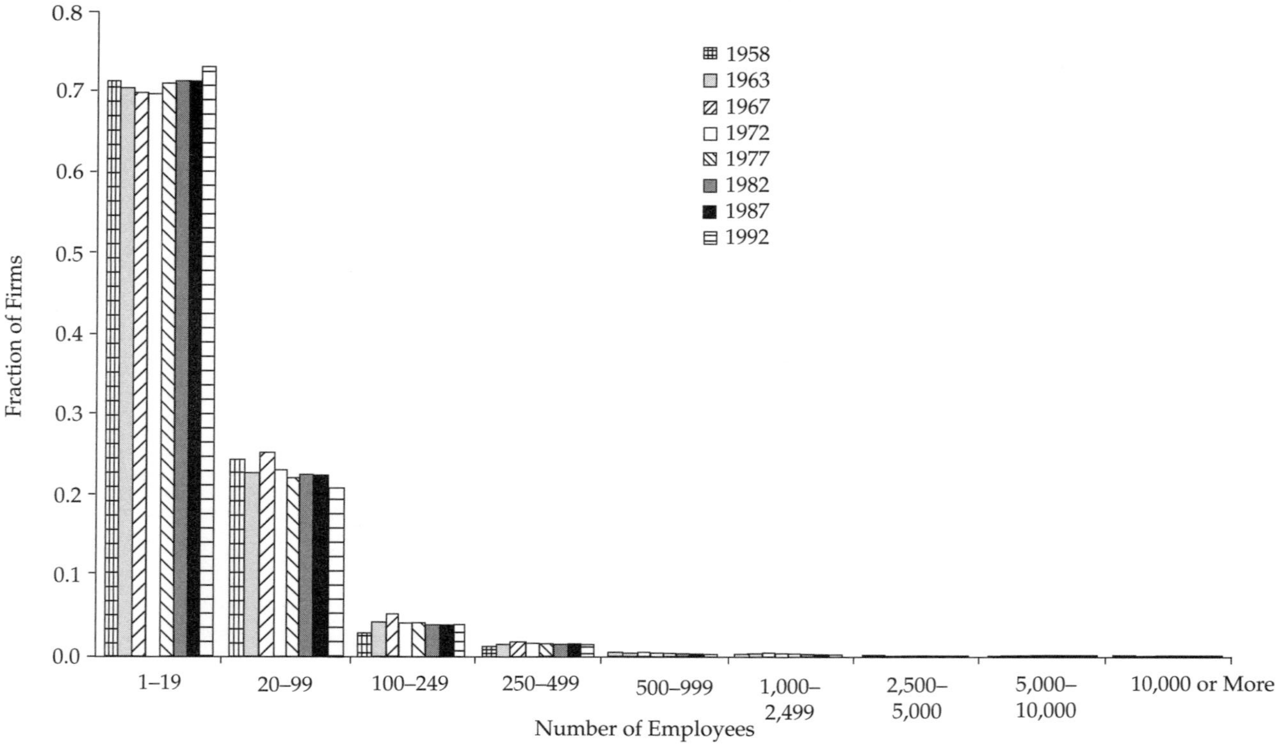

Source: U.S. Bureau of the Census, Enterprise Statistics (1958 to 1992).

Figure 5.4   Size Distribution of Employment, by Size of Firm in Number of Employees, 1958 to 1992

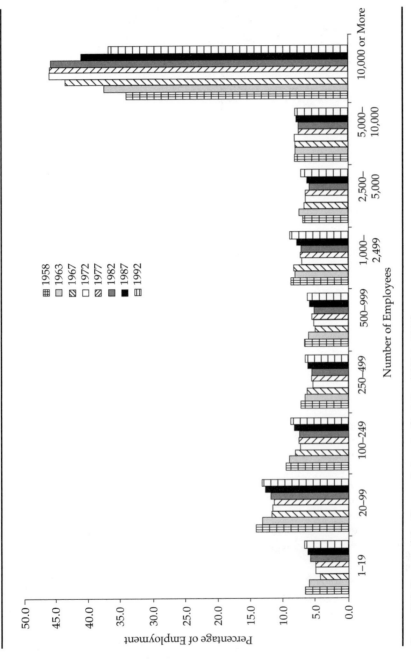

Source: U.S. Bureau of the Census, Enterprise Statistics (1958 to 1992).

Table 5.7   Dispersion of Employment, by Employee Size Class for
Establishments, Two-Digit Manufacturing Industries,
1967 and 1992

SIC	Industry	Coefficient of Variation			Gini Coefficient		
		1967	1992	Change, 1967–1992	1967	1992	Change, 1967–1992
	All manufac- turing industries	4.75	4.33	−0.42	0.828	0.796	−0.032
20	Food and kindred products	2.72	2.49	−0.23	0.745	0.762	0.017
21	Tobacco products	2.80	2.79	−0.01	0.796	0.755	−0.041
22	Textile mill products	2.20	1.81	−0.39	0.715	0.641	−0.074
23	Apparel and other textile products	2.24	2.31	0.07	0.697	0.692	−0.005
24	Lumber and wood products	3.39	2.51	−0.88	0.773	0.743	−0.030
25	Furniture and fixtures	3.00	3.05	0.05	0.775	0.771	−0.004
26	Paper and allied products	1.99	1.86	−0.13	0.682	0.654	−0.029
27	Printing and publishing	4.92	4.38	−0.53	0.814	0.775	−0.039
28	Chemicals and allied products	3.95	3.83	−0.12	0.833	0.796	−0.037
29	Petroleum and coal products	3.48	3.01	−0.46	0.818	0.823	0.005
30	Rubber and miscella- neous plastics products	3.58	2.34	−1.23	0.799	0.691	−0.107
31	Leather and leather products	1.78	2.21	0.43	0.702	0.727	0.025

Table 5.7   *Continued*

SIC	Industry	Coefficient of Variation			Gini Coefficient		
		1967	1992	Change, 1967–1992	1967	1992	Change, 1967–1992
32	Stone, clay, and glass	3.27	2.40	−0.87	0.771	0.602	−0.169
33	Primary metal industries	3.58	2.85	−0.74	0.818	0.677	−0.140
34	Fabricated metal products	3.35	2.68	−0.67	0.762	0.648	−0.114
35	Industrial machinery and equipment	4.85	4.66	−0.18	0.842	0.781	−0.062
36	Electronic and electrical equipment	3.42	3.31	−0.11	0.836	0.791	−0.045
37	Transportation equipment	4.32	4.78	0.46	0.902	0.863	−0.039
38	Instruments and related products	4.36	3.73	−0.62	0.855	0.841	−0.014
39	Miscellaneous industries	3.40	3.27	−0.13	0.780	0.775	−0.004

Source: Authors' computations from U.S. Bureau of the Census, Census of Manufacturing (1967 to 1992).

from which it follows that:

$$\Delta e_t = \Sigma (\Delta s_t)e_{jt} + \Sigma s_{jt} \Delta e_j, \tag{5.2}$$

where Δs_j is the change in s over the period and Δe is the change in e over the period. Several alternative choices of weights are available for the decomposition: beginning-of-the-period, end-of-the-period, and average period weights. The last set, given by $(e_{j1} + e_{j2})/2$ and $(s_{j1} + s_{j2})/2$, has the advantage of allowing an exact decomposition. Our results are therefore shown only for average period weights.[8]

Before we show the decompositions, it is first of interest to see how the distribution of the number of establishments (or firms) and employment among manufacturing industries has changed over time.

We begin with the Census of Manufacturing data. As shown in table 5.8, there has been a clear shift in the distribution of establishments away from low-tech industries and toward medium-tech and high-tech industries. The share of total establishments in food and kindred products fell almost by half between 1967 and 1992, and the share in textiles, apparel, lumber and wood products, chemicals, and stone, clay, and glass products also declined noticeably. In contrast, the proportion of establishments in printing and publishing increased by over five percentage points, and the proportion in both industrial machinery and rubber and miscellaneous plastics products by over two percentage points. Increases were also found in fabricated metal products, electronics and electrical equipment, transportation equipment, and instruments and related products. Over this twenty-five-year period, the total number of manufacturing establishments grew by 21 percent.

Changes in the distribution of employment among two-digit manufacturing industries are roughly similar. Relatively large declines of the share of total manufacturing employment are found in textiles and apparel, leather and leather products, and stone, glass, and clay products, as well in primary metals and electronics and electrical equipment. Interestingly, the share employed in food products remained relatively unchanged. Relatively large increases occurred in printing and publishing, rubber and plastic products, and instruments and related products, as well as in lumber and wood products. Between 1967 and 1992, total employment in manufacturing fell by 8.3 percent.

The composition of manufacturing employment can also be tabulated from the Enterprise Statistics, in this case for both establishments and firms.[9] The results are roughly similar, though the data now begin in 1958 instead of 1967. There is again a very sizable shift of establishments—and especially of firms—out of food products, as well a moderate decline in the employment share. Declines in establishment, firm, and employment shares are also found for textiles, apparel, lumber and wood products, and leather and leather products. There are big increases in the establishment, firm, and employment shares in printing and publishing between 1958 and 1992, and modest increases in rubber and plastic products, fabricated metal products, industrial machinery and equipment, and instruments and related products. The results for the other industries are either mixed or reflect relatively small changes. Between 1958 and 1992, the total number of establishments grew by 25 percent, the total number of firms by 17 percent, and total employment by 19 percent (although it declined from 1967 to 1992).[10]

We now turn to the results on the decompositions, which are shown in table 5.9. Panel A is based on establishment data from the Census of Manufacturing. Over the entire 1967 to 1992 period, the average establishment size in total manufacturing declined by 14.8 employees. Roughly speaking, all of the decline (107 percent) was attributable to declines in average establishment sizes within industries (the within-industry effect). In other words, if the distribution of establishments among industries had remained unchanged over the period, the over-all average establishment size would have fallen by 15.9 employees (instead of by 14.8 employees). Shifts in the distribution of establishments among industries (the between-industry effect) contributed virtually nothing to the change in the average size within total manufacturing. Actually, these shifts slightly favored industries with above-average establishment size.

As we look across five-year periods, the only notable departure from this pattern occurs from 1967 to 1972. During this period, the average establishment size in manufacturing fell by 2.8 employees. If the distribution of establishments among industries had remained constant over the period, the average size would have fallen by much more—by 4.9 employees. However, industries with above-average establishment sizes grew in relative terms, and this between-industries effect led to an increase in the average establishment size in manufacturing of 2.0 employees.

Panel B in table 5.9 is again based on establishment size, but this time using data from the Enterprise Statistics. Over the 1972 to 1992 period as a whole, average establishment size in total manufacturing fell by 6.0 employees, about half as much as recorded in the census data of panel A. But once again, the within-industry effect is totally dominant, accounting for 117 percent of the total decline. In other words, if the distribution of establishments among industries had not changed over the period, overall average establishment size would have fallen by 7.0 employees (instead of the actual 6.0 employees). As we have by now come to expect, the period before 1972 was different. Between 1958 and 1963, average establishment size in total manufacturing increased, and changes in average size in specific industries accounted for 79 percent of the change. During the 1963 to 1972 period (recall that establishment data are not available for 1967), average size in total manufacturing again rose. But in this case, average establishment size at the industry level fell, offsetting the positive effect on overall average size from the relative growth of industries with larger establishments.

Panel C in table 5.9 shows the same sorts of results on the basis of

(Text continues on p. 162.)

Table 5.8 Distribution of Establishments, Firms, and Employment, by Two-Digit Manufacturing Industry, 1958, 1967, and 1992

| | | Census of Manufacturing | | | | Enterprise Statistics | | | | | |
| | | Establishments | | Employment | | Establishments | | Number of Firms | | Employment | |
SIC	Industry	1967	1992	1967	1992	1958	1992	1958	1992	1958	1992
20	Food and kindred products	10.7%	5.6%	9.1%	8.9%	14.4%	7.1%	13.2%	4.9%	11.8%	9.8%
21	Tobacco products	0.1	0.0	0.4	0.2	0.2	0.2	0.1	0.0	0.6	0.7
22	Textile mill products	2.3	1.6	5.1	3.6	2.5	1.7	2.4	1.5	5.8	3.5
23	Apparel and other textile products	8.6	6.2	7.5	5.8	8.1	5.6	10.4	6.6	5.4	5.2
24	Lumber and wood products	12.1	9.7	3.1	3.9	9.8	7.5	13.1	10.3	3.4	3.1
25	Furniture and fixtures	3.3	3.1	2.4	2.8	2.9	2.8	3.7	3.3	1.9	2.7
26	Paper and allied products	1.9	1.7	3.5	3.7	1.7	2.1	1.4	1.3	3.4	4.3
27	Printing and publishing	12.4	17.6	5.7	8.8	9.7	14.9	12.7	18.7	5.5	9.0
28	Chemicals and allied products	3.9	3.2	4.7	5.0	4.4	4.7	3.2	2.4	5.6	7.0
29	Petroleum and coal products	0.6	0.6	0.8	0.7	7.5	2.7	0.4	0.3	3.4	1.8

30	Rubber and miscellaneous plastics products	2.1	4.3	2.9	5.3	2.0	4.5	1.5	3.9	2.4	4.6
31	Leather and leather products	1.2	0.5	1.8	0.6	1.7	0.6	1.5	0.6	2.2	0.4
32	Stone, clay, and glass	5.1	4.4	3.3	2.8	4.5	4.2	4.7	3.7	3.7	2.9
33	Primary metal industries	2.2	1.8	7.1	3.9	2.6	2.6	1.9	1.6	4.1	4.1
34	Fabricated metal products	9.0	9.8	7.4	8.0	7.1	8.4	8.5	10.0	6.4	6.9
35	Industrial machinery and equipment	12.4	14.5	10.3	10.3	9.5	12.8	10.4	15.5	9.0	10.1
36	Electronic and electrical equipment	3.5	4.6	10.4	8.5	3.7	5.2	2.5	4.4	8.5	7.5
37	Transportation equipment	2.5	3.0	10.1	9.7	2.4	5.6	2.2	2.9	12.3	9.2
38	Instruments and related products	1.5	3.1	2.2	5.4	1.5	3.1	1.2	3.0	1.6	5.2
39	Miscellaneous industries	4.6	4.6	2.3	2.2	3.9	3.7	5.0	5.0	2.6	1.9
	Nondurables	43.9	41.4	41.5	42.7	52.2	44.2	46.8	40.2	46.3	46.4
	Durables	56.1	58.6	58.5	57.3	47.8	55.8	53.2	59.8	53.7	53.6
	Total	100.0	100.0	100.0	100.0	100.0	100.0	100.0	100.0	100.0	100.0
	Total number (in thousands)	305.7	370.9	18,492	16,949	373.8	465.7	263.9	307.7	16,261	19,258

Source: Authors' computations from the U.S. Bureau of the Census, Census of Manufacturing, establishments (1967 to 1992), and Enterprise Statistics, establishments and firms (1958 to 1992).

Table 5.9 Decomposition of the Change in Average Establishment or Firm Size in Total Manufacturing, by Period, 1958 to 1992

	1958–1963	1963–1967	1967–1972	1972–1977	1977–1982	1982–1987	1987–1992	1967–1992
A. Census of Manufacturing: establishment data								
Actual change	—	—	-2.82	-4.89	-1.64	-1.79	-3.66	-14.80
Within industry	—	—	-4.85	-4.68	-1.43	-1.25	-3.65	-15.86
Between industry	—	—	2.03	-0.21	-0.21	-0.53	-0.02	1.06
Memo: percentage decomposition								
Actual change	—	—	100%	100%	100%	100%	100%	100%
Within industry	—	—	172	96	87	70	100	107
Between industry	—	—	-72	4	13	30	0	-7
B. Enterprise Statistics: establishment data[a]								
Actual change	2.12	—	1.14	-0.94	-2.74	1.20	-3.52	-6.00
Within industry	1.67	—	-1.06	-1.52	-2.36	1.22	-3.53	-7.02
Between industry	0.45	—	2.20	0.58	-0.38	-0.02	0.00	1.02

Memo: percentage decomposition								
Actual change	100%	100%	100%	100%	100%	100%	100%	100%
Within industry	79	—	−93	161	86	101	100	117
Between industry	21	—	193	−61	14	−1	0	−17
C. Enterprise Statistics: firm data								
Actual change	7.07	20.05	−6.25	−2.87	−4.39	−5.12	−8.15	−26.78
Within industry	6.39	20.33	−5.34	−3.83	1.31	−3.97	−7.97	−25.98
Between industry	0.68	−0.28	−0.90	0.96	−5.69	−1.15	−0.18	−0.81
Memo: percentage decomposition								
Actual change	100%	100%	100%	100%	100%	100%	100%	100%
Within industry	90	101	86	133	−30	77	98	97
Between industry	10	−1	14	−33	130	23	2	3

Sources: Authors' computations from the U.S. Bureau of the Census, Census of Manufacturing, establishments (1967 to 1992), and Enterprise Statistics, establishments and firms (1958 to 1992). See equation 5.2.

[a] For the Enterprise Statistics, establishment data for the year 1967 are not available. As a result, the time periods for panel B of the table are 1963 to 1972 instead of 1967 to 1972, and 1972 to 1992 instead of 1967 to 1992.

Note: Totals may not add up due to rounding error.

firm data drawn from the Enterprise Statistics. In both the 1958 to 1963 and 1963 to 1967 periods, average firm size in total manufacturing increased, and this change was almost completely ascribable to changes in firm size at the industry level. Average firm size in total manufacturing declined in each of the next five periods, and the within-industry effect was again the dominant cause. The only exception is the 1977 to 1982 period, when firm size rose, on average, at the industry level, led mainly by food products and tobacco products. This increase, in turn, may be attributable to the frenetic merger and acquisition activity during this time. However, in this case, industry growth favored industries with firm sizes smaller than average; that tendency led to a net decline in mean firm size in total manufacturing over the period. Over the entire period of 1967 to 1992, average firm size in total manufacturing fell by 26.8 employees, and this change was again almost entirely due to the within-industry effect.

Thus, according to all three data sources, changes in establishment (or firm) size at the industry level accounted for almost the entire change in average establishment (or firm) size in total manufacturing over the entire period, and for most subperiods as well. Therefore, we can comfortably focus on developments within two-digit industries in the next section, where we look for the causes of changes in average establishment (or firm) size in manufacturing.

Factors Affecting Downsizing in Manufacturing

In this section, we consider the influences responsible for changes in the size distribution of both establishments and firms within manufacturing industries. Using the downsizing hypotheses reiterated at the start of this chapter, we divide our explanatory variables into four groups: measures of technological activity; measures of capital formation; measures of international competition; and institutional and structural variables.[11]

To assess the correlations between technology and downsizing, we use three standard indicators of technological activity: the rate of total factor productivity (TFP) growth; the ratio of research and development expenditures to gross domestic product (GDP); and the number of scientists and engineers engaged in R&D as a share of total employment. Figure 5.5 displays the percentage change in average establishment and firm sizes and the average rates of TFP and labor productivity growth for total manufacturing by census period. It should be noted at the outset that this figure (like the next three) is meant only to provide some general indications about trends. The statistical relation between downsizing and these other variables is based on formal regression analysis involving pooled cross-sectional, time-

Figure 5.5   Change in Average Establishment and Firm Size and TFP and
Labor Productivity Growth, Total Manufacturing, 1958–1997

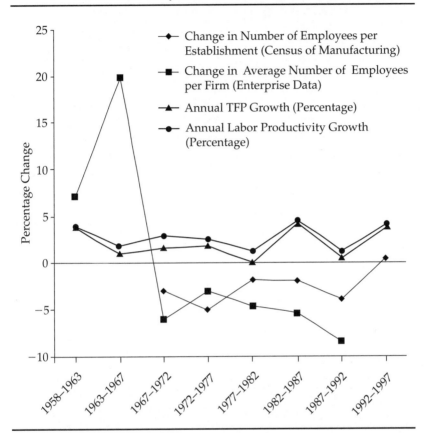

Sources: U.S. Bureau of the Census, Census of Manufacturing, establishments (1967 to
1997) , Enterprise Statistics, firms (1958 to 1992); and U.S. National Income and Product
Accounts (see the data appendix to chapter 5 for details).

series data for the twenty two-digit SIC industries. There are no clear
connections between productivity and size, at least at the level of total
manufacturing. Productivity (both TFP and labor productivity) growth
was very high during the first upsizing period, 1958 to 1963, but
much lower during the second upsizing period, 1963 to 1967. Downsizing occurred during the 1977 to 1982 period, when productivity
growth was very low, but also continued during the 1982 to 1987
period, when productivity grew very rapidly. Productivity growth
was also quite high in the 1992 to 1997 period, when average establishment size increased.

Figure 5.6 shows the relationship (or rather the lack thereof) between changes in R&D investment (by two different measures) and

Figure 5.6   Change in Average Establishment and Firm Size and R&D Intensity, Total Manufacturing, 1958 to 1997

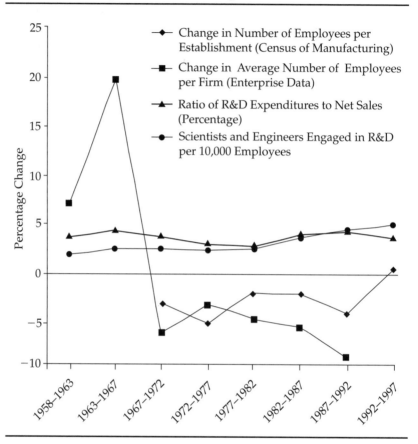

Sources: U.S. Bureau of the Census, Census of Manufacturing, establishments (1967 to 1997), Enterprise Statistics, firms (1958 to 1992); and National Science Foundation (see the data appendix to chapter 5 for details).

firm or establishment size for total manufacturing by census period. Here again, there does not seem to be a clear correspondence between downsizing and R&D activity. R&D expenditures as a share of net sales increased during the upsizing years 1958 to 1963 and 1963 to 1967, and then fell off over the next three periods as downsizing replaced upsizing. However, R&D activity then picked up after 1982, while downsizing continued (and even accelerated in terms of changes in firm size). In contrast, the number of scientists and engineers employed in R&D per employee has risen almost continuously over time since the 1958 to 1963 period—through both upsizing and downsizing periods.

The scope of investment by businesses in capital (plant and equipment) may also influence average establishment size. The variables used here to measure this capital intensity are: the annual growth of the ratio of *total capital* to total employment; the annual growth of the ratio of *equipment and machinery* to total employment; and the annual growth in the ratio of various measures of *information technology (IT) capital*, such as office, computing, and accounting (OCA) equipment, and OCA plus communications equipment (OCACM), as a ratio to total employment. These IT variables are used because computers (and information technology in general) may play a particularly important role in the changes in establishment and firm size, as we suggested above in hypotheses 1 and 4.

As figure 5.7 shows, the growth of total capital per worker was at its highest level during the periods 1967 to 1972 and 1977 to 1982, when downsizing was occurring. But it was also at one of its lowest points from 1982 to 1987, when downsizing was also occurring. The growth of equipment per worker was at its highest level in the 1963 to 1967 period, which was one of substantial upsizing, and at its second highest level in 1977 to 1982, a downsizing period. The growth of OCA per worker was largest from 1963 to 1967 (an upsizing period), 1972 to 1977, 1977 to 1982 (both downsizing periods), and 1992 to 1997 (another upsizing period). In sum, there is no obvious correlation, positive or negative, in the data.

The intensification of international competition—as measured by the change in the ratio of manufacturing exports to total manufacturing output and the change in the ratio of manufacturing imports to total manufacturing output over the period—may also affect the average size of both firms and establishments. Industries competing in international product markets and those competing against imports may be forced to reduce their size in order to cut costs, as we suggested above in hypothesis 3 (foreign competition compels domestic industry to downsize by trimming labor "fat"). Greater unionization may also reduce the degree of downsizing by restricting employers' flexibility to restructure the workplace substantially utilizing new technology.

As shown in figure 5.8, the change in export intensity was at its highest point over the 1987 to 1992 period (a significant downsizing period) and next highest from 1972 to 1977 and 1977 to 1982 (also downsizing periods). Import intensity grew most rapidly over the 1982 to 1987 period (also a downsizing period), followed by 1967 to 1972 (another downsizing period) and 1992 to 1997 (an upsizing period). The average unionization rate in total manufacturing has been falling rather steadily over time, at least from the 1960s (the earliest data available), while over these years the pace of downsizing of firm size has been increasing. However, changes in average establishment size do not show the same steady trend over time.

**Figure 5.7   Change in Average Establishment and Firm Size and the
Growth in Capital Intensity, Total Manufacturing, 1958 to 1997**

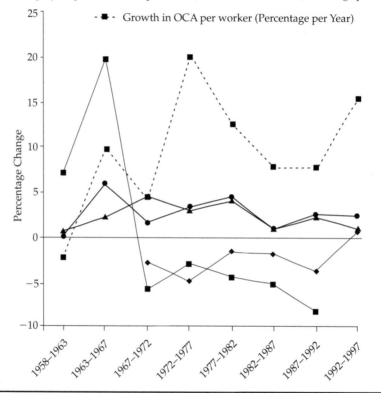

Sources: U.S. Bureau of the Census, Census of Manufacturing, establishments (1967 to
1997), Enterprise Statistics, firms (1958 to 1992); and Bureau of Economic Analysis (see
the data appendix to chapter 5 for details).

Regression Analysis of Downsizing in Manufacturing

We next turn to regression analysis to sort out the effects of these
disparate variables. Our regressions use pooled time-series, cross-
sectional data consisting of twenty industry observations in each of
the six or seven five-year time periods. We estimate what amounts to
a fixed-effects model, in which the average establishment size in an
industry is an unchanging function of the *levels* of these variables,
plus an industry-specific effect that is constant over time. Because our

Figure 5.8   Change in Average Establishment and Firm Size, the Change in Export and Import Intensity, and Union Density, Total Manufacturing, 1958 to 1997

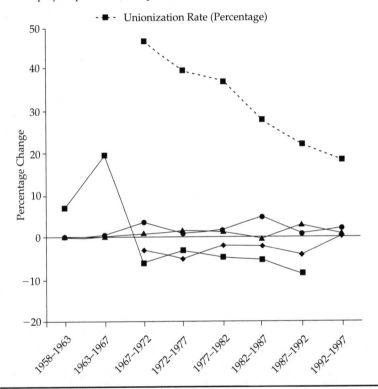

—◆— Change in Number of Employees per Establishment (Census of Manufacturing)

—■— Change in Average Number of Employees per Firm (Enterprise Data)

—▲— Change in Ratio of Exports to Total Sales (Percentage Points)

—●— Change in Ratio of Imports to Net Sales (Percentage Points)

- ■ - Unionization Rate (Percentage)

Sources: U.S. Bureau of the Census, Census of Manufacturing, establishments (1967 to 1997), Enterprise Statistics, firms (1958 to 1992); U.S. National Income and Product Accounts; and U.S. Department of Labor (see the data appendix to chapter 5 for details).

regression uses the first difference of this equation (actually, the percentage change in mean establishment size at the industry level), the industry-specific constant should wash out. (However, we will still test explicitly for the existence of industry effects.) The error terms are assumed to be independently distributed but may not be identically distributed; therefore, we use the White (1980) procedure for a heteroskedasticity-consistent covariance matrix in the estimation.

Table 5.10 shows our full results for the case where the dependent

Table 5.10   Regressions of Percentage Change in Mean Number of Employees per Establishment, on Selected Variables

Independent Variables	Specification					
	(1)	(2)	(3)	(4)	(5)	(6)
Constant	0.058*	0.045#	0.040	0.041	−0.001	0.014
	(2.29)	(1.95)	(1.65)	(1.56)	(0.03)	(0.55)
Annual rate of TFP growth	−0.176	−0.276	−0.227	−0.258	−0.209	−1.710
	(0.66)	(1.14)	(0.91)	(1.04)	(0.89)	(0.71)
Ratio of industry R&D to net sales (period average)	−0.301	−0.749#	−0.870*	−0.771#	−0.670#	−0.066#
	(0.73)	(1.92)	(2.10)	(1.94)	(1.85)	(1.71)
Period change in ratio of exports to gross output	−1.788**	−1.128*	−1.105*	−1.096*	−1.023*	−1.149*
	(3.28)	(2.18)	(2.13)	(2.08)	(2.06)	(2.27)
Period change in ratio of imports to gross output	−0.305*	−0.054	−0.056	−0.053	0.029	−0.092
	(2.26)	(0.40)	(0.20)	(0.39)	(0.22)	(0.70)
Unionization rate (period average)[a]	−0.142*	−0.097#	−0.107#	−0.094#	−0.078	−0.083
	(2.32)	(1.70)	(1.85)	(1.69)	(1.43)	(1.49)
Growth in employment[b]	—	2.133**	2.348**	2.148**	2.473**	2.229**
		(4.79)	(4.63)	(4.77)	(5.61)	(5.09)
Growth in total capital per worker	—	—	0.385	—	—	—
			(0.90)			
Growth in OCA per worker[c]	—	—	—	0.028	—	—
				(0.33)		
Profit share[d] (one-period lag)	—	—	—	—	0.199**	—
					(3.20)	
Profit rate[e] (one-period lag)	—	—	—	—	—	0.117**
						(2.52)
R^2	0.18	0.33	0.33	0.33	0.38	0.36
Adjusted-R^2	0.15	0.29	0.29	0.28	0.34	0.32
Standard error	0.0967	0.0883	0.0883	0.0886	0.0847	0.0862
Sample size	116	116	116	116	116	116

Source: U.S. Bureau of the Census, Census of Manufacturing (various years).
Note: The sample consists of pooled cross-section, time-series data, with observations on each of the twenty manufacturing industries in 1967 to 1972, 1972 to 1977, 1977 to 1982, 1982 to 1987, 1987 to 1992, and 1992 to 1997 (sixteen industries). The absolute value of the t-statistic is shown in parentheses below the coefficient estimate. See the data appendix for sources.
[a]Unionization rate: share of employees covered by union contracts.
[b]Employment is based on FTEEs and capital on net capital stock.
[c]OCA: net stocks of office, computer, and accounting.
[d]Profit share: ratio of net profits to net national income, average over the period.
[e]Profit rate: ratio of net profits to net capital stock, averaged over the period.
#Significant at the 10 percent level (two-tailed test).
*Significant at the 5 percent level (two-tailed test).
**Significant at the 1 percent level (two-tailed test).

variable is the percentage change in average *establishment* size as measured in the Census of Manufacturing data. There are, of course, general issues of timing, dynamics, and causality when considering the variables that influence changes in business size (and also the effects of business size change on other variables such as productivity growth). It should be noted that in table 5.10 the change in average establishment size (like most of the variables in the table) is entered contemporaneously. The reason is that our data, which are typically entered as percentage changes, usually entail five-year intervals. If we were to lag the data in order to reduce any potential bias from simultaneity, we would generally be looking for the effects, say, of changes in an independent variable between 1972 and 1977 on changes in the dependent variable between 1977 and 1982. That lag seems rather long, and indeed, our experiments with lagged variables generally provided meager correlations. (For this same reason, good instruments were not available.)

The most significant variable by far is the growth rate of industry employment. Its coefficient is positive and uniformly significant at the 1 percent level. A comparison of specifications 1 and 2 also indicates that the adjusted-R^2 statistic jumps from 0.18 to 0.31 when this variable is added to the regression equation.[12] This result, which is confirmed in everything that follows, supports our uncomplicated hypothesis of chapter 4: changes in average enterprise size are directly associated with changes in overall industry employment. When industry employment falls, average establishment size declines, and conversely.[13]

With regard to the effects of technological progress on downsizing, the most salient result is that (the five-year average of) industry R&D spending as a percentage of net sales has a consistently negative effect on the growth of average establishment size. And its coefficient is significant at the 5 or 10 percent level in all cases except one. This result is consistent with the predictions of hypothesis 1 (technological change favors smaller business enterprises). The regressions were repeated using the number of scientists and engineers engaged in R&D per one thousand employees as the measure of R&D intensity instead of R&D spending. The coefficient of this variable is also negative, but it is significant in only three of the six cases (results not shown).

However, the coefficient of the growth rate of TFP per se, while consistently negative, is not significant in any of the regressions in table 5.10. Similarly, the coefficient of the growth rate of labor productivity is also negative but not significant (results not shown). We also tried lagging both TFP growth and labor productivity growth one period, but in neither case was the coefficient significant (results not shown).

In contradistinction to the predictions of hypothesis 4 (downsizing occurs when capital is substituted for labor), there is no evidence whatever that the capital-labor ratio has increased more rapidly in industries that have downsized more. In fact, the coefficient of the growth rate of total capital per worker is positive, though not significantly so (see specification 3 in table 5.10). Similarly, the coefficient of the growth rate of OCA per worker is positive but not significant (specification 4). These findings appear to contradict the predictions of hypothesis 4. The coefficient of the growth rate of OCACM per worker is also positive but not significant, as is that of the growth rate of total equipment per worker (results not shown).

With regard to the trade variables, the change in the ratio of imports to total output has a uniformly negative coefficient. Its coefficient is significant at the 5 percent level in specification 1, before industry employment growth is included, but it is not significant when this variable is included. These results are mildly supportive of the predictions of hypothesis 3 (foreign competition compels domestic industry to downsize by trimming labor "fat"). They indicate that import competition tends to induce downsizing, perhaps through the substantial effects on plant-level efficiency. Moreover, a comparison of specifications 1 and 2 suggests that the main effect of import competition is to reduce overall employment within the industry: the (negative) coefficient drops by more than 50 percent when industry employment is added to the regression. However, the theory of contestable markets suggests that the effects of import competition on establishment size may be underestimated here because import intensity by itself does not fully capture *potential* competition from foreign suppliers of an industry's product.

Changes in export orientation (as measured by the ratio of exports to total output) have a negative coefficient that is significant at the 1 percent level in one case and at the 5 percent level in the other five cases. The power of this effect is a bit of a surprise—the coefficients are much larger than those of imports. This finding strongly suggests that competition for foreign markets induces firms to cut costs and therefore to downsize.

The unionization rate, somewhat surprisingly, has a consistently negative coefficient, which is significant at the 5 percent level in one case (when industry employment growth is not included), at the 10 percent level in three cases, and not significant in the other two cases (when profitability is included). Thus, consistent with hypothesis 5 about the breakdown of the social contract, the evidence weakly indicates that unionized companies are *more* apt to cut back plant size than those that are not unionized. Part of this effect may be attributable to the higher wages paid to unionized workers and the consequent pressure on firms to reduce labor costs. A comparison of specifications 1 and 2 suggests that the union effect acts mainly at the industry level, however, leading to reductions in overall industry employment. Moreover, when we control for profitability, the coefficient of the unionization variable falls by about 20 percent and becomes statistically insignificant.

In specification 5 we include the lagged profit share as an additional independent variable, and in specification 6 we include the lagged profit rate. (See the data appendix to this chapter for details on measurement.) The coefficients of both variables are positive and significant at the 1 percent level. The results thus suggest that lower profitability in one period leads companies to reduce their plant size in the succeeding period. This suggestion provides support for hypothesis 3, in that low profitability may lead to greater pressure to reach the most efficient enterprise size by "trimming fat."[14]

The best fit, as measured by the adjusted-R^2 statistic and the standard error of the regression, is provided by the fifth specification. This equation includes TFP growth, R&D expenditures as a share of net sales, the change in both export and import intensity, the unionization rate, the lagged profit share, and the growth in industry employment.

All of the regressions were repeated using persons engaged in production (PEP) instead of full-time equivalent employees (FTEE) as the measure of employment. (See data appendix for definitions.) The regression results were almost identical.[15]

The same set of regressions was repeated for the percentage change in average *firm* size derived from the Enterprise Statistics. The results are shown in table 5.11. We again use the pooled time-series, cross-sectional data set, consisting of twenty industry observations in as many five-year time periods as we have. With the Enterprise Statistics, that means adding the two periods 1958 to 1963 and 1963 to 1967 but losing the 1992 to 1997 period.[16] As a result, differences between these new results and those of table 5.9 may be due either to the fact that determinants of changes in employment at the firm level differ from those at the establishment level or to the different time periods. We will try to sort out these two possibilities.

As in the establishment-level regressions, the most significant variable is the growth in industry employment, which has the predicted positive coefficient of similar magnitude to what we found in table 5.10. Industry R&D spending as a percentage of net sales again has a consistently negative effect on the change in mean firm size, but in this case its coefficient is uniformly insignificant. However, this apparent difference between firms and establishments turns out to be a

Table 5.11   Regressions of Percentage Change in Mean Number of
Employees per Firm, on Selected Variables

Independent Variables	Specification				
	(1)	(2)	(3)	(4)	(5)
Constant	0.125**	0.076#	0.141**	0.057	0.031
	(4.58)	(1.89)	(4.46)	(1.62)	0.90
Annual rate of TFP growth	−1.362*	−0.976	−1.550*	−1.067#	−0.866
	(2.29)	(1.54)	(2.49)	(1.82)	(1.50)
Ratio of industry R&D to net sales (period average)	−0.227	−0.684	−0.075	−0.271	−0.220
	(0.27)	(0.77)	(0.09)	(0.33)	(0.27)
Period change in ratio of exports to gross output	−4.194**	−4.658**	−5.045**	−4.818**	4.604**
	(3.94)	(3.73)	(4.02)	(3.97)	(3.88)
Period change in ratio of imports to gross output	−0.274	−0.299	−0.259	−0.199	−0.387
	(0.88)	(0.96)	(0.83)	(0.65)	(1.30)
Growth in employment	2.224*	2.860**	2.041*	2.447**	2.163**
	(2.55)	(3.02)	(2.29)	(2.87)	(2.62)
Growth in total capital per worker	—	1.553	—	—	—
		(1.60)			
Growth in OCA per worker	—	—	−0.168	—	—
			(1.00)		
Profit share (one-period lag)	—	—	—	0.355**	—
				(2.97)	
Profit rate (one-period lag)	—	—	—	—	0.346**
					(3.97)
R^2	0.25	0.27	0.26	0.30	0.33
Adjusted-R^2	0.22	0.24	0.23	0.27	0.30
Standard error	0.213	0.211	0.213	0.207	0.202
Sample size	140	140	140	140	140

Source: U.S. Bureau of the Census, Enterprise Statistics (1958 to 1992).
Note: The sample consists of pooled cross-section, time-series data, with observations on each of the twenty manufacturing industries in 1958 to 1963, 1963 to 1967, 1967 to 1972, 1972 to 1977, 1977 to 1982, 1982 to 1987, and 1987 to 1992. The absolute value of the t-statistic is shown in parentheses below the coefficient estimate. See the data appendix to chapter 5 for sources and table 5.10 note for key.
#Significant at the 10 percent level (two-tailed test).
*Significant at the 5 percent level (two-tailed test).
**Significant at the 1 percent level (two-tailed test).

period effect. When the same regression is run on the five periods 1967 to 1972, 1972 to 1977, 1977 to 1982, 1982 to 1987, and 1987 to 1992, the coefficient of R&D spending is again found to be negative and significant at either the 5 or 10 percent level.

As before, the coefficient of TFP growth is consistently negative, but it is now significant at the 5 percent level in two of the five cases, at the 10 percent level in one case, and insignificant in the other two cases. A similar result is found for the coefficient of the growth of labor productivity. Also, just as in the establishment-level regressions, the coefficient of the growth in total capital per worker is positive but not significant, while the coefficient of the growth of OCA per worker is actually negative but not significant (specifications 2 and 3). This latter result conflicts with the conjecture that computerization may lead to easier coordination among establishments and thus to greater economies of scale and scope at the firm level. Computerization, in turn, may result in more establishments per firm and thus in higher employment per firm, while it can still reduce economies of scale at the establishment level and lead to smaller establishment sizes.

As before, the change in the ratio of imports to total sales has a uniformly negative coefficient. But again, this variable is not significant in any case. The change in export intensity also has a negative coefficient and is once again highly significant—at the 1 percent level in every case. The unionization rate, as before, has a consistently negative coefficient, but it is now not even remotely significant. We have excluded this variable from table 5.11 since it is shown empirically to be unimportant and data for it are available only beginning in 1967. The lagged profit share and the lagged profit rate again have positive coefficients. As before, the coefficients of both are significant at the 1 percent level (specifications 4 and 6).

In general, the results in table 5.11 on firms are quite similar to those in table 5.10 on establishments. Thus, we can conclude that the influences that affect changes in establishment size are generally the same as those that affect changes in firm size.

Regression Analysis of Changes in the Dispersion of Establishment Size

Next we look at changes in the dispersion of employment among size classes by two-digit industry. We use the pooled cross-sectional time-series data set from the Census of Manufacturing for twenty industry observations in 1967 to 1972, 1972 to 1977, 1977 to 1982, 1982 to 1987, and 1987 to 1992.[17] As before, the error terms are assumed to be independently distributed but may not be identically distributed, so we use the White (1980) procedure for a heteroskedasticity-consistent co-variance matrix in the estimation.

The only significant variables in these regressions turn out to be our measures of growth in information technology investment per worker. Their coefficients are negative, indicating that greater invest-ment in computers reduces dispersion in employment by size class within an industry.

The results of our regressions are shown in table 5.12. The first dependent variable is the change in the Gini coefficient (CHNGGINI), and the second is the change in the coefficient of variation (CHNGCV). The only significant variables in these two regressions are the growth in OCA per worker and the growth of OCACM per worker. (The latter result is very similar to the former and is not shown.) Their coefficient is negative, indicating that greater investment in OCA (or OCACM) leads to smaller dispersion in employment by size class within an industry. In contrast, the growth in total capital and the growth in total equipment per worker have positive coefficients that are not significant (results not shown). The coefficients of the change in the import share are all positive but not significant, while those of the change in the export share are of mixed sign but again not signifi-cant. The lagged profit share and the lagged profit rate have positive but insignificant coefficients (results not shown).

Since OCA investment is not a significant determinant of downsiz-ing but does have a significant effect on dispersion, it is possible that its main effect is reduction in the shares of employment in both very small and very large establishments—that is, promotion of regression toward the mean. However, as we see in the third column of table 5.12, the growth of OCA per worker actually has a positive and sig-nificant effect on the share of total employment in establishments of nineteen or fewer employees (CHEST20), as does the growth in OCACM per workers (not shown). The growth of total industry em-ployment is negatively associated with the share of employment in small establishments, as might be expected, but its coefficient is not significant. As in the case of changes in overall dispersion, none of the other variables is statistically significant.

On the other hand, the growth in OCA per worker is negatively and significantly associated with the share of employment in estab-lishments of one thousand or more employees, as is R&D intensity. However, none of the other variables proves significant.

Conclusions

In the main, we find that the variables responsible for changes in business establishment size are essentially the same as those that af-

Table 5.12   Regressions of the Change in the Dispersion of Employment, on Selected Variables

Independent Variables	CHNGGINI[a]	CHNGCV[b]	CHNGEST20[c]	CHNGEST1000[d]
Constant	0.009	−0.049	−0.001	0.000
	(0.87)	(0.49)	(0.16)	(0.01)
Annual rate of	−0.024	−0.207	0.033	0.068
TFP growth	(0.23)	(0.21)	(0.49)	(0.47)
Ratio of industry	0.034	0.362	−0.030	−0.395[#]
R&D to net sales (period average)	(0.23)	(0.25)	(0.31)	(1.90)
Period change in	−0.024	0.036	−0.040	0.173
ratio of exports to gross output	(0.12)	(0.02)	(0.31)	(0.63)
Period change in	0.006	0.466	0.023	0.032
ratio of imports to gross output	(0.13)	(0.98)	(0.74)	(0.47)
Unionization rate	−0.023	0.119	0.008	−0.024
(period average)	(1.03)	(0.56)	(0.53)	(0.78)
Growth in	−0.023	−0.123	−0.172	0.343
employment	(0.14)	(0.07)	(1.56)	(1.44)
Growth in OCA	−0.098**	−0.695*	0.041*	−0.079[#]
per worker	(3.05)	(2.22)	(2.08)	(1.86)
R^2	0.11	0.07	0.10	0.10
Adjusted-R^2	0.04	0.01	0.03	0.04
Standard error	0.0314	0.306	0.0204	0.0440
Sample size	100	100	100	100

Note: The sample consists of pooled cross-section, time-series data, with observations on each of the twenty manufacturing industries in 1967 to 1972, 1972 to 1977, 1977 to 1982, 1982 to 1987, and 1987 to 1992. The absolute value of the t-statistic is shown in parentheses below the coefficient estimates. See the data appendix to chapter 5 for sources and table 5.9 note for key. Establishment size data are from the U.S. Bureau of the Census, Census of Manufacturing.
[a]CHNGGINI: Change in the Gini coefficient for the average number of employees per establishment by industry size class.
[b]CHNGCV: Change in the coefficient of variation for the average number of employees per establishment by industry size class.
[c]CHNGEST20: Change in the percentage of employment in size classes nineteen or fewer employees.
[d]CHNGEST1000: Change in the percentage of employment in size classes one thousand or more employees.
[#]Significant at the 10 percent level (two-tailed test).
*Significant at the 5 percent level (two-tailed test).
**Significant at the 1 percent level (two-tailed test).

fect firm size. This finding is reassuring since more data, and more recent data, are available for establishments than for firms.[18] In both cases, the most powerful effect is contributed by growth in overall industry employment. These results support chapter 4's uncomplicated hypothesis that changes in average establishment and firm size are directly and positively related to gains in overall industry employment. This may perhaps be viewed primarily as a short-term or cyclical effect. However, changes in overall industry employment do not appear to be directly related to changes in the dispersion of employment among size classes.

Turning to the effects of new technology, we find that industry R&D spending as a percentage of net sales has a consistently negative effect on the growth in mean establishment and firm size—at least in the post-1967 period—as posited in hypothesis 1. The likely reason is that the new technology that grows out of R&D investment has been making smaller industrial units more viable—that is, it has been reducing economies of scale. This may be viewed primarily as a long-term effect. On the other hand, R&D intensity does not appear to affect the dispersion of employment among different size classes, except the share of employment in very large establishments, where the effect is negative. Moreover, contemporaneous and lagged TFP and labor productivity growth are not significant determinants of the change in establishment size, nor of the dispersion of employment among size classes. However, TFP and labor productivity growth, as hypothesized, do appear to result in smaller firm size. This last result was also consistent with our newspaper sample of firms.

In contrast to the predictions of hypothesis 4, the growth in total capital per worker, the growth of OCA per worker, the growth of OCACM per worker, and the growth of total equipment per worker all have positive but insignificant effects on changes in average establishment and firm size. The results for OCA (and OCACM) per worker, in particular, do not support the argument that information technology may lead to downsizing on the establishment level but upsizing on the firm level.

However, the growth in OCA (and OCACM) per worker does appear to have a significant negative effect on changes in the overall dispersion of employment among different size classes. In fact, it is the only consistently significant variable. The results support the argument that greater investment in OCA (and OCACM) leads to less dispersion in employment by size class within an industry. Interestingly, the growth of OCA (and OCACM) per worker is positively related to the change in the share of employment in very small establishments, but negatively related to the change in the share of employment in very large establishments. These results suggest that information technology reduces economies of scale at the establishment level. On the other hand, the growth in total capital per worker and the growth in total equipment per worker do not exert any significant effects on the dispersion of employment among size classes.

Changes in imports as a share of total sales have a uniformly negative effect on growth in both establishment and firm size, but the effect is not significant. These results may be interpreted as weakly consistent with the predictions of hypothesis 3: import competition tends to induce downsizing, perhaps by forcing establishments to get rid of unnecessary layers of management and staff. The main effect is attained through reduction in overall employment within the industry. However, as we have noted before, contestable-markets theory suggests that the effects of import competition on both establishment and firm size may be underestimated because import intensity does not fully capture the influence of potential competition.

On the other hand, changes in export intensity consistently have a very significant negative effect on both establishment and firm size. These results suggest that competition for foreign markets induces firms to cut costs and therefore to downsize. Increases in export intensity do not, however, affect the overall dispersion of employment by size class or the share of employment in either small or large establishments.

The unionization rate has a consistently negative effect on establishment size, and it is generally significant. It has virtually no effect on firm size. Consistent with hypothesis 5 (the breakdown of the social contract), the evidence indicates that unionized industries are *more* apt to downsize—perhaps to get rid of more expensive union labor. Unionization, moreover, appears to be unrelated to changes in the dispersion of employment by size class.

The lagged profit share and lagged profit rate have positive and significant effects on both average establishment and average firm size. Our results suggest that lower profitability in one period leads companies to downsize in the succeeding period, as predicted by hypothesis 3 on foreign competition and "fat" trimming. This result is also consistent with the finding from our newspaper sample that downsizing firms underperformed in terms of profitability relative to the national average. However, profitability is not significantly related to changes in the overall dispersion of establishments by size class.

In brief, our econometric study of the determinants of downsizing (and upsizing) in manufacturing finds considerable support for the simple idea that expanding industries tend to upsize while contracting industries downsize (chapter 4's hypothesis); for the notion that at least since 1967 technology has favored smaller enterprises (hypotheses 1 and 2); and for the idea that falling profits put pressure on firms to downsize (hypothesis 3). We also find support for the idea that foreign competition, at least in terms of export markets, pushes firms to downsize (hypothesis 3). However, we did not find that unions are an effective impediment to downsizing (hypothesis 5) or that faster capital (or IT capital) formation leads to downsizing by substituting capital for labor (hypothesis 4).

Data Appendix: Definitions and Sources

National Income and Product Accounts Employment Data

Full-time equivalent employees (FTEE) equals the number of employees on full-time schedules plus the number of employees on part-time schedules converted to a full-time basis. FTEE is computed as the product of the total number of employees and the ratio of average weekly hours per employee for all employees to average weekly hours per employee on full-time schedules. Persons engaged in production (PEP) equals the number of full-time and part-time employees plus the number of self-employed persons. Unpaid family workers are not included. (*Source:* U.S. Department of Commerce, Bureau of Economic Analysis, *National Income and Product Accounts* [NIPA].)

NIPA Employee Compensation

Employee compensation includes wages and salaries and employee benefits. (*Source:* NIPA).

Net Stock of Fixed Reproducible Tangible Wealth

Capital stock figures are based on chain-type quantity indexes for net stock of fixed capital in 1992 dollars, year-end estimates. Equipment and structures, including information technology (IT) equipment, are for the private (nongovernment) sector only. Information processing and related equipment includes: computers and peripheral equipment; other office and accounting machinery; communication equipment; instruments; and photocopying and related equipment. (*Source:* U.S. Department of Commerce, Bureau of Economic Analysis, *Fixed Reproducible Tangible Wealth;* for technical details, see U.S. Department of Commerce, Bureau of Economic Analysis 1993.)

Total Factor Productivity Growth

Total factor productivity growth (TFPGRTH) for sector j is defined as:

$$TFPGRTH_j = \pi_j = Y^*_j - \alpha_j L^*_j - (1 - \alpha_j) K^*_j,$$

where Y^*_j is the annual rate of output growth, L^*_j is the annual growth in labor input, K^*_j is the annual growth in capital input in sector j, and α_j is the average share of employee compensation in GDP over the period in sector j (the Tornqvist-Divisia index). We measure output using GDP in constant dollars, the labor input using FTEEs or PEPs, and the capital input by the fixed nonresidential net capital stock (in 1992 dollars).

Research and Development

Research and development expenditures performed by industry include company, federal, and other sources of funds. Company-financed R&D performed outside the company is excluded. Industry series on R&D and full-time equivalent scientists and engineers engaged in R&D per full-time equivalent employee run from 1957 to 1997. (*Source:* National Science Foundation; for technical details, see National Science Foundation 1996.)

Export and Import Data

GDO is gross domestic output (net sales). (*Sources:* U.S. input-output data for years 1947, 1958, 1963, 1967, 1972, 1977, 1982, 1987, 1992, and 1997 provided on computer tape, diskette, or the Internet by the U.S. Department of Commerce, Bureau of Economic Analysis.)

Percentage of Labor Force Covered by Unions

Estimates for 1953 to 1983 are the annual average number of dues-paying members reported by labor unions. Estimates for 1983 to 1997 are annual averages from the Current Population Survey (CPS). Data exclude the numbers of professional and public employee associations. (*Sources:* U.S. Department of Labor 1979; U.S. Department of Labor 1990; Jacobs 1998. Sources for the industry-level data include, in addition to the above, Kokkelenberg and Sockell 1985; Hirsch and Macpherson 1993, accompanying data files; and U.S. Department of Labor, Bureau of Labor Statistics, Office of Employment Projections, output and employment database.)

Profit Share and Profit Rate

Data are from the U.S. Department of Commerce, Bureau of Economic Analysis, *National Income and Product Accounts* and *Net Stock of Fixed Reproducible Tangible Capital Accounts*. The key is:

PBT: Corporate profits before tax.

PI: Proprietors' income.

PTI: Gross property-type income, defined as the sum of corporate profits, the profit portion of proprietors' income, rental income of persons, net interest, capital consumption allowances, business transfer payments, and the current surplus of government enterprises less subsidies. Proprietors' income includes both labor income and a return on capital. The labor portion is estimated by multiplying the number of self-employed workers by the average employee compensation of salaried workers. The profit portion is the residual part of proprietors' income.

CCCA: Corporate capital consumption allowance.

NCCA: Noncorporate capital consumption allowance.

GDP: Current dollar gross domestic product.

COMP: Compensation of employees, which consists of wage and salary accruals, employer contributions for social insurance, and other labor income.

NNI: Net national income, defined as COMP + PTI − CCCA − NCCA.

NETK: Current-cost net stock of fixed, reproducible, tangible, nonresidential, private capital stock.

Net profit rate, private economy = (PTI − CCCA − NCCA)/NETK.

Net profit share = (PTI − CCCA − NCCA)/NNI.

Chapter 6

Upsizing in the Retail and Service Industries: Causes and Correlates

C HAPTER 5 focused on the determinants of the pace of downsizing within manufacturing, the sector of the U.S. economy for which statistical data are most abundant. However, as we noted in chapter 4, not only does the manufacturing sector account for but a small proportion of total U.S. employment, it is also highly atypical in terms of changes in firm (or establishment) size. Roughly speaking, we saw that the downsizing phenomenon is prevalent *only* in manufacturing industries; outside of manufacturing, *upsizing* is the norm. So, in this short chapter, we turn to the rest of the economy, or at least to those few nonmanufacturing industries for which we were able to assemble the requisite data. And we focus on explanations of upsizing rather than of downsizing. As far as possible, we try to replicate precisely the statistical tests on manufacturing data presented in chapter 5 in order to facilitate comparisons.

Unfortunately, while the nonmanufacturing sectors constitute the preponderance of the U.S. economy, whether measured by output or employment, they are relatively data-poor compared to manufacturing. This paucity of data is just one manifestation of a broader problem that economists have been bemoaning for decades: the U.S. government's data collection systems concentrate too much on agriculture and manufacturing and not enough on, for example, trade and services. When we tried to piece together comparable time series for the explanatory variables utilized in the regression analysis of chapter 5—measures of technology, capital, profitability, and so forth—we found (not to our surprise) that several of the data series were either unavailable or available on only a sketchy basis (for example, for only some years or only a few industries). Many entire industries analyzed in chapter 4 had to be omitted from the analysis of this chapter. Thus, the findings here are necessarily supported by far fewer data points than those of chapter 5 and therefore must be interpreted with a great deal of caution.[1] The analysis is meant to be no more than exploratory; it is mainly designed to see whether the determinants of *upsizing* outside of manufacturing look similar to or different from the determinants of *downsizing* within manufacturing. We will therefore make frequent comparisons with the results in chapter 5.

What we find here, in brief, is that the list of variables that are significant explanatory factors for upsizing *outside* manufacturing is quite similar to the list of variables that are significant in explaining downsizing *within* manufacturing. That includes the industry's growth rate of employment, its export or import intensity, and, to some extent, its profitability. However, in some cases, the signs of the relevant coefficients are the opposite of what we found for manufacturing. For example, there is a hint in the data that less profitable firms tend to *upsize* in nonmanufacturing whereas they tend to *downsize* in manufacturing. One possible explanation for these disparate results is, once again, a kind of regression toward the mean. The (smaller) firms in the retail and service sectors may raise their efficiency when they grow larger, while the (larger) firms in manufacturing may improve efficiency by getting smaller.

Limitations Imposed by the Data

To remind the reader, the main variables used in the regression analysis of the last chapter were total industry employment, research and development expenditures, the rate of technological progress as measured by total factor productivity growth, various measures of capital per worker, various measures of export and import intensity, unionization, and profitability. The following is a brief synopsis of the empirical findings for manufacturing:

- Total industry employment was the most significant regressor, with a positive coefficient consistently between 2 and 3—meaning that each percentage point of industrywide employment growth raised firm or establishment size by 2 to 3 percent.

- The two measures of technical progress (R&D spending and TFP growth) were sometimes significant and sometimes not. But their coefficients were consistently *negative,* indicating that faster technical change leads to more downsizing.

- The ratio of exports (more than imports) to output was another important regressor, also with a negative coefficient. Thus, export-competing industries downsize more.

- The two measures of capital per worker were not significant.

- Profitability was highly significant, whether measured by the profit rate or the profit share. The *positive* coefficients mean that downsizing tends to occur where and when profits are low.

- Higher unionization rates were associated with more downsizing, but the coefficients were not always significant.

Of this list of right-hand variables, only one, R&D expenditures, was totally unavailable in the nonmanufacturing industries that we study in this chapter. However, we were able to construct the alternative measure of technological change, TFP growth, in essentially the same way as was done for manufacturing.[2]

The more serious data limitations were sectoral. Not a single one of the right-hand variables utilized in chapter 5 was available (or could be constructed) for *every* industry studied in chapter 4. Even where variables were available, the time series had gaps and never extended over the entire period 1953 to 1992 covered by the Enterprise Statistics. Thus, the analysis in this chapter is limited to the period 1967 to 1992 and to the industries listed in table 6.1. As can be seen, most of the data come from retailing (that is, the entire retail sector, without any more-detailed, two-digit breakdown), wholesaling, and four particular service industries.

For each of these industries and time periods, we created time series for the previously listed determinants of the percentage change in firm (or establishment) size that replicated the variables used in chapter 5.

Correlates of Changes in Firm and Establishment Size

With so little data, some readers may harbor justifiable skepticism about the validity of the implications of the multiple regressions we report in this chapter. Before doing so, we therefore look briefly at the simple correlations in the data. Which variables correlate well, and with what sign, with changes in firm or establishment size?

With one exception, all the right-hand variables that we use in our regressions are available for the full data set. Pooling both the cross-sectional and time-series aspects of the data set, we have just forty-two observations for firms and thirty-eight observations for establishments. The lone exception is the unionization rate, which is missing for two of the service industries (motion pictures and miscellaneous repair services) listed in table 6.1, accounting for five observations. Thus, we display the correlations in two ways: with and without the unionization rate.

Fortunately, the *qualitative* results do not depend on whether union-

Table 6.1   Availability of Nonmanufacturing Data, 1967 to 1992

EIC	Industry or Sector	Data Availability
50	Retail trade	1967–1992
51	Wholesale trade	1967–1992
70	Hotels and other lodging	1967–1992
72	Personal services	1967–1992
73	Business services	1967–1992
75	Automotive repair, parking	1967–1992
76	Miscellaneous repair	1972–1982
78	Motion pictures	1967–1982
79	Amusement and recreation	1967–1982
80	Health services	1982–1992
81	Legal services	1972–1982

Source: Authors' compilation.
Note: The table pertains to firms. For establishment data, replace 1967 with 1963 (there are no establishment data for 1967) and omit the health services and legal services industries.

ization is included or excluded. But a few quantitative results do. For example, when the two industries lacking data on unionization are dropped, the simple correlation between changes in *establishment* size and changes in the industry's capital-to-labor ratio falls from -0.13 to -0.35, and the simple correlation with the ratio of OCA capital (office, computer, and accounting machines) to labor's share falls from 0.35 to 0.12. These are large changes; it appears that the capital stock behavior of the two industries are atypical. The other changes reported in tables 6.2 and 6.3 seem relatively minor by comparison.

In the case of changes in firm size, the growth of total industry employment appears to be the most promising regressor, but none of the correlations is very high. In the case of changes in establishment size, employment growth again displays the highest consistent correlation, but depending on whether or not the unionization variable is used, one of the two capital stock measures also correlates well.

Econometric Analysis of Changes in Firm and Establishment Size

Simple correlations, of course, are not always good indicators of the marginal effects of a particular independent variable *holding other determinants of upsizing constant.* For that, we must turn to multiple regression analysis, ever mindful of the handicaps imposed by the paucity of data.

Before getting enmeshed in the details of the regressions reported in tables 6.4 through 6.7, we can make four broad observations. First,

Table 6.2   Simple Correlations with Changes in Firm Size

Variable	Without Unionization	With Unionization
Employment growth	.31	.27
Total factor productivity (TFP) growth	.22	.26
Total capital per worker	−.26	−.22
Office, computer and accounting machines (OCA) capital per worker	.02	.03
Export share	−.20	−.06
Import share	.01	.01
Profit share	−.21	−.23
Profit rate	.14	.13
Unionization	—	.18
Number of observations	42	37

Source: Authors' compilation.

most of the qualitative results turn out the same whether we analyze changes in firm size or establishment size, and that is just what we found in chapter 5 for manufacturing industries. Second, in terms of which variables are significant determinants of changes in unit size and which are not, the results presented in tables 6.4 through 6.7 are broadly similar to those we found for manufacturing in the previous chapter. Third, there are some notable sign differences, however, as

Table 6.3   Simple Correlations with Changes in Establishment Size

Variable	Without Unionization	With Unionization
Employment growth	.31	.43
Total factor productivity (TFP) growth	.11	.08
Total capital per worker	−.35	−.13
Office, computer, and accounting machines (OCA) capital per worker	.12	.35
Export share	−.09	.04
Import share	.15	.10
Profit share	−.21	−.17
Profit rate	−.18	−.12
Unionization	—	.09
Number of observations	38	33

Source: Authors' compilation.

will become clear shortly. And fourth, the goodness of fit of these regressions—which is modest—is roughly comparable to those in chapter 5. The lower levels of statistical significance are therefore clearly a consequence of the much smaller sample sizes: we now have roughly 30 percent as many observations as in the manufacturing regressions.

Table 6.4 begins by displaying our results for changes in *firm* size, with the unionization variable *excluded*. We focus on these as our central results for three reasons. First, as stated previously, we believe that firms are a more interesting unit of analysis than establishments. Still, because changes in establishment size may reveal more about the imprint of technology, we do not want to focus on firms exclusively. Second, this choice gives us the largest possible sample size— forty-two observations. Third, the unionization variable turns out to be insignificant anyway.

Although symbols in the table indicate statistical significance at the 1 percent, 5 percent, and 10 percent levels (using two-tailed tests), we concentrate on the 10 percent level in our discussion of the results. With so few degrees of freedom, 10 percent should be a sufficiently stern criterion.

In regression 1, all three variables—TFP growth and both the export and import shares—are significant. Unlike the manufacturing regressions reported in table 5.12, however, TFP growth here has a *positive* sign—indicating that more rapid technological change leads to *larger* rather than *smaller* firms. Remember that the typical firm in trade and services is much smaller than the typical manufacturing firm, and that the trends are toward smaller firm size in manufacturing and larger firm size in trade and services. So this different finding again seems consistent with our (highly tentative) hypothesis that computer technology may lead to regression toward the mean—that very small firms grow larger while large firms shrink. But given the lack of statistical significance of TFP growth in the other regressions in table 6.4, this support for our hypothesis is weak indeed. With so little data, regression 1 gives us little more than a hint.

The export and import shares are significant not only in regression 1 but consistently throughout table 6.4, with a *negative* coefficient (generally between −0.2 and −0.3) on exports and a *positive* coefficient (usually between 0.5 and 0.7) on imports. In the corresponding manufacturing regressions, the regressions used percentage changes in the export and import shares. But that is inadvisable here because a number of the import and export figures are close to zero, giving rise to erratic percentage changes.[3] The import share is, in fact, one of the two strongest regressors in the table, and its positive coefficient means that industries tend to upsize faster when they face more import competition. That makes sense if larger size is the route to greater effi-

Table 6.4   Regressions Explaining Percentage Change in Mean Number of Employees per Firm, without Unionization Rate

Independent Variables	(1)	(2)	(3)	(4)	(5)	(6)	(7)
Constant	.016**	.012*	.014*	.023	.012*	.038*	.013*
	(2.92)	(2.16)	(2.20)	(1.62)	(1.98)	(2.16)	(2.16)
TFP growth[a]	.300*	.167	—	—	—	—	—
	(1.96)	(0.78)					
Growth in total capital/FTEE[b]	—	—	—	−.117	—	—	—
				(1.02)			
Growth in OCA/ FTEE[c]	—	—	—	—	−.013	—	—
					(0.38)		
Exports/GDO[d]	−.291*	−.245*	−.212*	−.190*	−.206*	−.211**	−.214*
	(2.49)	(1.96)	(2.51)	(2.53)	(2.44)	(2.78)	(2.43)
Imports/GDO[e]	.740*	.686*	.591**	.609**	.584*	.450*	.593*
	(2.61)	(2.58)	(3.14)	(2.95)	(2.65)	(2.19)	(3.07)
Profit share[f]	—	—	—	—	—	−.086*	—
						(1.90)	
Profit rate[g]	—	—	—	—	—	—	.002
							(0.33)
Growth in FTEE[h]	—	.249	.367**	.303*	.431*	.423**	.350**
		(1.43)	(3.74)	(2.30)	(2.01)	(3.72)	(2.99)
R^2	.14	.16	.15	.16	.16	.22	.15
Standard error	.0306	.0306	.0304	.0306	.0306	.0295	.0308
Sample size	42	42	42	42	42	42	42

Note: The sample consists of pooled cross-section, time-series data, with observations on each of the eleven service and retail industries in 1967 to 1972, 1972 to 1977, 1977 to 1982, and 1987 to 1992. The absolute value of the t-statistic is shown in parentheses below the coefficient estimate. See the data appendix to chapter 5 for sources. The data for the mean number of employees per establishment are taken from the U.S. Bureau of the Census, Enterprise Statistics.
[a] Average annual rate of TFP growth, based on full-time equivalent employees (FTEE) and net capital stock.
[b] Annual rate of growth in the ratio of the gross stock of total capital to FTEE.
[c] Annual rate of growth in the ratio of the gross stock of office, computer and accounting machinery (OCA) to FTEE.
[d] Ratio of industry exports to industry gross domestic output (GDO) beginning of period.
[e] Ratio of industry imports to industry GDO, beginning of period.
[f] Ratio of net profits to net national income, beginning of period.
[g] Ratio of net profits to net capital stock, beginning of period.
[h] Annual growth rate of FTEE, by industry and period.
*Significant at the 10 percent level (two-tailed test).
*Significant at the 5 percent level (two-tailed test).
**Significant at the 1 percent level (two-tailed test).

ciency in retail and service industries. But as we have noted, that technological hypothesis is itself an unproven conjecture. The negative sign on the export share is puzzling; more export-oriented industries apparently tend to downsize. But it corresponds to what we found for manufacturing.

Regression 2 adds industry employment growth, which, the reader will remember, was the most important determinant of changes in firm (or establishment) size in chapter 5. The R^2 moves up only slightly, and the standard error of the regression is virtually unchanged. Surprisingly, employment growth does not appear to be a significant determinant of changes in firm size in retailing and services, despite the high simple correlation reported in table 6.2.

But the reason behind this unexpected finding is that employment growth and TFP growth turn out to be highly correlated in this sample ($\rho = 0.60$). (They were not so strongly correlated in the manufacturing data.) When we drop TFP growth, which is insignificant in regression 2 anyway, employment growth becomes highly significant (see regression 3 and others). Nonetheless, its coefficients in the other regressions in table 6.4 are much smaller than the corresponding coefficients in the manufacturing regressions. This echoes the finding in chapter 4 that changes in overall industry employment were less important determinants of firm size outside of manufacturing than they were in manufacturing.

As just mentioned, regression 3 drops the (insignificant) TFP growth variable. The coefficients change slightly, except for that of employment growth, which rises by about half and becomes highly significant. Thus, the rest of the regressions in table 6.4 use employment growth rather than TFP growth.[4]

In regressions 4 and 5 we experiment with two alternative measures of the capital-labor ratio, one using total capital and the other using just OCA machinery. Neither comes close to statistical significance. This finding (or nonfinding) is consistent with the manufacturing results.

Finally, regressions 6 and 7 experiment with two alternative measures of profitability: the profit share (that is, profits divided by income) and the profit rate (profits divided by capital). The former is significant, and it raises the R^2 from 0.16 to 0.22. The latter does not matter at all. But notice that the coefficient is negative, meaning that more profitable firms tend to downsize while less profitable ones tend to upsize. In the case of manufacturing, we found just the opposite: it was the less profitable firms that tended to downsize. Once again, the reconciliation may be that, while downsizing typically improves efficiency in manufacturing, upsizing more often improves efficiency in services and trade.

On balance, regression 6 seems to be the best equation in the table. It tells us that, other things being equal, the firms are likely to upsize more if they are in faster-growing industries, have a high import intensity (but a low export intensity!), and have a lower profit share.

Table 6.5 shows the corresponding regressions when the unionization variable is included. (The sample size drops to thirty-seven.) We

Table 6.5 **Regressions of Percentage Change in Mean Number of Employees per Firm, with Unionization Rate**

Independent Variables	(1)	(2)	(3)	(4)	(5)	(6)	(7)
Constant	−.002	−.001	.008	.014	−.007	.033*	.005
	(0.18)	(0.09)	(0.62)	(1.00)	(−0.26)	(1.85)	(0.39)
TFP growth	.430*	.304	—	—	—	—	—
	(2.20)	(0.89)					
Growth in total capital/FTEE	—	—	—	−.167	—	—	—
				(1.07)			
Growth in OCA/FTEE	—	—	—	—	−.032	—	—
					(0.65)		
Exports/GDO	−.665*	−.737*	−.749*	−.604*	−.858*	−.752*	−.762*
	(1.96)	(2.17)	(2.26)	(2.00)	(2.19)	(2.09)	(2.27)
Imports/GDO	1.559*	1.730*	1.713*	1.486*	1.933*	1.575*	1.736*
	(2.26)	(2.47)	(2.51)	(2.40)	(2.57)	(2.17)	(2.51)
Unionization rate	.148	.111	.049	.119	.140	.022	.064
	(1.22)	(0.72)	(0.40)	(0.73)	(0.67)	(0.24)	(0.49)
Profit share	—	—	—	—	—	−.082*	—
						(1.79)	
Profit rate	—	—	—	—	—	—	.006
							(0.65)
Growth in FTEE	—	.206	.447**	.332*	.609*	.495**	.405
		(0.71)	(4.74)	(2.54)	(2.04)	(4.23)	(3.46)
R^2	.18	.20	.16	.19	.22	.23	.17
Standard error	.0317	.0320	.0321	.0322	.0315	.0313	.0325
Sample size	37	37	37	37	37	37	37

Note: The sample consists of pooled cross-section, time-series data, with observations on each of the eleven service and retail industries in 1967 to 1972, 1972 to 1977, 1977 to 1982, and 1987 to 1992. The absolute value of the t-statistic is shown in parentheses below the coefficient estimate. See the data appendix to chapter 5 for sources, and table 6.4 for definitions of variables.
*Significant at the 10 percent level (two-tailed test).
*Significant at the 5 percent level (two-tailed test).
**Significant at the 1 percent level (two-tailed test).

have emphasized the table 6.4 results because the industry's unionization rate itself is never a significant determinant of firm size. Moreover, the qualitative results in table 6.5 are just the same as those in table 6.4. In particular, employment growth seems to be a far better regressor than TFP growth.[5] The only difference worth mentioning is quantitative: the coefficients on the export and import variables are two to four times as large when unionization is included (which leaves out the motion picture and miscellaneous repair industries) as when it is excluded.

Tables 6.6 and 6.7 turn from firms to establishments, still using the data from the Enterprise Statistics. We argued earlier that the results for firms were the more interesting. But for certain issues—for exam-

Table 6.6   Regressions Explaining Percentage Change in Mean Number of Employees per Establishment, Without Unionization Rate

Independent Variables	(1)	(2)	(3)	(4)	(5)	(6)	(7)	(8)
Constant	.013*	.002	.002	.001	.003	.001	.007	.004
	(2.48)	(0.46)	(0.31)	(0.22)	(0.29)	(0.19)	(0.55)	(0.37)
TFP growth	.123	−.046	—	—	—	—	—	—
	(0.78)	(0.27)						
Growth in total capital/FTEE	—	—	—	—	−.021	—	—	—
					(0.26)			
Growth in OCA/FTEE	—	—	—	—	—	.009	—	—
						(1.51)		
Exports/GDO	−.093#	−.017	−.027	—	—	—	—	—
	(1.83)	(0.23)	(0.52)					
Imports/GDO	.359#	.289	.319#	.274#	.286#	.256#	.242#	.283#
	(1.93)	(1.60)	(2.00)	(1.85)	(1.72)	(2.03)	(1.43)	(1.93)
Profit share	—	—	—	—	—	—	−.019	—
							(0.63)	
Profit rate	—	—	—	—	—	—	—	−.009
								(0.45)
Growth in FTEE	—	.441**	.420**	.427**	.417**	.392**	.421**	.423**
		(2.90)	(3.35)	(3.61)	(2.93)	(3.10)	(3.37)	(3.27)
R²	.05	.22	.22	.22	.22	.26	.22	.22
Standard error	.0211	.0193	.0191	.0188	.0191	.0185	.0190	.0191
Sample size	38	38	38	38	38	38	38	38

Note: The sample consists of pooled cross-section, time-series data, with observations on each of the eleven service and retail industries in 1963 to 1972, 1972 to 1977, 1977 to 1982, and 1987 to 1992. The absolute value of the t-statistic is shown in parentheses below the coefficient estimate. See the data appendix to chapter 5 for sources, and table 6.4 for definitions of variables.
#Significant at the 10 percent level (two-tailed test).
*Significant at the 5 percent level (two-tailed test).
**Significant at the 1 percent level (two-tailed test).

ple, the effects of technological change on business size—the establishment may be the more pertinent unit of analysis. In any case, when we move from firms to establishments, the sample sizes shrink by four because we lose the data on the health and legal services industries. Furthermore, the first period of observation becomes the nine-year period 1963 to 1972 instead of the five-year period 1967 to 1972.[6]

Table 6.6 reports results for the larger sample *without* the unionization variable. Now overall employment growth is by far the most important regressor, just as we found in the manufacturing regressions in chapter 5. When employment growth is added to the equation in regression 2, the R^2 jumps from 0.05 to 0.22 and both exports and imports lose significance. Since TFP growth is not significant in this or in any other variant of the regression, we drop it in the remainder of table 6.6. Similarly, regression 3 shows that the export variable is insignificant, and that result is also general. So the remaining regressions in table 6.6 omit both TFP growth and the export share. Regressions 5 and 6 show that neither measure of the capital stock is significant, although OCA capital comes close (t-ratio = 1.5; p-value = 0.14). Neither profitability variable even approaches statistical significance (see regressions 7 and 8).

Arguably, regression 6 is the best specification in table 6.6. It explains changes in average establishment size by overall industry employment growth and import intensity, with OCA capital intensity playing a minor role. The positive (though small) coefficient on the import-share variable means that industries tend to upsize more if they face more import competition.

Adding the unionization variable, which costs us five observations, leads to the regressions in table 6.7. We focus on the table 6.6 results because unionization, once again, is insignificant in all specifications. Apart from that, the qualitative results correspond closely to what we found in table 6.6, except that the export variable is now usually significant and hence is included in all the regressions. However, at least one quantitative change is large enough to bear mentioning: the magnitudes of the import and export coefficients are vastly larger in the regressions that include the unionization variable—just as we found with the firm-level data.

Conclusions

We cannot expect to learn much from thirty to forty pooled, time-series, cross-section observations. There seem to be only three robust findings.

Table 6.7 Regressions Explaining Percentage Change in Mean Number of Employees per Establishment, with Unionization Rate

Variables	(1)	(2)	(3)	(4)	(5)	(6)	(7)
Constant	.008	.007	.003	.003	.007	.009	.004
	(0.72)	(0.58)	(0.36)	(0.27)	(0.74)	(0.59)	(0.27)
TFP growth	.149	−.135	—	—	—	—	—
	(0.81)	(0.57)					
Growth in total capital/FTEE	—	—	—	.023	—	—	—
				(0.22)			
Growth in OCA/ FTEE	—	—	—	—	.009	—	—
					(1.17)		
Exports/GDO	−.301	−.560*	−.563*	−.582*	−.453	−.564*	−.557*
	(1.09)	(2.10)	(2.10)	(2.12)	(1.56)	(2.05)	(2.17)
Imports/GDO	0.802	1.464*	1.487*	1.514*	1.244*	1.451*	1.478*
	(1.43)	(2.67)	(2.67)	(2.68)	(2.01)	(2.58)	(2.68)
Unionization rate	.039	−.066	−.042	−.053	−.072	−.041	−.045
	(0.51)	(0.85)	(0.74)	(0.61)	(1.15)	(0.77)	(0.67)
Profit share	—	—	—	—	—	−.019	—
						(0.57)	
Profit rate	—	—	—	—	—	—	−.003
							(0.12)
Growth in FTEE	—	.619**	.543**	.558**	.491**	.531**	.540**
		(3.68)	(4.65)	(3.63)	(4.00)	(4.07)	(4.20)
R^2	.06	.32	.31	.31	.34	.31	.31
Standard error	.0229	.0198	.0197	.0200	.0195	.0199	.0200
Sample size	33	33	33	33	33	33	33

Note: The sample consists of pooled cross-section, time-series data, with observations on each of the eleven service and retail industries in 1963 to 1972, 1972 to 1977, 1977 to 1982, and 1987 to 1992. The absolute value of the t-statistic is shown in parentheses below the coefficient estimate. See the data appendix to chapter 5 for sources, and table 6.4 for definitions of variables.
*Significant at the 10 percent level (two-tailed test).
*Significant at the 5 percent level (two-tailed test).
**Significant at the 1 percent level (two-tailed test).

The first is obvious: both firms and establishments seem to upsize more when their industry is growing more rapidly (as measured by total employment). Second, upsizing seems to be more pronounced in industries that compete more heavily with imports. Third, and surprisingly, business units in more export-oriented industries appear to upsize less.

Neither technological improvement (as measured by TFP growth) nor capital intensity (measured two ways) nor profitability (also measured two ways) shows a robust connection to upsizing, although firms (not establishments) with a lower profit share do seem to upsize more.

Perhaps the most interesting finding—though it is only suggestive—is the result that lower profitability leads to increased upsizing, with its implication that technical change may have increased the relative efficiency of firms of intermediate size throughout the economy.

Chapter 7

A Closer Look at U.S. Manufacturing: The Consequences of Downsizing

W E HAVE examined the fairly abundant evidence on the actual magnitude of downsizing (and sometimes upsizing) in
the manufacturing sector of the economy (chapter 4) and
sought to throw light on its causes (chapter 5). We also investigated
the rather paltry, but persuasive, evidence of upsizing in the rest of
the economy (chapters 4 and 6). In this chapter, we focus again on
manufacturing (since that is where most of the downsizing has occurred) to consider downsizing's consequences for the companies in
that industry. We look at downsizing's effect on the productivity of
manufacturing firms and on the competitiveness of American products. We also consider downsizing's effect on firms' profitability and
investigate the common misperception that downsizing increases a
company's share price in the stock market.

In addition, we look into downsizing's consequences for both the
structure of work and employee compensation. As we argued in chapters 1 and 4, downsizing per se may simply be an excuse or a veil for
the restructuring of job patterns within an establishment or firm.
Thus, we may find a relationship between changes in establishment
or firm size and the occupational composition of jobs within an industry. Moreover, downsizing may also be a means of bringing about
wage cuts, particularly if downsizing depletes the ranks of more senior employees or reduces the number of higher-paid jobs in an industry. Reductions in firm size may also lower wages simply through
the well-documented employer-size effect on wages: larger firms tend
to pay higher wages simply by virtue of being larger, and smaller

firms tend to pay lower wages (see, for example, Masters 1969; Mellow 1981; Idson 1999).

Although this chapter sheds light on a wide variety of related issues, the central story that emerges is straightforward and dramatic. First, on average, downsizing in the manufacturing sector has *not* contributed to better productivity performance, contrary to what is frequently claimed. Nevertheless, downsizing *has* contributed to higher profits. (However, according to the results of our newspaper sample, firms that downsized did outperform the national average in terms of productivity growth, but underperformed in terms of profitability.) Further, because downsizing has tended to depress wages and workers' total compensation, we can ask whether one of the central consequences of downsizing has been a transfer of income from labor to capital. Finally, and curiously, despite its stimulus to profits, downsizing by a firm has been associated with a *decline* in the price of its stock, not a rise, perhaps because investors take downsizing as management's response to prospects of trouble ahead. We had not expected this picture of the consequences of downsizing, but the evidence provides strong support for this interpretation of it.

Our analysis also provides evidence on the validity of two of our six downsizing hypotheses, especially hypothesis 3 (downsizing is stimulated by increased foreign competition that forces firms to trim "fat"). But the fact that downsizing has not led to increased productivity in manufacturing seems to conflict with this hypothesis. The evidence in this chapter does, however, seem to be consistent with hypothesis 5 (downsizing is at least partly a breakdown of the social contract between capital and labor), in that firms that formerly did not pressure labor to accept the minimum compensation levels permitted by the market have reversed this worker-friendly policy under the pressure of increased competition or a change in management attitudes.

Review of the Literature on the Economic Effects of Downsizing

Before turning to the details of our own analysis, we begin with a capsule review of previous research findings. As we indicated in chapter 5, there is now a fairly sizable literature on some of the economic consequences of downsizing. Two papers that have examined the effects of downsizing on productivity are Baily, Bartelsman, and Haltiwanger (1996b) and Collins and Harris (1999). Martin Neil Baily, Eric Bartelsman, and John Haltiwanger (1996b) investigated why average labor productivity declines during recessions and increases during booms. They found that plants that permanently downsize (those that end up smaller in the long run) contribute disproportionately to the cyclical pattern of productivity. Specifically, productivity tends to decline in plants that are downsizing—at least during aggregate downswings in the economy. Alan Collins and Richard Harris (1999) used the methods designed by Baily, Bartelsman, and Haltiwanger to investigate the effects of downsizing on productivity trends in the British motor vehicle industry over the period 1974 to 1994. They found that productivity growth was indeed higher in those plants that successfully downsized, but that those plants that were unsuccessful at downsizing tended to have among the worst productivity growth records. Unsuccessful downsizers accounted for a significant part of the overall decline in productivity after 1989 in this industry.

David Gordon (1996) was among the first to argue that downsizing can reduce wages and salaries. He contended that a critically important source of falling wages has been U.S. corporations' increasingly aggressive stance in relations with their employees, their mounting power to gain the upper hand in labor struggles, and the shifts in the institutional environment that this increasing power has helped foster. Two papers provide some evidence on this. Peter Capelli (1998) looked at job losses associated with shortfalls in demand, downsizing, and subsequent financial performance. His results indicate, among other things, that downsizing reduces labor costs per employee. Reza Espahbodi, Teresa John, and Gopala Vasudevan (2000) examined the performance of 118 firms that downsized between 1989 and 1993. They found that operating performance improved significantly after the downsizing and, in particular, that these firms were able to reduce labor costs.

Several papers have investigated the reaction of stock prices to downsizing. The evidence is mixed. John Abowd, George Milkovich, and John Hannon (1990) used an event-study method to determine whether the human resource decisions of firms (such as staffing) announced in the *Wall Street Journal* between 1980 and 1987 discernibly affected either the level or variation of shareholder return. They found no consistent pattern of increased or decreased valuation in response to any of five categories of announcements of staff reduction, even after controlling for the probable effect of such announcements on total compensation costs.[1] In a similar study, Steven Abraham (1999) used an event-study method to assess the effects of layoff announcements on shareholder returns. Abraham also used the *Wall Street Journal* to identify 368 firms that had announced layoffs in 1993 or 1994. The results showed that layoff announcements induced a decrease in the shareholder returns from firms that made the announcements. Dan Worrell, Wallace Davidson, and Varinder Sharma (1991) tested the reaction of the securities market to announcements of 194 layoffs.

They found that adverse preannouncement reactions occurred when pessimistic hints about firms preceded layoff announcements, and also that announcements of large or permanent layoffs elicited stronger negative responses than other announcements. Michael Gombola and George Tsetsekos (1992) argued that a permanent plant closing provides evidence about a firm's entire financial condition—in particular, that an out-of-date plant could not be sold and the firm had no alternatives. Unless investors already knew the true value of the plant, a closing announcement could be expected to be followed by a decline in stock price. Gombola and Tsetsekos found confirmation of this hypothesis in their data analysis. R. E. Caves and Matthew Krepps (1993) also examined the stock market reaction to announcements of corporate downsizing between 1987 and 1991. Using disaggregated manufacturing industries data for 1967 through 1986, they found that shareholders reacted favorably to downsizings that involved white-collar layoffs and related reorganizations.

Finally, one paper indirectly looked at the effects of downsizing on employment restructuring. Randy Ilg (1996) examined the quality of employment growth, using earnings as the measure of job quality, for a group of ninety major industries and occupations. The findings reinforced the conclusion drawn from previous U.S. Bureau of Labor Statistics research that employment growth has been greater for occupation-industry cells at the top and bottom of the earnings distribution than for those in the middle. While downsizing and restructuring have led to the displacement of many managers and professionals, considerable growth still has occurred within these occupations. In fact, three-quarters of the net job growth between 1989 and 1995 occurred in the managerial and professional specialty occupations.

Thus, the literature on the economic effects of downsizing corroborates at least some of the key findings in this chapter—for example, the disappointing productivity outcomes for downsizing firms and downsizing's compression of wages. In the rest of the chapter, we describe our investigation of the economic consequences of downsizing in manufacturing, providing graphs on trends in profitability, occupational change, and wage growth and summarizing our regression results on the consequences of downsizing for key variables.

Descriptive Statistics on Profitability, Occupational Change, and Wage Levels

In chapter 5, we presented descriptive statistics on trends in productivity in the U.S. manufacturing sector. We begin here by showing the changes in average establishment and firm sizes and the changes in both the average rate of profit and the average profit share for total

**Figure 7.1   Change in Average Business Size and Profitability,
1958 to 1997**

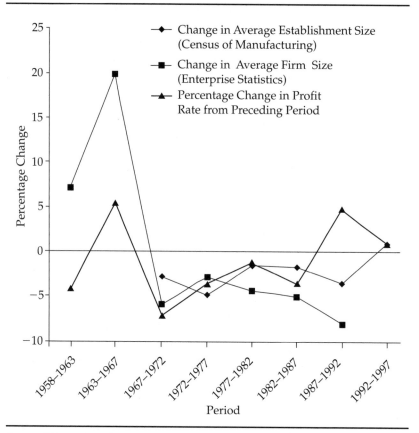

Sources: U.S. Bureau of the Census, Census of Manufacturing, establishments (1967 to 1997), Enterprise Statistics, firms (1958 to 1992); and U.S. National Income and Product Accounts (see the data appendix to chapter 5 for details).

manufacturing from the preceding census period (see figures 7.1 and 7.2). There appears to be a somewhat direct relation between the three sets of statistics, at least at the level of total manufacturing. Changes in both the profit rate and the profit share were highest during the period 1987 to 1992, when both establishments and, particularly, firms experienced pronounced downsizing, and lowest from 1967 to 1972, a period of modest downsizing.

Figure 7.3 shows trends in the average real market value of firms in total manufacturing. The data are from the University of Chicago's Center for Research in Security Prices (CRSP) Market Capitalization database, which includes a sample of firms in almost all two-digit industries. Average market value is computed as the ratio of the total

Figure 7.2   Change in Average Business Size and Profit Share, 1958 to 1997

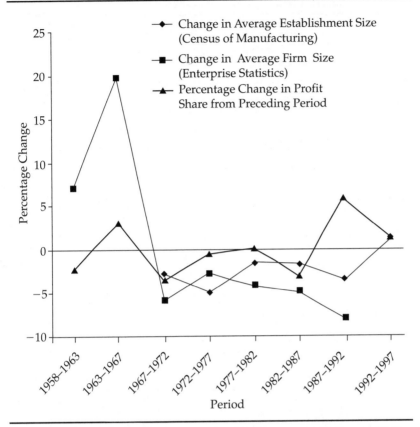

Sources: U.S. Bureau of the Census, Census of Manufacturing, establishments (1967 to 1997), Enterprise Statistics, firms (1958 to 1992); and U.S. National Income and Product Accounts (see the data appendix to chapter 5 for details).

market capitalization in a two-digit manufacturing industry (deflated by the consumer price index [CPI]), divided by the number of firms in that industry. The index is somewhat imperfect since it does not correct for mergers, acquisitions, or divestitures.

Stock values fluctuate much more widely than do the other industry-level variables. During the two upsizing periods 1958 to 1963 and 1963 to 1967, the average market value of firms in total manufacturing rose by 27 and 48 percent, respectively. During the first downsizing period, 1967 to 1972, it rose by only 14 percent, and during the next downsizing period, 1972 to 1977, it fell precipitously, by 43 percent. (This was true for the Standard & Poor's 500 stock index as well.) Between 1977 and 1982, another downsizing period, average market value in manufacturing inched up by 3 percent. However,

Figure 7.3   Change in Average Business Size and Stock Market Valuation, 1958 to 1997

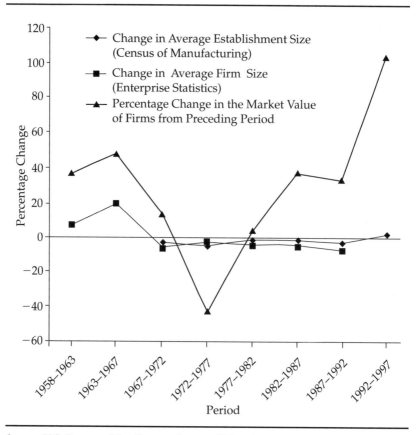

Sources: U.S. Bureau of the Census, Census of Manufacturing, establishments (1967 to 1997), Enterprise Statistics, firms (1958 to 1992); and CRSP (see the text for details).

during the next two periods, 1982 to 1987 and 1987 to 1992, in which both average firm and establishment size fell, average market values rose by 37 and 32 percent, respectively. In the 1992 to 1997 period, when average establishment size increased very modestly, the average stock valuation in manufacturing boomed (as it did for the Standard & Poor's 500 stock index), more than doubling in value. If anything, it appears that stock values rise faster during upsizing periods than during downsizing.

Our next variable of interest is a measure of the degree to which the occupational structure shifts over time. For this, we employ an index of similarity. First we define:

M = occupation-by-industry employment coefficient matrix, where m_{ij} shows the employment of occupation i in industry j as a share of total employment in industry j

Our employment data are for 267 occupations and 64 industries, and we obtained them from the decennial Census of Population for the years 1950, 1960, 1970, 1980, and 1990 (for details, see Wolff 1996). The standard similarity index for industry j between two time periods 1 and 2 is given by:

$$SI_{12} = \frac{\Sigma_i \, m_{ij1} m_{ij2}}{[\Sigma_i \, (m_{ij1})^2 \, \Sigma_i \, (m_{ij2})^2]^{1/2}} \qquad (7.1)$$

The index SI is the cosine of the angle between two vectors and varies from 0 (when the two vectors are orthogonal) to 1 (when the two vectors are identical). The index of occupational dissimilarity, DIOCCUP, is defined as:

$$DIOCCUP = 1 - SI \qquad (7.2)$$

Descriptive statistics for DIOCCUP are shown in figure 7.4. It should be noted at the outset that this variable is based on decennial census data, so that it is available only for 1960, 1970, 1980, and 1990, while the Census of Manufacturing data are available for 1953, 1963, 1972, 1982, and 1992. Despite this slight misalignment, the results are suggestive. The DIOCCUP index for total manufacturing dropped from 0.061 in the period 1960 to 1970 to 0.041 in the period 1970 to 1980, but then surged to 0.090 in the 1980s, its highest level of the three decades. These results confirm anecdotal evidence about the substantial degree of industrial restructuring during the 1980s. Average firm size in total manufacturing rose by 13.8 employees from 1963 to 1972 but then fell by 7.3 employees in from 1972 to 1982 and by another 13.3 employees in the period 1982 to 1992. Changes in the average number of employees per establishment were fairly comparable between the two later periods: −6.5 in the 1972 to 1982 period and −5.4 in the 1982 to 1992 period. On the surface, there is not much correspondence between the degree of firm or establishment downsizing and the degree of occupational change, at least at the level of total manufacturing.

Figure 7.4 also shows the change in the share of managers in total employment for total manufacturing. This variable is also computed from the decennial census data, so that it is available only for 1960, 1970, 1980, and 1990. Moreover, since it is hard to separate out "mid-

Figure 7.4   Changes in Average Establishment and Firm Size and Changes in Occupational Composition, 1960 to 1990

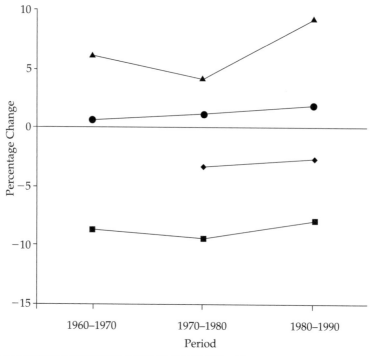

Sources: U.S. Bureau of the Census, Census of Manufacturing, establishments (1967 to 1997), Enterprise Statistics, firms (1958 to 1992); and Census of Population (1960 to 1990) (see text for details).

dle" managers from total managers and administrators, the data are based on all managers and administrators in the occupational classification (see "Managerial Occupations in Manufacturing" in the appendix). The census data show a steady rise in the share of managers in total employment over this period, from 4.7 percent in 1960 to 5.3 percent in 1970, 6.3 percent in 1980, and 8.0 percent in 1990. Here too there does not appear to be much of a relation between changes in firm or establishment size and changes in the managerial share in total employment.

Our last variable of interest is the change in average employee pay. This is defined in two ways: first, as average wages and salaries per

**Figure 7.5   Change in Average Establishment and Firm Size and
Employee Compensation, 1958 to 1997**

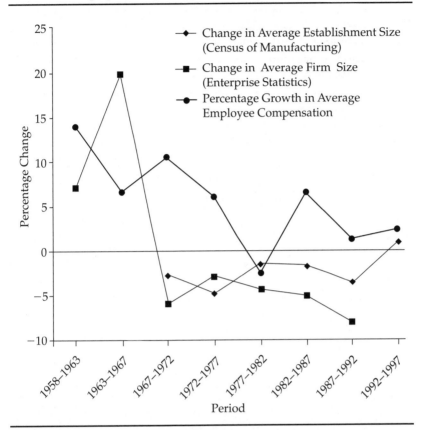

Sources: U.S. Bureau of the Census, Census of Manufacturing, establishments (1967 to 1997), Enterprise Statistics, firms (1958 to 1992); and U.S. National Income and Product Accounts (see the data appendix to chapter 5 for details).

full-time equivalent employee (FTEE); and second, as the average employee compensation, including wages and salaries and employee benefits per FTEE. Both wages and salaries and employee compensation are deflated by the CPI to obtain employee pay in constant dollars.

Figure 7.5 shows the percentage change in employee pay for the Census of Manufacturing periods. (Changes in wages and employee compensation are highly correlated.) Here we do see a somewhat closer correspondence between patterns of upsizing and downsizing and the growth in pay than between changes in average size and the preceding set of variables. During the two upsizing periods 1958 to

1963 and 1963 to 1967, there were robust gains in pay, with average compensation rising by 13.9 and 6.6 percent, respectively. During the first downsizing period, 1967 to 1972, average compensation growth continued at a brisk pace (10.5 percent), but in the next downsizing period, 1972 to 1977, the growth in average compensation fell off by 6.0 percent. Over the next three periods, all characterized by downsizing, gains in average employee compensation declined to −2.6 percent, then rebounded to 6.4 percent, but subsequently collapsed to 1.2 percent. During the period 1992 to 1997, when average establishment size rose slightly, the growth in average compensation once again recovered, to 2.2 percent.

Regression Analysis of the Effects of Downsizing in Manufacturing

We turn next to regression analysis to evaluate the effects of downsizing on our key variables. Once again, we use the pooled time-series, cross-sectional data set, consisting of twenty industry observations in each of the six or seven five-year time periods. As before, the error terms are assumed to be independently distributed but may not be identically distributed, and we use the White (1980) procedure for a heteroskedasticity-consistent covariance matrix in the estimation.

A few words should again be said about timing, dynamics, and causality when considering the effects of changes in business size on factors such as productivity growth and profitability. In chapter 5's analysis of the causes of downsizing, we generally entered the variables contemporaneously (with the exception of profitability, which was entered with a lag of one period). For example, productivity growth was assumed to affect changes in average business size over the same period (say, 1977 to 1982). The main reason is that the data typically cover five-year periods, so that entering an independent variable with a one-period lag would suggest that an event five to ten years before the current period would induce changes in average business size. The lag seems rather long to us, and experiments with lagged variables did not generally produce significant results.

On the other hand, it is quite likely that a change in average business size over one period can cause changes in some other variable in the subsequent period—for example, in real wages. In this case, the independent variable—changes in business size—measures an event that occurs over one period and its consequences may be felt in the next period. Moreover, in two cases, productivity growth and changes in profitability, the independent variables used in chapter 5 become the dependent variable here. This is not inconsistent. For example, a change in productivity in one period may induce changes in business size (either contemporaneously or with a lag), and changes in business size in one period may subsequently induce changes in productivity in the next period. In addition, for these two variables, the inclusion of lagged changes in business size as an independent variable prevents simultaneity bias from arising in the equations used here and the corresponding equations in chapter 5.

Productivity Growth

Results are shown in table 7.1 for the first of our dependent variables, total factor productivity (TFP) growth. The first variable of interest is the constant term, which is interpreted as the pure rate of technological progress. Its value ranges from 0.9 percent to 1.5 percent per year. These values are typical for most estimates of TFP growth in manufacturing.

The next variable of interest is industry research and development (R&D) expenditures as a percentage of net sales. A large literature, beginning with Mansfield (1965), has now almost universally established a positive and significant effect of R&D expenditures on productivity growth (for reviews of the literature, see Griliches 1979, 1992; Mohnen 1992). Following Zvi Griliches (1980) and Edwin Mansfield (1980), we can interpret the coefficient of this variable as the rate of return of R&D, under the assumption that the (average) rate of return to R&D is equalized among sectors. The coefficient of the ratio of R&D expenditures to net sales is significant in all specifications, at either the 10 percent level or the 5 percent level. The estimated rate of return to R&D ranges from 0.22 to 0.32. These estimates are about average for previous work on the subject (for a review of previous studies, see, for example, Mohnen 1992).[2]

Next we consider the effects of international trade on TFP growth. The change in import intensity has a positive coefficient, which is generally significant at the 5 percent level (occasionally at the 10 percent level). These results are consistent with the predictions of hypothesis 3 and indicate that import competition has an important effect on plant-level efficiency and tends to increase overall industry productivity. On the other hand, the change in export intensity has a negative coefficient, but the coefficient is not significant except in one instance where it is (marginally) significant at the 10 percent level.

We look next at the effects of changes in the size distribution of establishments (and firms) on productivity growth. As we suggested earlier, downsizing may be a mechanism that increases establishment (or firm) productivity as unnecessary labor is shed. Moreover, we would expect that the effects of downsizing on efficiency would occur with a lag, since there are immediate adjustment costs associated with any major restructuring of a firm or establishment. However, the results (shown in specifications 2 and 3) do not indicate any direct asso-

Table 7.1 Regressions of TFP Growth,[a] on Downsizing Variables

Independent Variables	Specification						
	(1)	(2)	(3)	(4)	(5)	(6)	(7)
Constant	0.015** (3.91)	0.012* (2.00)	0.012** (2.74)	0.009 (1.55)	0.009 (1.53)	0.010# (1.70)	0.015* (2.49)
Ratio of industry R&D to net sales (period average)	0.253* (2.20)	0.247# (1.79)	0.244* (2.01)	0.221# (1.72)	0.221# (1.79)	0.273# (1.69)	0.324* (2.01)
Period change in ratio of exports to gross output	−0.336# (1.91)	−0.322 (1.43)	−0.265 (1.43)	−0.178 (0.08)	−0.157 (0.68)	−0.307 (1.39)	−0.365 (1.56)
Period change in ratio of imports to gross output	0.074* (1.99)	0.079# (1.68)	0.078* (2.00)	0.082# (1.81)	0.090* (1.99)	0.072# (1.70)	0.078# (1.70)
Percentage change in mean employment per establishment (one-period lag)[b]	—	−0.032 (0.82)	—	—	—	—	—
Percentage change in mean employment per firm (one-period lag)[c]	—	—	−0.013 (1.09)	—	—	—	—
CHGINI (one-period lag)[d]	—	—	—	−0.241# (1.91)	—	—	—
CHNGCV (one-period lag)[e]	—	—	—	—	−0.027* (2.00)	—	—

	(1)	(2)	(3)	(4)	(5)	(6)	(7)
CHEST20 (one-period lag)[f]	—	—	—	—	—	0.322	—
						1.51	
CHEST1000 (one-period lag)[g]	—	—	—	—	—	—	0.148
							(1.57)
R^2	0.055	0.066	0.067	0.095	0.098	0.087	0.085
Adjusted-R^2	0.037	0.027	0.040	0.056	0.060	0.049	0.046
Standard error	0.0335	0.0392	0.0341	0.0386	0.0384	0.0387	0.0388
Sample size	160	100	140	100	100	100	100
Period	1953–1997	1972–1997	1963–1997	1972–1997	1972–1997	1972–1997	1972–1997

Note: The sample consists of pooled cross-section, time-series data, with observations on each of the twenty manufacturing industries. The full set of census periods is: 1958 to 1963, 1963 to 1967, 1967 to 1972, 1972 to 1977, 1977 to 1982, 1982 to 1987, 1987 to 1992, and 1992 to 1997 (sixteen industries). Actual periods for each regression are indicated. The absolute value of the t-statistic is shown in parentheses below the coefficient estimate. See the data appendix to chapter 5 for sources.

[a]TFP growth: Average annual rate of total factor productivity growth, based on FTEEs and net capital stock.

[b]Mean number of employees per establishment: Data are from the Census of Manufacturing, 1967 to 1997. Percentage change is over the census period.

[c]Mean number of employees per enterprise: Data are from the Enterprise Statistics, 1958 to 1992. Percentage change is over the census period.

[d]CHGINI: Change in the Gini coefficient for the average number of employees per establishment by industry size class. Data are from the Census of Manufacturing.

[e]CHNGCV: Change in the coefficient of variation for the average number of employees per establishment by industry size class. Data are from the Census of Manufacturing.

[f]CHEST20: Change in the percentage of employment in size classes of nineteen or fewer employees. Data are from the Census of Manufacturing.

[g]CHEST1000: Change in the percentage of employment in size classes of one thousand or more employees. Data are from the Census of Manufacturing.

*Significant at the 10 percent level (two-tailed test).

*Significant at the 5 percent level (two-tailed test).

**Significant at the 1 percent level (two-tailed test).

ciation of lagged changes in average establishment or firm size with industry productivity. Indeed, the coefficients are (perversely) negative, though, as we indicated, not statistically significant.[3]

On the other hand, lagged changes in the dispersion of employment among different manufacturing size classes have a negative effect on TFP growth (specifications 4 and 5). The coefficients are significant at the 10 percent level for the change in the Gini coefficient and at the 5 percent level for the change in the coefficient of variation. This result is what we would expect, since as inefficient large establishments and inefficient small ones are eliminated from the industry, overall dispersion in employment should fall and overall productivity within the industry should rise. This result is also consistent with our argument in chapter 3 that, as plants (or firms) move away from both the downward and upward sloping portions of their average cost curves toward the flat-bottomed middle, overall efficiency in the industry should increase, as should productivity.

Unfortunately, this result is not as clear-cut as we would like, since, as shown in the last two regressions (specifications 6 and 7), lagged changes in the share of employees working in small establishments (fewer than twenty employees) is positively related to TFP growth, as are lagged changes in the share of employees employed in very large establishments (one thousand or more). However, in this case, while the coefficients of these two variables are positive, both coefficients are insignificant.

We also used the annual rate of labor productivity growth as the dependent variable. In this case, we include one additional independent variable, the rate of growth of total capital per worker, since increases in capital intensity will, other things being equal, raise labor productivity. The results are very similar to those for TFP growth. (These results are not shown in a table.) The coefficient of R&D intensity remains significant (at the 5 or 10 percent level), and the estimated rate of return to R&D falls in the range of 0.23 to 0.33. The coefficient of the change in the share of imports in total sales remains positive and significant at the 5 or 10 percent level.

The coefficients of lagged changes in average establishment or firm size are now positive but, again, not statistically significant (t-ratios of 0.13 and 0.42, respectively). The coefficient of the lagged change in the Gini coefficient is, as before, negative but in this case not significant (a t-ratio of 1.55), while the coefficient of the lagged change in the coefficient of variation is also negative and significant at the 5 percent level. The coefficients of both the lagged change in the share of employees working in establishments of fewer than twenty employees and the lagged change in the share of employees working in establishments of one thousand or more employees remain positive but not statistically significant (t-ratios of 0.94 and 1.51, respectively).

Profitability and Market Value

Next we investigate the effects of downsizing on both profitability and the market value of companies. We use the same sample as in the analysis of productivity trends. There is less of a theoretical basis for the choice of possible determinants of firm profitability and stock valuation than there is of productivity growth. However, as we argue in hypothesis 5, we would expect that profitability within an industry would depend on, among other things, the unionization rate, the degree of import penetration, and the concentration ratio.

The first dependent variable is the change in the average industry profit rate between the previous period and the current period (see table 7.2). This is essentially a fixed-effect model, where the average profit rate of an industry is a function of the levels of these variables and an industry-specific effect. Our regression uses the first difference of this equation, so that the industry effect should, in principle, wash out.[4] In the first specification, we include only the unionization rate for the industry and its change in import intensity. The coefficient of the unionization rate is negative, as expected, and significant at the 1 percent level. The coefficient of the change in import intensity is, also as expected, negative but not significant.

In the next specifications, we add variables reflecting changes in the size distribution of establishments and firms. We do find, as predicted, that downsizing has a positive effect on profitability. The coefficient of the percentage change in average establishment size lagged one period is negative and significant at the 5 percent level, while the coefficient of the percentage change in average firm size lagged one period is also negative but now significant at the 1 percent level (see specifications 2 and 3).

We also find that changes in the dispersion of employment among different manufacturing size classes are positively associated with changes in profitability. The coefficient of the lagged change in the Gini coefficient is positive and significant at the 10 percent level, while the coefficient of the lagged change in the coefficient of variation is positive and significant at the 5 percent level. The results indicate that as establishment size regresses to the mean, overall industry profitability rises. On the other hand, neither the lagged change in the share of employees working in small establishments nor that in the share of employees employed in very large establishments is statistically significant.

It is also worth noting that when variables reflecting changes in the size distribution of employment within the industry are added to the regression, the coefficient of the unionization rate remains negative and significant, though the significance level drops to the 5 or 10 percent level. The coefficient of the period change in import intensity also remains negative but is not significant in any specification.[5]

Table 7.2 Regressions of the Change in the Profit Rate,[a] on Downsizing Variables

Independent Variables	Specification						
	(1)	(2)	(3)	(4)	(5)	(6)	(7)
Constant	0.025	0.022	0.024	0.025	0.029	0.020	0.021
	(1.36)	(1.12)	(1.38)	(1.21)	(1.45)	(0.95)	(1.00)
Unionization rate[b] (period average)	−0.136**	−0.127*	−0.122*	−0.104#	−0.118#	−0.107#	−0.109#
	(2.77)	(2.11)	(2.57)	(1.73)	(1.97)	(1.77)	(1.78)
Period change in ratio of imports to gross output	−0.097	−0.123	−0.144	−0.076	−0.101	−0.090	−0.072
	(1.06)	(1.27)	(1.62)	(0.80)	(1.06)	(0.92)	(0.74)
Percentage change in mean employment per establishment (one-period lag)	—	−0.183*	—	—	—	—	—
		(2.29)					
Percentage change in mean employment per firm (one-period lag)	—	—	−0.101**	—	—	—	—
			(3.29)				

	(1)	(2)	(3)	(4)	(5)	(6)	(7)
CHGINI (one-period lag)	—	—	—	0.430# (1.68)	—	—	—
CHNGCV (one-period lag)	—	—	—	—	0.061* (2.26)	—	—
CHEST20 (one-period lag)	—	—	—	—	—	0.381 (0.94)	—
CHEST1000 (one-period lag)	—	—	—	—	—	—	-0.049 (0.26)
R^2	0.065	0.084	0.144	0.061	0.082	0.043	0.034
Adjusted-R^2	0.049	0.055	0.122	0.032	0.054	0.013	0.004
Standard error	0.0801	0.0807	0.0770	0.0817	0.0808	0.0825	0.0829
Sample size	120	100	120	100	100	100	100
Period	1967–1997	1972–1997	1967–1992	1972–1997	1972–1997	1972–1997	1972–1997

Sources: U.S. Bureau of the Census, Census of Manufacturing (1967 to 1997), and Enterprise Statistics (1958 to 1992).
Note: See table 7.1 notes for a description of the sample and estimation technique and the definitions of variables.
ᵃChange in profit rate: Change in the ratio of net profits to net capital stock between the current period and the previous period.
ᵇUnionization rate: Share of employees covered by union contracts.
#Significant at the 10 percent level (two-tailed test).
*Significant at the 5 percent level (two-tailed test).
**Significant at the 1 percent level (two-tailed test).

Our next dependent variable is the change in the profit share within an industry between the previous and current periods. This is also a fixed-effect model, where the average profit share of an industry is a function of the levels of various variables and an industry-specific effect. The results are shown in table 7.3. They are similar to those for the change in the average profit rate within the industry, but less robust. As in the profit rate regressions, the coefficient of the unionization rate is negative and the coefficient of the change in import intensity is negative, but in this case neither is statistically significant. The coefficients of both the percentage change in average establishment size lagged one period and the percentage change in average firm size lagged one period are negative, as before (see specifications 2 and 3). However, only the coefficient of the percentage change in average firm size is now significant, and its significance level is only 10 percent.

As in the profit rate regressions, the coefficient of the lagged change in the Gini coefficient is positive, and the coefficient of the coefficient of variation lagged one period is positive. However, neither is statistically significant (specifications 4 and 5). Moreover, neither the lagged change in the share of employees working in small establishments nor that in the share of employees in very large establishments is statistically significant.

The third dependent variable in this group is the percentage change in the average market value of firms within an industry, deflated by the CPI. In the case of stock market valuation, there is little theory to guide us. We did use the same two independent variables as in the analysis of the change in the profit rate and the change in the profit share. Although the coefficients of the change in import intensity proved statistically insignificant, we did find that unionization is a powerful explanatory variable. Its coefficient is uniformly negative and significant at the 1 percent level (see table 7.4). The stock market appears to put a negative valuation on the presence of unions, presumably because of their depressing effect on the profit rate.

Our major finding is that the coefficient of the percentage change in mean employment per establishment is positive and significant at the 1 percent level. In other words, contrary to popular belief, downsizing is associated with a *drop* in stock values, not a rise. This result holds only for the contemporaneous change in mean employment size. The coefficient of the percentage change in mean employment per establishment lagged one period is virtually zero (see specification 3).[6] We also find that the coefficient of the percentage change in mean employment per firm is positive but significant at only the 10 percent level (specification 4). None of the other variables measuring changes in the size distribution of establishments within the industry is statistically significant (specifications 5 through 8).

This regression finding on the relation between changes in the market valuation of firms and downsizing does not establish the *direction* of causation. It is possible that firms downsize when their stock values fall, thus creating a positive correlation between changes in average market value and changes in establishment size. It is also possible that when a firm gets into trouble, not only does its stock value fall, but it downsizes in response to falling profits. It may also be true that the market does not reward downsizing—that is, when layoffs occur, investors may take it as a sign of trouble and sell off the company's stock.[7]

Changes in Occupational Composition

Next we come to the effects of downsizing on the composition of industry employment. Table 7.5 shows the regression results for the dependent variable DIOCCUP, which is a measure of the overall change in industry employment composition. In this case, none of the coefficients of variables reflecting changes in the average size of establishments or firms or their size distribution is statistically significant, with one exception: the coefficient of the change in the share of employees in very large establishments is negative and significant at the 10 percent level. The implication here is that, as employment in very large establishments declines, the degree of occupation change rises.

Several other interesting results emerge. First, TFP growth has a positive influence on the change in the job structure, though the coefficient of the variable is not significant. Second, industry expenditures on R&D generally have a positive association with changes in job structure, though here too the coefficient is not significant. Third, the degree of unionization in an industry appears to inhibit changes in job composition. Its coefficient is significant at the 10 percent level in six of the seven cases and at the 5 percent level in the other case.

The second dependent variable is the change in the share of managers in total industry employment (see table 7.6). In this case, changes in both the average establishment size and the average firm size are negatively associated with changes in the managerial share of employment. The coefficient of the latter variable is significant at the 5 percent level, while that of the former is not significant. This result is contrary to the predictions of hypothesis 6 on "blue-collarization," since it indicates that industries that downsize more experience relatively greater increases, rather than decreases, in the share of managers in total employment. The coefficients of the other variables, which measure changes in the size distribution of employment by size class, are not statistically significant.

There are several other interesting results. First, industries with more rapid rates of TFP growth tend to have lower increases in the

(Text continues on p. 222.)

Table 7.3 Regressions of the Change in the Profit Share,[a] on Downsizing Variables

Independent Variables	Specification						
	(1)	(2)	(3)	(4)	(5)	(6)	(7)
Constant	0.029	0.028	0.029	0.029	0.031	0.026	0.025
	(1.64)	(1.41)	(1.63)	(1.44)	(1.57)	(1.31)	(1.25)
Unionization rate (period average)	−0.065	−0.064	−0.057	−0.052	−0.069	−0.054	−0.058
	(1.34)	(1.09)	(1.18)	(0.89)	(1.00)	(0.91)	(0.99)
Period change in ratio of imports to gross output	−0.054	−0.083	−0.080	−0.057	−0.069	−0.065	−0.046
	(0.60)	(0.87)	(0.89)	(0.61)	(0.74)	(0.69)	(0.49)
Percentage change in mean employment per establishment (one-period lag)	—	−0.100	—	—	—	—	—
		(1.28)					
Percentage change in mean employment per firm (one-period lag)	—	—	−0.057#	—	—	—	—
			(1.81)				

CHGINI (one-period lag)	—	—	—	0.179 (0.72)	—	—	—
CHNGCV (one-period lag)	—	—	—	—	0.030 (1.16)	—	—
CHEST20 (one-period lag)	—	—	—	—	—	0.221 (0.56)	—
CHEST1000 (one-period lag)	—	—	—	—	—	—	-0.158 (0.88)
R^2	0.016	0.027	0.044	0.016	0.024	0.014	0.019
Adjusted-R^2	0.005	0.010	0.018	0.007	0.007	0.003	0.010
Standard error	0.0791	0.0791	0.0783	0.0795	0.0792	0.0796	0.0794
Sample size	120	100	120	100	100	100	100
Period	1967–1997	1972–1997	1967–1992	1972–1997	1972–1997	1972–1997	1972–1997

Sources: U.S. Bureau of the Census, Census of Manufacturing (1967 to 1997), and Enterprise Statistics (1958 to 1992).

Note: See table 7.1 notes for a description of the sample and estimation technique and the definitions of variables.

[a]Change in profit share: Change in the ratio of net profits to GDP between the current period and the previous period.

#Significant at the 10 percent level (two-tailed test).

*Significant at the 5 percent level (two-tailed test).

**Significant at the 1 percent level (two-tailed test).

Table 7.4 Regressions of the Percentage Change in the Average Market Value[a] of Firms, on Downsizing Variables

Independent Variables	Specification							
	(1)	(2)	(3)	(4)	(5)	(6)	(7)	(8)
Constant	0.632**	0.615**	0.669**	0.457**	0.445**	0.449**	0.457**	0.449**
	(5.97)	6.00	(5.49)	(4.20)	(4.06)	(4.06)	(4.18)	(4.06)
Unionization rate (period average)	−1.195**	1.010**	−1.439**	−0.900**	−0.891**	−0.881**	−0.856**	−0.871**
	(3.92)		(3.79)	(3.02)	(2.94)	(2.92)	(2.86)	(2.87)
Percentage change in mean employment per establishment	—	1.702**	—	—	—	—	—	—
Percentage change in mean employment per establishment (one-period lag)	—	—	−0.006	—	—	—	—	—
			(0.01)					
Percentage change in mean employment per firm	—	—	—	0.286#	—	—	—	—
				(1.71)				

CHGINI	—	—	—	—	−0.477 (0.34)	—	—	—
CHNGCV	—	—	—	—	—	0.040 (0.27)	—	—
CHEST20	—	—	—	—	—	—	−2.691 (1.25)	—
CHEST1000	—	—	—	—	—	—	—	0.258 (0.25)
R^2	0.115	0.218	0.130	0.102	0.082	0.095	0.095	0.081
Adjusted-R^2	0.108	0.204	0.112	0.084	0.063	0.077	0.076	0.062
Standard error	0.502	0.477	0.551	0.502	0.448	0.445	0.445	0.448
Sample size	120	116	100	100	100	100	100	100
Period	1967–1997	1967–1997	1972–1997	1967–1992	1967–1992	1967–1992	1967–1992	1967–1992

Sources: U.S. Bureau of the Census, Census of Manufacturing (1967 to 1997), and Enterprise Statistics (1958 to 1992).

Note: See table 7.1 notes for a description of the sample and estimation technique and the definitions of variables.

ªChange in the average market value: Percentage change in the average market value of firms within the industry between the current period and the previous period (*Source*: CRSP database).

#Significant at the 10 percent level (two-tailed test).

*Significant at the 5 percent level (two-tailed test).

**Significant at the 1 percent level (two-tailed test).

Table 7.5 Regressions of DIOCCUP^a on Downsizing Variables

Independent Variables	Specification						
	(1)	(2)	(3)	(4)	(5)	(6)	(7)
Constant	0.082**	0.088**	0.082**	0.088**	0.087**	0.091**	0.083**
	(5.68)	(4.62)	(5.64)	(4.55)	(4.54)	(4.76)	(4.49)
TFP growth	0.278	0.308	0.322	0.292	0.290	0.303	0.380
	(1.29)	(1.25)	(1.47)	(1.18)	(1.18)	(1.25)	(1.57)
Ratio of industry R&D to net sales (period average)	−0.075	0.140	−0.045	0.126	0.128	0.071	0.012
	(0.42)	(0.52)	(0.25)	(0.47)	(0.47)	(0.26)	(0.05)
Unionization rate (period average)	−0.060$^#$	−0.093$^#$	−0.040$^#$	−0.098$^#$	−0.097$^#$	−0.091$^#$	−0.112*
	(1.81)	(1.88)	(1.91)	(1.88)	(1.99)	(1.88)	(2.33)
Percentage change in mean employment per establishment	—	0.029	—	—	—	—	—
		(0.57)					
Percentage change in mean employment per firm	—	—	0.018	—	—	—	—
			(1.09)				
CHGINI	—	—	—	−0.011	—	—	—
				(0.06)			

CHNGCV	—	—	—	—	−0.005 (0.30)	—	—
CHEST20	—	—	—	—	—	−0.281 (1.06)	—
CHEST1000	—	—	—	—	—	—	−0.214[*] (1.73)
R^2	0.093	0.167	0.111	0.160	0.162	0.184	0.223
Adjusted-R^2	0.047	0.077	0.050	0.045	0.071	0.096	0.139
Standard error	0.0418	0.0448	0.0417	0.0449	0.0449	0.0443	0.0432
Sample size	60	40	60	40	40	40	40
Period	1963–1992	1972–1992	1963–1992	1972–1992	1972–1992	1972–1992	1972–1992

Sources: U.S. Bureau of the Census, Census of Manufacturing (1967 to 1997), and Enterprise Statistics (1958 to 1992).

Note: The sample consists of pooled cross-section, time-series data, with observations on each of the twenty manufacturing industries for census periods 1963 to 1972, 1972 to 1982, and 1982 to 1992. Actual periods for each regression are indicated. The absolute value of the t-statistic is shown in parentheses below the coefficient estimate. See table 7.1 notes for definitions of variables.

[a]DIOCCUP: Dissimilarity index for the occupational distribution of employment by industry.

[#]Significant at the 10 percent level (two-tailed test).

[*]Significant at the 5 percent level (two-tailed test).

[**]Significant at the 1 percent level (two-tailed test).

Table 7.6 Regressions of CHGMGR,[a] on Downsizing Variables

Independent Variables	Specification						
	(1)	(2)	(3)	(4)	(5)	(6)	(7)
Constant	0.016**	0.013**	0.016**	0.012**	0.013**	0.013**	0.012**
	(5.87)	(3.64)	(6.16)	(3.54)	(3.81)	(3.54)	(3.52)
TFP growth	−0.076#	−0.101*	−0.092*	−0.088#	−0.091*	−0.095*	−0.081#
	(1.92)	(2.26)	(2.37)	(1.94)	(2.05)	(2.08)	(1.78)
Ratio of industry R&D to net sales (period average)	0.123**	0.182**	0.112**	0.188**	0.187**	0.189**	0.170**
	(3.79)	(3.70)	(3.53)	(3.80)	(3.81)	(3.71)	(3.38)
Unionization rate (period average)	−0.018**	−0.011	−0.017**	−0.006	−0.009	−0.010	−0.011
	(3.02)	(1.26)	(2.88)	(0.62)	(1.01)	(1.06)	(1.32)
Percentage change in mean employment per establishment	—	−0.013	—	—	—	—	—
		(1.39)					
Percentage change in mean employment per firm	—	—	−0.067*	—	—	—	—
			(2.27)				
CHGINI	—	—	—	0.041	—	—	—
				(1.14)			

CHNGCV	—	—	—	—	0.042 (1.34)	—	—
CHEST20	—	—	—	—	—	0.063 (0.13)	—
CHEST1000	—	—	—	—	—	—	-0.034 (1.48)
R^2	0.270	0.336	0.330	0.324	0.334	0.301	0.340
Adjusted-R^2	0.233	0.264	0.284	0.251	0.262	0.226	0.269
Standard error	0.0076	0.0081	0.0074	0.0082	0.0081	0.0083	0.0081
Sample size	60	40	60	40	40	40	40
Period	1963–1992	1972–1992	1963–1992	1972–1992	1972–1992	1972–1992	1972–1992

Sources: U.S. Bureau of the Census, Census of Manufacturing (1967 to 1997), and Enterprise Statistics (1958 to 1992).
Note: The sample consists of pooled cross-section, time-series data, with observations on each of the twenty manufacturing industries for census periods 1963 to 1972, 1972 to 1982, and 1982 to 1992. Actual periods for each regression are indicated. The absolute value of the t-statistic is shown in parentheses below the coefficient estimate. See table 7.1 notes for definitions of variables.
ᵃCHGMGR: Change in the share of managers in total industry employment over the period.
*Significant at the 10 percent level (two-tailed test).
*Significant at the 5 percent level (two-tailed test).
**Significant at the 1 percent level (two-tailed test).

share of managers in total employment. The coefficient of TFP growth is significant at the 5 percent level in four of the seven cases and at the 10 percent level in the other three cases. Second, industries with greater R&D intensity experience increases in managerial employment. The coefficient of R&D intensity is significant at the 1 percent level in all seven cases. This result may reflect both the greater coordination associated with a greater level of research activity and a reduction in production-worker employment induced by the new technology contributed by research activity. Third, more unionized industries also tend to have smaller increases in their managerial share. In this case, the coefficient of the unionization rate is significant in only two of the seven cases (those that cover the full 1962 to 1992 period).

Employee Compensation

Our next two variables are changes in employee remuneration. The first of these is the percentage change in average wages and salaries per FTEE, and the second is the percentage change in employee compensation, including wages, salaries, and fringe benefits, per FTEE. This is another fixed-effect model, where average employee remuneration is posited to be a function of the levels of various variables and an industry-specific effect. Our regressions essentially use the first difference of this equation, so that the industry effect should fall out.

We do not have very many other independent variables for the analysis. Ideally, we would like to control for changes in the average human capital or skill level of employees within an industry. However, these data are not available. We do, however, have information on the degree of unionization within an industry. This allows us to control for the well-documented wage differential between union and non-union workers (see, for example, Lewis 1963, 1986). We also control for the concentration ratio of the industry, using the period average Gini coefficient. This accords with numerous findings in the literature that, other things being equal, more concentrated industries pay higher wages than those that are less concentrated (see, for example, Weiss 1966; Pugel 1980).

The results for the percentage change in average wages and salaries are shown in table 7.7. The unionization rate, as predicted, has a uniformly positive effect on the change in average earnings, but it is not statistically significant in any case. The concentration ratio also has the predicted positive association with earnings growth. It is significant at the 10 percent level in two cases but not significant in the others.

Our main finding is that the percentage changes in both the average number of employees per establishment and the average number of employees per firm have a positive effect on wage growth. The coefficients are significant at the 1 percent level in both cases (specifications 2 and 4). These results establish that downsizing leads to a reduction in average wages and salaries. The coefficient of the percentage change in the average number of employees per establishment lagged one period is also positive and significant at the 1 percent level (specification 3). By and large, however, the results are stronger for a contemporaneous association between the contraction in firm or plant size and a decline in wage growth. The result that there is a positive and significant association between change in firm and establishment size and wage growth survives the inclusion of both period and industry effects. (The coefficient remains significant at the 5 or 1 percent level.)

We also find that changes in the dispersion of employment among different size classes within manufacturing are positively associated with wage growth. The coefficient of the change in the Gini coefficient is significant at the 10 percent level, and that of the change in the coefficient of variation is significant at the 5 percent level (specifications 5 and 6). The results indicate that regression to the mean in terms of establishment size (that is, a reduction in the dispersion of employment among size classes) is associated with a decline in wage growth. Interestingly, an increase in the share of total employment in both very small and very large establishments appears to be associated with a reduction in wage growth, but the coefficients are not statistically significant (specifications 7 and 8).

The results for the second of the two variables, growth in average employee compensation (the sum of wages and salaries and employee benefits), are shown in table 7.8. The results are, if anything, stronger than for the growth in just wages and salaries. The concentration ratio has the expected positive sign and is statistically significant in all but one case. The coefficients of the percentage change in mean number of employees per establishment and per firm remain positive and significant at the 1 percent level. The coefficients of the change in both the Gini coefficient and the coefficient of variation remain positive and are now both significant at the 5 percent level. The coefficient of the change in the share of employment in very small establishments has the expected negative sign (smaller establishments provide lower compensation) and is now significant at the 10 percent level. The coefficient of the share of employment in very large establishments is now positive but still insignificant.

Our last variable is the annual change in unit labor cost. Unit labor cost is defined as the ratio of employee compensation (in 1992 dollars) to output (also in 1992 dollars). It is the ratio of real compensa-

(Text continues on p. 228.)

Table 7.7 Regressions of the Percentage Change in Average Wages and Salaries,[a] on Downsizing Variables

Independent Variables	Specification							
	(1)	(2)	(3)	(4)	(5)	(6)	(7)	(8)
Constant	-0.091	-0.114	-0.066	-0.098	-0.075	-0.072	-0.070	-0.087
	(1.09)	(1.43)	(0.77)	(1.28)	(0.92)	(0.89)	(0.84)	(1.05)
Unionization rate (period average)	0.031	0.041	0.021	0.022	0.041	0.029	0.036	0.029
	(0.67)	(0.91)	(0.39)	(0.52)	(0.89)	(0.64)	(0.78)	(0.62)
Concentration ratio[b]	0.137	0.173#	0.116	0.162#	0.117	0.118	0.112	0.132
	(1.26)	(1.69)	(1.04)	(1.70)	(1.08)	(1.10)	(1.03)	(1.20)
Percentage change in mean employment per establishment	—	0.189**	—	—	—	—	—	—
		(2.95)						
Percentage change in mean employment per establishment (one-period lag)	—	—	0.171**	—	—	—	—	—
			(2.61)					
Percentage change in mean employment per firm	—	—	—	0.108**	—	—	—	—
				(4.06)				

CHGINI	—	—	—	—	0.358# (1.67)	—	—	—
CHNGCV	—	—	—	—	—	0.047* (2.13)	—	—
CHEST20	—	—	—	—	—	—	−0.470 (1.40)	—
CHEST1000	—	—	—	—	—	—	—	−0.072 (0.46)
R^2	0.023	0.104	0.096	0.166	0.050	0.067	0.043	0.069
Adjusted-R^2	0.003	0.076	0.060	0.140	0.020	0.040	0.013	0.025
Standard error	0.0685	0.0659	0.0640	0.0636	0.0678	0.0672	0.0681	0.0688
Sample size	100	100	80	100	100	100	100	100
Period	1967–1992	1967–1992	1972–1992	1967–1992	1967–1992	1967–1992	1967–1992	1967–1992

Sources: U.S. Bureau of the Census, Census of Manufacturing (1967 to 1997), and Enterprise Statistics (1958 to 1992).

Note: See table 7.1 notes for a description of the sample and estimation technique and the definitions of variables.

a Percentage change in average wages and salaries within the industry between the current and preceding period.

b Concentration ratio: Gini coefficient for the size distribution of employment by size class, averaged over the period.

Significant at the 10 percent level (two-tailed test).

* Significant at the 5 percent level (two-tailed test).

** Significant at the 1 percent level (two-tailed test).

Table 7.8 Regressions of the Percentage Change in Average Employee Compensation,[a] on Downsizing Variables

Independent Variables	Specification							
	(1)	(2)	(3)	(4)	(5)	(6)	(7)	(8)
Constant	−0.135	−0.158#	−0.112	−0.142#	−0.115	−0.116	−0.107	−0.137
	(1.61)	(1.94)	(1.32)	(1.83)	(1.39)	(1.41)	(1.28)	(1.62)
Unionization rate (period average)	0.059	0.069	0.002	0.051	0.073	0.058	0.067	0.061
	(1.27)	(1.52)	(0.04)	(1.16)	(1.58)	(1.26)	(1.43)	(1.29)
Concentration ratio	0.208#	0.243*	0.191#	0.224*	0.182#	0.188#	0.175	0.211#
	(1.90)	(2.28)	(1.73)	(2.20)	(1.69)	(1.75)	(1.60)	(1.91)
Percentage change in mean employment per establishment	—	0.183**	—	—	—	—	—	—
		(2.82)						
Percentage change in mean employment per establishment (one-period lag)	—	—	0.191**	—	—	—	—	—
			(2.93)					
Percentage change in mean employment per firm	—	—	—	0.109**	—	—	—	—
				(4.02)				

	(1)	(2)	(3)	(4)	(5)	(6)	(7)	(8)
CHGINI	—	—	—	0.474* (2.20)	—	—	—	—
CHNGC	—	—	—	—	0.050* (2.25)	—	—	—
CHEST2	—	—	—	—	—	—	−0.633# (1.88)	—
CHEST1000	—	—	—	—	—	—	—	0.049 (0.31)
R^2	0.057	0.130	0.125	0.193	0.103	0.105	0.091	0.058
Adjusted-R^2	0.038	0.102	0.091	0.168	0.075	0.077	0.063	0.029
Standard error	0.0692	0.0669	0.0631	0.0644	0.0679	0.0679	0.0684	0.0696
Sample size	100	100	80	100	100	100	100	100
Period	1967–1992	1967–1992	1972–1992	1967–1992	1967–1992	1967–1992	1967–1992	1967–1992

Sources: U.S. Bureau of the Census, Census of Manufacturing (1967 to 1997), and Enterprise Statistics (1958 to 1992).

Note: See table 7.1 notes for a description of the sample and estimation technique and the definitions of variables.

ᵃPercentage change in average employee compensation within the industry between the current period and the previous period.

#Significant at the 10 percent level (two-tailed test).

*Significant at the 5 percent level (two-tailed test).

**Significant at the 1 percent level (two-tailed test).

tion per worker to labor productivity. Its change over time thus reflects changes in employee compensation and changes in labor productivity. The results for this variable are shown in table 7.9.

The key result for labor costs is that the coefficients of the percentage change in mean number of employees per establishment and per firm are positive and significant at the 5 percent level. Thus, downsizing leads to reductions in unit labor costs. The main mechanism is through a reduction in pay rather than an increase in productivity. The coefficient of the percentage change in the average number of employees per establishment lagged one period is also positive but significant at only the 10 percent level. On the other hand, changes in the dispersion of employment among different size classes within manufacturing do not seem to bear directly on unit labor costs.

The unionization rate, as expected, is positively related to changes in unit labor costs (through its positive effect on wages), but its coefficient is not statistically significant in any case. The concentration ratio also has a positive association with changes in unit labor costs since, as found earlier, more concentrated industries tend to experience higher growth in employee remuneration. Its coefficient is significant at the 1 percent level in seven of the eight cases and at the 5 percent level in the other. Expenditures on R&D, in contrast, lead to reductions in unit labor costs, mainly through their effect on productivity. The coefficient of this variable is significant at the 5 percent level in seven of the eight cases and at the 10 percent level in the other.

Conclusions

In this chapter, we investigated the consequences of downsizing (and upsizing) in the U.S. manufacturing sector, focusing on its effects on productivity growth, profitability and market value, occupational composition, and employee compensation.

First, for productivity growth, our results do not indicate that lagged changes in average establishment or firm size have any direct association with industry productivity. Indeed, the coefficients are (perversely) negative, though not statistically significant. These results are broadly consistent with the findings of Baily, Bartelsman, and Haltiwanger (1996b) and Collins and Harris (1999), who found that downsizing is generally associated with a lowering of productivity growth.

On the other hand, we find that lagged changes in the dispersion of employment among different manufacturing size classes tend to diminish total factor productivity growth, with coefficients that are significant at the 5 or 10 percent level. This result suggests that as inefficient small and large establishments are eliminated from the industry, overall dispersion in employment falls and overall industry productivity increases. This result is also consistent with our argument in chapter 3 that, as plants (or firms) move toward the flat-bottomed middle part of their average cost curves, overall efficiency in the industry, as well as productivity, should increase.

We also find, as do most previous studies on productivity, that the coefficient of the ratio of R&D expenditures to net sales is significant. The estimated rate of return to R&D ranges from 0.22 to 0.32. The change in import intensity also has a positive coefficient, and its coefficient is significant at the 5 or 10 percent level. These results are consistent with the predictions of hypothesis 3 that import competition increases plant-level efficiency and overall industry productivity.

Turning to the effects of downsizing on profitability, we find very strong effects. The coefficients of the lagged percentage change in both average establishment size and average firm are negative and statistically significant. The results support the plausible hypothesis that downsizing leads to increased profitability. We also find that changes in the dispersion of employment among different size classes are positively associated with changes in profitability. These results indicate that as establishment size regresses to the mean within an industry, overall industry profitability rises. When the regressions are replicated for the change in the average profit share within an industry, the signs of these variables remain unchanged but are generally less significant. We also find that the unionization rate has a negative effect on the average industry profit rate, and that its coefficient is highly significant, indicating that the presence of unions in an industry reduces profitability.

Our next topic was the effect of downsizing on the percentage change in the average market value of firms within an industry. We find that the coefficient of the percentage change in mean employment per establishment is positive and highly significant. Contrary to popular belief, downsizing is associated with a fall in stock values, not a rise. This result holds only for the contemporaneous change in mean employment size. This result is also consistent with some of the previous literature on the subject, which found a negative relation between downsizing and stock price changes (see Worrell, Davidson, and Sharma 1991; Gombola and Tsetsekos 1992; Abraham 1999). The regression finding does not establish the direction of causation—whether downsizing leads to falling stock values or falling stock values induce firms to downsize. Unionization is found to be inversely related to market value gains, and its coefficient is highly significant. The results suggest that the stock market has a negative valuation of the presence of unions, presumably because of their depressing effect on profit rates.

We also looked at the effects of downsizing on employment restructuring. While changes in the size distribution of employment appear to have little effect on overall changes in the occupational com-

Table 7.9 Regressions of the Annual Growth in Unit Labor Costs,[a] on Downsizing Variables

Independent Variables	Specification							
	(1)	(2)	(3)	(4)	(5)	(6)	(7)	(8)
Constant	-0.141**	-0.144**	-0.156**	-0.138**	-0.143**	-0.142**	-0.139**	-0.141**
	(3.17)	(3.31)	(2.91)	(3.18)	(3.17)	(3.15)	(3.05)	(3.15)
Ratio of Industry R&D to net sales (period average)	-0.393*	-0.340*	-0.356#	-0.350*	-0.398*	-0.394*	-0.391*	-0.401*
	(2.38)	(2.09)	(1.81)	(2.16)	(2.38)	(2.37)	(2.35)	(2.39)
Unionization rate (period average)	0.022	0.027	0.040	0.020	0.021	0.022	0.022	0.021
	(0.95)	(1.21)	(1.28)	(0.91)	(0.88)	(0.95)	(0.97)	(0.90)
Concentration ratio	0.164**	0.167**	0.178*	0.160**	0.166**	0.164**	0.161**	0.163**
	(2.65)	(2.77)	(2.39)	(2.65)	(2.66)	(2.64)	(2.56)	(2.63)
Percentage change in mean employment per establishment	—	0.076*	—	—	—	—	—	—
		(2.39)						
Percentage change in mean employment per establishment (one-period lag)	—	—	0.066#	—	—	—	—	—
			(1.79)					

	Percentage change in mean employment per firm							
CHGINI	—	—	—	0.033* (2.41)	—	—	—	—
CHNGCV	—	—	—	—	−0.037 (0.35)	−0.001 (0.14)	—	—
CHEST20	—	—	—	—	—	—	−0.049 (0.30)	—
CHEST1000	—	—	—	—	—	—	—	−0.029 (0.38)
R^2	0.104	0.156	0.136	0.156	0.106	0.105	0.105	0.106
Adjusted-R^2	0.076	0.120	0.090	0.120	0.068	0.067	0.068	0.068
Standard error	0.0329	0.0321	0.0357	0.0321	0.0330	0.0331	0.0331	0.0331
Sample size	100	100	80	100	100	100	100	100
Period	1967–1992	1967–1992	1972–1992	1967–1992	1967–1992	1967–1992	1967–1992	1967–1992

Sources: U.S. Bureau of the Census, Census of Manufacturing (1967 to 1997), and Enterprise Statistics (1958 to 1992).
Note: See table 7.1 notes for a description of the sample and estimation technique and the definitions of variables.
ᵃUnit labor cost: employee compensation in 1992 dollars per unit of output in 1992 dollars.
*Significant at the 10 percent level (two-tailed test).
*Significant at the 5 percent level (two-tailed test).
**Significant at the 1 percent level (two-tailed test).

position of employment, changes in average firm size are found to be significantly related to changes in the share of managers in total industry employment. However, this effect, contrary to the predictions of hypothesis 6 about "blue-collarization," is negative—that is, managerial employment as a share of total employment tends to *increase* as firms downsize. The result implies that nonmanagerial employees— clerical, sales, and blue-collar workers—absorb the brunt of the effects of downsizing. These results on the share of managerial employment are consistent with Ilg's (1996) findings.

We also find that TFP growth is positively but not significantly associated with changes in job structure and negatively related to increases in the share of managers in total employment. On the other hand, industry expenditures on R&D have a strong positive association with changes in the share of management in employment. More unionized industries tend to have less change in job structure and lower increases in their managerial share.

Our final topic was the effect of downsizing on growth in employee costs. We found that the change in both the average number of employees per establishment and the average number of employees per firm has a positive effect on growth in both average wages and salaries and average employee compensation, with highly significant coefficients. These results confirm our hypothesis that downsizing leads to a reduction in average employee remuneration. We also found that a decrease in the dispersion of employment among different size classes within manufacturing is negatively related to growth in both wages and salaries and total employee compensation. The results indicate that regression to the mean in terms of establishment size is associated with a decline in the growth of average employee remuneration. Further, we found that the concentration ratio has the predicted positive association with earnings and compensation growth and is generally statistically significant in the case of changes in employee compensation. The unionization rate, as expected, is positively associated with growth in employee compensation but, surprisingly, is not statistically significant.

As a consequence, downsizing at both the establishment level and the firm level leads to reductions in unit labor costs. Similar findings were reported by Capelli (1998) and Espahbodi, John, and Vasudevan (2000). However, changes in the dispersion of employment among size classes do not seem to affect unit labor costs. R&D expenditures tend to reduce unit labor costs through their effect on productivity. Industry concentration is also positively associated with increases in unit labor costs, mainly through its association with wage increases.

Thus, we end up with a relatively simple and coherent, if somewhat surprising, assessment of the average effects of downsizing in

U.S. manufacturing companies. Leaving out many details, downsizing firms typically increase their profitability by decreasing their unit labor costs. But downsizing does not achieve these cuts in unit labor costs by raising productivity. Instead, downsizing firms somehow manage to squeeze wages. And perhaps ironically, this transformation of what were once wages into profits does not seem to enhance a downsizing firm's stock market valuation. This last result is curious and may reflect the market's assessment that the profit gains are transitory. It is also possible that the market views downsizing either as a public admission that a firm is already in more trouble than was previously recognized or as an indicator of trouble down the road.

Appendix

Table 7A.1   List of Managerial Occupations in Manufacturing, 1970

Occupation Number	Occupation Name	1970 Census Code
62	Bank officers and financial managers	201, 202
63	Buyers and shippers: farm, wholesale, retail	203, 205
64	Credit people	210
65	Funeral directors and embalmers	211, 165
66	Health administrators	212
67	Construction inspectors, public administrators	213
68	Inspectors, except construction, public administrators	215
69	Managers and superintendents, buildings	216
70	Office managers, n.e.c.	220
71	Ship officers, pilots, and pursers	221
72	Administrators, public administrators, n.e.c.	222
73	Officials of lodges, societies, and unions	223
74	Postmasters and mail superintendents	224
75	Purchasing agents and buyers, n.e.c.	225
76	Railroad conductors	226
77	Restaurant, cafeteria, and bar managers	230
78	Sales managers and department heads, retail	231
79	Sales managers, except retail trade	233
80	School administrators, college, elementary, secondary	235, 240
81	Managers and administrators, n.e.c.	245

Source: Authors' compilation.

Chapter 8

Downsizing and Increasing Turbulence in the Labor Market

As we saw in chapters 4 and 5, the 1980s were a period of rapid downsizing in manufacturing.[1] No other sector of the economy displayed consistent downsizing; in fact, in the services and retail trade sectors, *upsizing* was the norm. Even in manufacturing, the overall tendency in changes in the size of company workforces was toward intermediate size as the larger firms shrank (or were replaced by smaller firms) and the smaller firms expanded. In this chapter, we investigate in greater depth the effects of downsizing on workers by examining whether these upheavals in company size were accompanied by greater churning in the labor market. Were there changes in job tenure (the length of time that workers stay in a particular job)? Were there changes in the rates at which workers shifted into different occupations or different industries?

There have been numerous studies of job tenure (particularly length of time with the same employer) in the last dozen years or so.[2] However, very few of these studies focused on the frequency with which workers switched to different occupations or different industries. It is this information that is more relevant for our discussion, since if downsizing really is a feature of corporate restructuring rather than a manifestation of an absolute reduction in employment (as we suggested in chapter 1), then it should show up in an increased pace of change in both the composition of jobs (that is, the occupations in which individuals are employed) and in employment by industry (the industries in which workers are employed). We will investigate whether industrial restructuring is directly related to changes in the occupational and industrial composition of employment (rather than to changes in job tenure within firms).

234

In this chapter, we concentrate on the experiences of individual workers rather than on establishments and firms (the focus of chapters 4 through 7).[3] Among other things, we look into the truth of the common understanding of the consequences of downsizing—the clichéd image of formerly well-paid manufacturing workers reduced to flipping burgers and washing dishes in fast-food establishments. There are no available statistical data that permit a systematic study of the consequences of downsizing for all the workers who thereby lost their jobs, so we turn to survey data from the University of Michigan's Panel Study on Income Dynamics (PSID) for our analysis. This data source (which covers the long-term employment histories of a representative sample of individual workers) enables us to focus on employees who underwent job changes for any reason, including being laid off, receiving a better job offer from another company, experiencing changes in tastes or job satisfaction, or being affected by changes in the supply of different kinds of labor. Unfortunately for our purposes, since many of the surveyed job changers undoubtedly switched employment voluntarily (possibly in response to a better job offer), our study of the survey data on employment transfers is likely to report greater well-being in the group of transferees than would have been the case had the data pertained only to involuntary job shifting in the wake of a downsizing move by employers. Furthermore, although downsizing was particularly common in manufacturing during the 1980s, data limitations of the panel study prevent us from focusing exclusively on manufacturing. Instead, we are forced to consider the experience of workers in all sectors of the economy.

Despite these limitations, the results of our analysis of the survey data do offer some illumination, and several findings bear mention at the outset. Investigating the occupational and industrial mobility of individuals over the time periods 1969 to 1980 and 1981 to 1992 in the United States, we find that workers did change both occupations and industries more frequently in the later period. Workers, on average, switched occupations 1.8 times in the earlier period and 2.1 times in the later, and they switched industries 0.8 and 1.2 times, respectively. Our results also indicate that older workers were less likely to shift occupation or industry,[4] as were better-paid men (but not better-paid women). On the other hand, the effect of education on frequency of job changes varied from one period to another. We also find that changes in occupation and changes in industry were associated with decreased earnings, although this effect lessened over time (from a 13 percent earnings reduction per occupational change for men in the 1972 to 1974 period to a 9 percent loss in the 1990 to 1992 period).

Turmoil in the Labor Market: Background

Over the last three decades, the U.S. economy has undergone substantial structural change. Employment has shifted from goods-producing to service-providing industries, and new information-based technology has been introduced at a rapidly increasing pace, necessitating sweeping adjustments in operations and organizational restructuring of firms. At the same time, American businesses have become more export-oriented, while facing increasing competition from imports. We can illustrate the degree of this structural change in the economy by looking at the shift in the (gross) composition of employment both among industries and among occupations. For example, using the 1970, 1980, and 1990 U.S. Census of Population Public Use Samples, we have calculated total employment in each of those years for 267 occupations and 64 industries (for details on the classification schemes, see Wolff 1996). Using what is called the Duncan and Duncan index (the absolute values of the change in the percentage of employment in each category summed across all occupations or all industries), we find evidence of rising turbulence in the labor market in the 1980s relative to the 1970s. On the basis of employment by occupation, the index increased from 20.1 in the 1970s to 26.3 in the 1980s; on the basis of employment by industry, it increased from 10.6 to 12.4 for those time periods.

Previous research on labor mobility has focused primarily on movement between jobs (employers/firms), the relationship between job seniority and earnings, and worker-firm matching. Only a few studies have investigated mobility among occupations and industries, as we do here. Furthermore, this literature has focused mainly on occupational choice and occupational attainment. Models of occupational choice have concentrated on new entrants to the labor markets in which education and family antecedents play a key role. Such studies include Robertson and Symons (1990), Orazem and Mattila (1986), Shaw (1986), Miller (1984), and Rosen (1972). These studies argue that the intensity of human capital investment in occupational skills (investment in education or other efforts to increase knowledge or skills) varies among occupations and individuals, and their results generally show that individuals do appear to change occupations in ways that are intended to maximize the present value of their investment.

However, some recent exceptions can be found in studies that consider the determinants of occupational and industrial changes. Nachum Sicherman and Oded Galor (1990) analyze occupational mobility in the United States, theoretically and empirically, by focusing on individual careers. They conclude that education helps to increase the probability of occupational upgrading. Barry Harper (1995) focuses on occupational "quits" in Britain as opposed to occupational upgrading. He finds, as we do, that young and more educated individuals are more likely to change occupations.

Although our main objective here is to investigate job changes between occupations and industries over time and by gender,[5] a related concern is the relationship between job tenure and occupational and industry switching. Theoretical and empirical studies of wage determination growing out of job-matching models have established that job changes slow down over time with job tenure.[6] These models deduce a positive correlation between wages and job tenure even if seniority itself does not exert a separate (positive) influence on wages. The positive relation between wages and job tenure is explained if match quality is job-specific; in other words, individuals are less likely to quit and less likely to be laid off or fired as job seniority increases. Thus, the quality of the job match will improve with job tenure, as should wages, and job tenure and wages will be positively associated with one another even with no increase in wage offers.[7]

Similarly, human capital models (see, for example, Becker 1962) predict a negative relation between job mobility and tenure. George Borjas (1981) and Jacob Mincer and Boyan Jovanovic (1981) analyze the relationships between job tenure, wages, and interfirm labor mobility that depend on investment in job-specific human capital. They find a strong association between job tenure and wages, a result they attribute to rises over time in the firm-specific component of wages within the firm. In contrast to these results, Derek Neal (1995), using the Displaced Workers Surveys (DWS),[8] shows that workers receive compensation for skills that are specific to their industry rather than completely general or firm-specific. Similarly, Daniel Parente (2000) and Neal (1999), using the National Longitudinal Survey of Youth (NLSY),[9] show that industry-specific (rather than firm-specific) human capital is what matters most for workers' wage profile. This would suggest that job matching not only is a process of finding a job match adapted to a fixed career choice but also entails the search for a good occupation and/or industry match.

Our Study: Data Sources and Methods

The data for our study are drawn from the University of Michigan's Panel Study of Income Dynamics, a representative sample of U.S. workers. The panel contains data for twenty-five years, from 1968 to 1992, the last year of data available at the time we started our study. We carry out two divisions of the panel. In the first, we divide the panel into two periods, one from 1969 to 1980 and the other from 1981 to 1992. In the second period, we divide the panel into four three-year periods, 1972 to 1974, 1978 to 1980, 1984 to 1986, and 1990 to 1992, in order to obtain larger sample sizes.

The samples are restricted to individuals who meet the following criteria: those who were heads of households or wives over twenty-five years of age at the beginning of each period; those who were employed or on temporary layoff at the time of the interview; and those who worked at least one thousand hours per year and reported being employed in an assigned occupation and industry. To focus the analysis on wage and salary workers, people who were self-employed in any year of the survey are excluded. We also discard government employees from the sample. These criteria reduce the original sample to 508 individuals for the 1969 to 1980 sample and 635 individuals for the 1981 to 1992 sample. For the 1972 to 1974, 1978 to 1980, 1984 to 1986, and 1990 to 1992 subsamples, the sample sizes are 1,761, 2,057, 2,143, and 2,409 individuals, respectively.

Information (variables) collected for all the samples include occupation of employment, industry of employment, real (inflation-adjusted) wages (hourly labor income), experience, tenure, marital status, years of schooling, race, and age. Wages in each year are deflated by the consumer price index (using 1990 as the base year).

Our main task is to measure and analyze the number of changes of occupation and industry on the basis of aggregate occupation and industry categories. To do that, we define an occupational or industrial change as a worker's shift from one aggregate occupation or industry to another, without unemployment interruptions. Therefore, we exclude exits from and entries into the labor force. Like Sicherman and Galor (1990), we assume that occupational change will be observed if there is a dramatic shift in the tasks performed by the worker.

We used the following occupational categories in the study:[10]

1. Professional, technical, and kindred workers
2. Managers and administrators, except farm-related
3. Clerical workers, sales workers, and kindred workers
4. Craftsmen, foremen, and kindred workers
5. Operatives and kindred workers
6. Laborers and service workers, farm labor
7. Farmers and farm managers
8. Miscellaneous (armed services, protective services, and so on)

The industry categories include:[11]

1. Agriculture, forestry, and fisheries
2. Mining
3. Construction
4. Manufacturing
5. Transportation, communications, and other
6. Wholesale and retail trade
7. Finance, insurance, and real estate
8. Business and repair services
9. Personal services
10. Entertainment and recreation services
11. Professional and related services

A number of caveats are in order. First, our research focuses on the total number of changes and does not take into account differences between voluntary and involuntary changes, because the PSID survey did not include questions that provide this information.[12] Second, we cannot distinguish between job changes between occupations and industries that are permanent and those in which workers switch jobs temporarily and then switch back to their previous occupation or industry. Finally, changes in occupation are examined without any consideration of changes in employment among firms or within firms.[13]

Descriptive Statistics

Table 8.1 shows the distribution of the number of changes of occupation in the two periods 1969 to 1980 and 1981 to 1992. The mean number of occupational changes increased between the two periods, from 1.8 to 2.1. It rose by roughly equal amounts for both men and women. The mode (the most frequently occurring number of occupational changes) is 2 for both men and women and for each time period.[14] The distribution tails off very quickly, with only about 20 percent of workers experiencing more than three occupational changes over either of the eleven-year periods.[15]

Table 8.1 shows slightly greater mobility of workers in the later period than the earlier one.[16] In the period 1969 to 1980, 38.0 percent of all workers experienced no change in occupation,[17] while for the 1981 to 1992 period the corresponding figure is 36.4 percent. This

Table 8.1 Distribution of Occupational Changes, 1969 to 1992

	Period	0	1	2	3	4	5	6	7	8	9	10	Mean
Men	1969–1980	35.6	13.2	17.9	14.4	7.5	5.9	3.5	0.9	0.9	0.0	0.0	1.87
	1981–1992	34.0	11.6	17.1	9.4	9.7	7.7	5.9	2.4	2.0	0.2	0.4	2.24
Women	1969–1980	50.0	14.3	16.7	3.6	6.0	3.6	4.8	1.2	0.0	0.0	0.0	1.36
	1981–1992	42.5	13.4	13.4	12.8	6.1	4.5	2.2	3.4	1.1	0.6	0.0	1.77
Total	1969–1980	38.0	13.4	17.7	12.6	7.3	5.5	3.7	1.0	0.8	0.0	0.0	1.79
	1981–1992	36.4	12.1	16.1	10.4	8.3	6.8	4.9	2.7	1.7	0.3	0.3	2.11

Source: Authors' compilation.

trend is clearer for women: 50 percent of the women experienced no change in occupation between 1969 and 1980, but only 42.5 percent did so between 1981 and 1992.

Men were considerably more mobile than women in both periods. In the first period, almost 36 percent of all male workers never changed occupation, while for women the corresponding figure is 50 percent. For the period 1981 to 1992, the figures for men and women who never changed occupation are 34 percent and 42.5 percent, respectively.

In table 8.2 we report the distribution of the number of changes in industry in the two periods, 1971 to 1980 and 1981 to 1992. The average number of industry changes increased between the two periods, from 0.78 to 1.18 among all workers. The mode, as with occupational changes, is 2 (except among women in the period 1971 to 1980). The distributions also tail off quickly, with about 15 percent of workers shifting industries more than three times over the period.[18]

Mobility among industries, like occupational mobility, increased between the periods 1971 to 1980 and 1981 to 1992, with 33 percent of all workers during the first and 40 percent during the second experiencing one or more changes in industry. Men had greater industry mobility than women in the 1980s, while the reverse was true in the 1970s.

It is also interesting to note that changes, either between occupations or between industries, tend to entail a move between occupations that are similar (for example, changes from professional workers to managers) or industries that are similar (for example, from one service sector to another service sector). Almost 90 percent of these changes were between occupations or industries that required "similar" skills. This observation suggests that general and specific human capital play an important role in determining the new kind of work that is pursued.

Table 8.3 presents means and standard deviations of real labor income[19] in the periods 1969 to 1980 and 1981 to 1992. The results are reported separately for individuals who stayed in the same occupation and/or industry in each period and for those who changed occupation and/or industry at least one time.

Our most striking result here is that the growth of hourly earnings has been substantially *larger* for changers than for stayers. This is true for both men and women and for both periods. On the surface at least, it appears that pecuniary motives are the main reason behind a worker's occupational or industry job change. These findings are also in accord with those reported by Mark Wilson and Carole Green (1990), who conclude that there exists a strong positive correlation between occupational mobility and changes in real labor earnings, even after

Table 8.2 Distribution of Changes in Industry, 1971 to 1992

	Period	0	1	2	3	4	5	6	7	8	9	10	Mean
Men	1971–1980	67.9	8.5	11.3	5.9	4.0	1.7	0.7	0.0	0.0	0.0	—	0.77
	1981–1992	57.0	7.2	14.0	6.6	7.7	3.1	2.2	1.3	0.7	0.2	0.0	1.31
Women	1971–1980	61.9	16.7	10.7	3.6	3.6	2.4	1.2	0.0	0.0	0.0	—	0.80
	1981–1992	68.7	7.8	11.7	3.9	3.9	0.6	1.7	0.6	1.1	0.0	0.0	0.84
Total	1971–1980	66.9	9.8	11.2	5.5	3.9	1.8	0.8	0.0	0.0	0.0	—	0.78
	1981–1992	60.3	7.4	13.4	5.8	6.6	2.4	2.0	1.1	0.8	0.2	0.0	1.18

Source: Authors' compilation.

Table 8.3 Percentage Change in Real Labor Earnings, by Changes in Occupation and Industry, 1969 to 1992

Variable or Situation	Men		Women	
	1969–1980	1981–1992	1969–1980	1981–1992
Occupation				
Change[a]	33.7	28.1	39.6	36.8
	(64.7)	(69.1)	(62.9)	(63.8)
No change	25.5	23.7	22.6	32.7
	(57.2)	(54.6)	(38.6)	(48.9)
Industry				
Change[a]	33.1	31.5	35.8	39.6
	(79.4)	(72.0)	(67.7)	(70.6)
No change	29.7	23.0	28.2	33.0
	(52.2)	(58.1)	(41.1)	(51.2)

Source: Authors' compilation.
Note: Standard deviations are in parentheses.
[a] At least one change.

controlling for personal characteristics and firm-specific human capital.

Second, not only are there striking differences in average hourly earnings between changers and stayers, but there are also differences in their volatility. The variance in hourly income was much greater for changers than for stayers. Third, earnings for men grew more rapidly during the period 1969 to 1980 than during 1981 to 1992. This is true for both changers and stayers. On the other hand, for women, earnings increased faster in the second period, except for women who changed occupation. Fourth, there was another significant difference between men and women: during the 1981 to 1992 period, women registered higher increases in real labor income than men did. This observation is partially consistent with the finding of Elizabeth Becker and Cotton Lindsay (1994) that women experience more rapid on-the-job earnings growth than men do.[20]

Are younger people inclined to change occupation or industry more frequently than older people? The results of table 8.4 generally confirm this by showing that changers are, on average, younger than stayers (except for women during the 1981 to 1992 period).[21] This result is consistent with the three-year period samples, in which younger workers, both male and female, tend to change occupation and industry more frequently than older workers. (These results are not shown in the table.) In terms of volatility, we do not observe a clear pattern.

The results for changes in industry are similar: younger people tend to change industry more frequently than older ones.[22] One plau-

Table 8.4 Average Age at Beginning of Period, by Changes in Occupation and Industry, 1969 to 1992

	Men		Women	
Variable or Situation	1969–1980	1981–1992	1969–1980	1981–1992
Occupation				
Change[a]	37.9	33.8	38.9	35.2
	(8.3)	(7.5)	(7.6)	(8.1)
No change	38.9	35.1	40.2	36.5
	(8.1)	(7.7)	(8.0)	(8.2)
Industry				
Change[a]	38.2	33.8	39.7	36.7
	(8.4)	(7.3)	(6.9)	(8.2)
No change	39.3	35.9	39.7	35.3
	(7.6)	(8.1)	(8.8)	(8.2)

Source: Authors' compilation.
Note: Standard deviations are in parentheses.
[a]At least one change.

sible explanation for this set of results is the fact that younger people have not accumulated the job-specific human capital that can increase the risk entailed in changing occupation or industry. Another possible reason is that education and job training of a more general variety occur when a person is young. The resulting general-purpose human capital makes it easier for young workers to switch occupation or industry. Other explanations may reflect younger workers' lower adjustment costs of changing jobs, lower "match quality" attributable to less intensive previous job search, and more learning about talents that make the individual better suited to another job.

There is clear evidence from table 8.5 that more-educated workers change occupation and industry more frequently throughout their working lives. During the period 1969 to 1980, the modal education of workers who underwent either occupational or industry changes was nine to twelve years in duration, while in the later period the mode was in the range of twelve to fifteen years of schooling. In the three-year samples, the results are similar, with male changers generally more educated than male stayers and female changers more educated than female stayers in every period.

Table 8.5 also reveals some important differences by educational attainment. First, average schooling among workers was higher in the later period than the earlier one, while the variance of years of schooling was lower. Second, male workers have, on average, more years of schooling than female workers in the later period among both changers and stayers, but this holds only for stayers in the earlier period.

Table 8.5   Average Years of Education at End of Period, by Changes in
Occupation and Industry, 1969 to 1992

Variable or Situation	Men		Women	
	1969–1980	1981–1992	1969–1980	1981–1992
Occupation				
Change[a]	11.0	13.1	11.2	12.1
	(3.3)	(2.8)	(2.0)	(1.7)
No change	11.3	12.7	11.0	12.5
	(3.1)	(2.6)	(2.6)	(1.7)
Industry				
Change[a]	10.9	13.0	11.4	12.3
	(3.2)	(2.4)	(2.1)	(1.7)
No change	11.8	12.6	10.8	12.3
	(3.0)	(3.2)	(2.6)	(1.7)

Source: Authors' compilation.
Note: Standard deviations are in parentheses.
[a]At least one change.

Possible explanations of these results are similar to those for age differences. In particular, more-educated workers change occupation or industry more frequently because their greater human capital (including general training) opens up a greater number of new job opportunities. This relation may be stronger in more recent years, with the advent of information technology, because of the more rapid restructuring of jobs that such computerization has induced.

Our Model of Occupation and Industry Job Changes: Specification and Estimation Issues

Our estimation proceeds in two stages. The first stage investigates the determinants of occupational and industry change. For this we used a logit regression whose dependent variable is a dummy variable with a value of 1 if a worker remains in the same occupation (or industry) for three or more years. The second stage examines the effects of occupational (or industry) change on earnings growth. For this we use a standard earnings function together with a variable (or variables) indicating whether the worker changed occupation (or industry). The variables are shown in table 8.6.

Our estimation was performed as follows. In each period an individual was taken to be in one of two states. Let no change of occupation or industry be denoted by value 1, and one or more changes by value 0. Let the value of being in state j be given by

Table 8.6 Descriptive Statistics, by Sex, 1972 to 1992

Variable	Men				Women			
	1972–1974	1978–1980	1984–1986	1990–1992	1972–1974	1978–1980	1984–1986	1990–1992
Education	11.054	11.791	12.719	12.992	11.596	11.782	12.400	12.758
	(3.422)	(2.857)	(2.517)	(2.378)	(2.570)	(2.160)	(2.043)	(1.979)
Experience	23.803	15.263	14.102	14.070	24.833	10.405	11.444	11.671
	(11.656)	(11.457)	(10.483)	(9.654)	(11.736)	(9.091)	(9.047)	(9.241)
Tenure	3.848	5.665	8.887	10.126	NA	4.885	7.612	8.986
	(1.505)	(7.002)	(8.165)	(8.352)		(5.297)	(6.409)	(7.136)
Age (at start)	40.878	37.888	35.992	39.367	42.429	38.250	37.545	40.841
	(10.350)	(11.652)	(10.068)	(8.798)	(10.754)	(11.732)	(10.819)	(9.550)
Married	0.921	0.887	0.818	0.875	0.665	0.682	0.747	0.704
	(0.270)	(0.318)	(0.386)	(0.331)	(0.472)	(0.469)	(0.435)	(0.456)
Race	1.380	1.384	1.320	1.301	NA	NA	1.378	1.368
	(0.769)	(0.710)	(0.692)	(0.630)			(0.669)	(0.646)
Number of changes in occupation	0.698	0.611	0.771	0.695	0.574	0.483	0.586	0.497
	(0.884)	(0.841)	(0.936)	(0.938)	(0.839)	(0.794)	(0.829)	(0.818)
Number of changes in industry	0.592	0.338	0.566	0.474	0.538	0.414	0.432	0.306
	(0.907)	(0.679)	(0.873)	(0.826)	(0.840)	(0.717)	(0.731)	(0.666)
Ln(wages)	2.598	2.613	2.633	2.620	2.134	2.136	2.216	2.295
	(0.540)	(0.498)	(0.515)	(0.556)	(0.524)	(0.468)	(0.498)	(0.513)

Source: Authors' compilation.

Note: Wages are at the end of the period. Standard deviations are reported in parentheses.

NA = Not available.

Table 8.7 Logit Estimates of the Probability of Remaining in the Same Occupation over the Three-Year Period

Variable	Men				Women			
	1972–1974	1978–1980	1984–1986	1990–1992	1972–1974	1978–1980	1984–1986	1990–1992
Constant	−0.958	−2.822	−3.267	−0.957	−0.881	1.245	0.130	−0.320
	(0.003)	(0.000)	(0.000)	(0.001)	(0.014)	(0.002)	(0.742)	(0.446)
Ln(real wage)	0.489	0.488	0.348	0.328	0.384	−0.195	−0.037	−0.062
	(0.000)	(0.000)	(0.000)	(0.000)	(0.000)	(0.089)	(0.694)	(0.501)
Age (at start)	−0.005	0.034	0.040	0.019	0.017	0.024	0.010	0.015
	(0.285)	(0.000)	(0.000)	(0.000)	(0.000)	(0.000)	(0.019)	(0.001)
Completed education	−0.024	0.034	0.047	−0.029	0.000	−0.085	−0.038	0.001
	(0.000)	(0.013)	(0.002)	(0.058)	(0.987)	(0.001)	(0.107)	(0.954)
Married	0.443	0.217	0.293	0.254	−0.231	0.012	0.251	0.218
	(0.000)	(0.034)	(0.001)	(0.006)	(0.025)	(0.910)	(0.010)	(0.018)
Race	0.007	0.035	0.136	−0.094	NA	NA	0.213	0.331
	(0.967)	(0.475)	(0.006)	(0.060)			(0.004)	(0.000)
χ^2	292.09	235.31	244.79	85.995	36.168	65.583	25.435	32.190
N	3,287	4,128	4,034	4,434	1,974	2,042	2,389	2,795

Source: Authors' compilation.
Note: Probability values are reported in parentheses. Dependent variable: change = 0; no change = 1.
NA = Not available.

$$V_i^j = \alpha + \beta X_i + \varepsilon_i \quad j = 0, 1, \tag{8.1}$$

where matrix X_i includes real wages, age, years of education, marital status, and race, while ε_i captures unobserved individual characteristics.

Table 8.7 reports the estimation results of the logit regression with the dependent variable indicating whether the individual changed occupation. We see that the probability of remaining in the same occupation is affected by several characteristics. First, men with higher wages are significantly more likely to stay in the same occupation than men with lower wages. This is also true for women in the period 1972 to 1974, but not for subsequent periods, when higher-paid women were more likely to switch occupation.

Second, the table indicates that, with the exception of the 1972 to 1974 period, older workers are significantly more likely to remain in the same occupation than younger workers. This result is consistent with those reported by Barry Harper (1995) for Britain and with Kathryn Shaw's (1986) model, which predicts that younger people are more likely to change occupations and that this probability will decline over time. Third, marriage increases the probability of staying (except for women in the 1972 to 1974 period).[23]

Fourth, schooling has no clear effect on whether an individual will change occupation. In the periods 1972 to 1974 and 1990 to 1992, more-educated men were less likely to stay in the same occupation. (Harper [1995] obtains the same result for Britain.) However, in the two middle periods, 1978 to 1980 and 1984 to 1986, more-educated men were more likely to stay in the same occupation. This result can perhaps be explained by two opposite effects of education on occupational mobility. More-educated workers may have a greater chance of finding the "right" occupation at the beginning of their working career and thus be less likely to change later on. On the other hand, more-educated workers have a larger stock of human capital (including general training) and a wider range of tasks that they can perform and may thus have better opportunities for switches of occupation (or industry).

Table 8.8 presents the logit estimates for changes of industry. The results are remarkably similar to the occupational change regressions, with one exception. More education for men significantly increases the likelihood of changing industry in the last three periods, while for women this is true in the first three periods.

Earnings Regressions

Our basic earnings model derives from the standard human capital model and is given by:

Table 8.8 Logit Estimates of the Probability of Remaining in the Same Industry over the Three-Year Period

	Men				Women			
Variable	1972–1974	1978–1980	1984–1986	1990–1992	1972–1974	1978–1980	1984–1986	1990–1992
Constant	−3.106	−2.868	−2.141	0.532	−1.631	−0.322	−0.531	−0.101
	(0.000)	(0.000)	(0.000)	(0.075)	(0.000)	(0.425)	(0.207)	(0.834)
Ln(real wage)	0.629	1.231	0.728	0.410	0.421	0.473	0.267	−0.178
	(0.000)	(0.000)	(0.000)	(0.000)	(0.000)	(0.000)	(0.008)	(0.097)
Age (at start)	0.007	0.027	0.036	0.012	0.035	0.035	0.038	0.035
	(0.080)	(0.000)	(0.000)	(0.003)	(0.000)	(0.000)	(0.000)	(0.000)
Completed education	0.028	−0.058	−0.050	−0.080	−0.019	−0.076	−0.084	0.003
	(0.029)	(0.000)	(0.002)	(0.000)	(0.399)	(0.006)	(0.001)	(0.920)
Married	0.303	0.424	0.124	−0.150	0.204	−0.343	0.383	0.395
	(0.000)	(0.000)	(0.158)	(0.149)	(0.052)	(0.002)	(0.000)	(0.000)
Race	−0.102	0.195	0.091	0.001	NA	NA	0.089	0.114
	(0.459)	(0.003)	(0.082)	(0.983)			(0.232)	(0.162)
χ^2	300.16	343.44	263.23	60.178	70.313	104.78	103.62	54.224
N	3,287	4,128	4,034	4,434	1,974	2,042	2,389	2,795

Source: Authors' compilation.
Note: Probability values are reported in parentheses. Dependent variable: change = 0; no change = 1.
NA = Not available.

$$\ln(w_{it}) = c + \gamma_1 Z_{it} + \gamma_2 N_{it} + \mu_i + v_{it}, \qquad (8.2)$$

where $\ln(w_{it})$ is the log of the hourly wages deflated by the consumer price index for individual i at time t, and Z_{it} is a standard set of regressors: years of education, experience, tenure, marital status, and race. Experience and tenure squared are also included in the model. The experience terms are incorporated to capture wage growth attributable to investment in general human capital, while the tenure terms capture wage growth attributable to investment in specific human capital. The variable N_{it} is the number of changes in occupation or industry over the time period. A similar variable was used by Audrey Light and Kathleen McGarry (1998) to measure job mobility. The term c denotes the constant of the regression, and γ_1 and γ_2 are vectors of coefficients.

The residual structure in the equation includes an unobserved time-invariant individual characteristic term (μ_i) and a white-noise term (v_{it}) that captures all other unobserved variables. Each component of the residual is assumed to be independently distributed with zero mean and variance equal to σ_μ^2 and σ_v^2, respectively. This structure is consistent with the mover-stayer model. (The argument is that personal characteristics induce high-productivity workers to avoid job change and low-productivity workers to undergo persistent job change.)

The tenure variable refers to a position with an employer (firm) rather than to an occupational position with the same employer. As many others point out (see, for example, Altonji and Shakotko 1987; Light and McGarry 1998), tenure is correlated with the error in the earnings equations. For example, tenure is likely to be correlated with μ_i because high-productivity workers presumably receive higher wages and thus are less likely to quit.

To avoid this problem, we use an instrumental variable that is a feasible generalized least-square estimator (IV/FGLS). The instrumental variables for the tenure variables T_{it} and T_{it}^2 are the deviations of the tenure variables around their means for the sample observations.[24] These instrumental variables are uncorrelated by construction with the error component of the earnings equation.

We estimate equation 8.2 both by ordinary least squares (OLS) and by IV/FGLS. If the error component is specified as v_{it}, the model should be estimated by OLS, while if the error structure is specified as $\mu_i + v_{it}$, the model should be estimated by IV/FGLS.

Tables 8.9 and 8.10 show the two sets of estimates for the earnings equation, including a term for the number of occupational changes. The results are very similar. Schooling has the expected positive coefficient and is highly significant. The return to education in terms of earnings is generally higher for women than for men (except for the

Table 8.9 Estimates of Earnings Equations, Including Changes in Occupation, by OLS, 1972 to 1992

Variable	Men				Women			
	1972–1974	1978–1980	1984–1986	1990–1992	1972–1974	1978–1980	1984–1986	1990–1992
Constant	1.184	1.390	1.061	0.825	1.066	0.773	0.714	0.427
	(20.030)	(31.498)	(23.097)	(15.528)	(19.867)	(18.778)	(14.091)	(8.140)
Education	0.073	0.078	0.100	0.117	0.099	0.097	0.100	0.130
	(32.060)	(32.729)	(38.761)	(39.358)	(32.581)	(31.890)	(30.223)	(37.771)
Experience	0.037	0.033	0.015	0.010	-0.008	0.018	0.024	0.011
	(15.176)	(15.622)	(9.618)	(6.502)	(-2.989)	(8.476)	(9.720)	(7.807)
Experience^2/10	-0.007	-0.006	-0.002	-0.001	0.002	-0.004	-0.007	-0.001
	(-15.18)	(-12.38)	(-5.741)	(-4.232)	(3.226)	(-6.745)	(-10.15)	(-6.465)
Tenure	0.050	0.009	0.025	0.035	NA	0.022	0.033	0.032
	(2.655)	(3.947)	(11.125)	(15.611)		(8.250)	(11.330)	(12.761)
Tenure^2/10	-0.001	-0.001	-0.004	-0.007	NA	-0.005	-0.005	-0.006
	(-0.054)	(-1.455)	(-5.605)	(-9.119)		(-4.577)	(-4.511)	(-6.800)
Married	0.181	0.150	0.104	0.112	0.017	0.035	0.031	0.022
	(7.562)	(7.541)	(6.238)	(5.474)	(1.075)	(2.519)	(1.928)	(1.630)
Race	-0.068	-0.078	-0.091	-0.110	NA	NA	-0.088	-0.075
	(-7.944)	(-8.626)	(-9.937)	(-10.27)			(-9.311)	(-7.623)
Number of changes in occupation	-0.084	-0.048	-0.023	-0.025	-0.037	0.023	0.030	0.0207
	(-10.70)	(-6.195)	(-3.300)	(-3.503)	(-4.498)	(2.933)	(3.820)	(2.596)
Error structure								
σ_v^2	0.188	0.172	0.167	0.199	0.206	0.170	0.175	0.180
N	3,287	4,093	3,976	4,371	1,974	2,014	2,345	2,736

Source: Authors' compilation.
Note: T-statistics are reported in parentheses.
NA = Not available.

1984 to 1986 period). Moreover, as found in other studies, the return to education rose over the four periods for both men and women.

Experience and tenure have the expected quadratic shape in almost all regressions (with the exception of the 1972 to 1974 regression for women, for which information on job tenure is lacking). In all cases (with the same exception), these variables are highly significant. On the other hand, as is well known in the labor economics literature, tenure is positively correlated with individual and job characteristics, and therefore OLS tenure estimates may be biased upward relative to estimates that take these characteristics into account. After we account for the correlation between tenure and the error component (individual effects) by using IV/FGLS, the coefficients for tenure decrease in all cases, though they remain statistically significant. Another interesting result is that in both sets of regressions the slope of the wage-tenure curve is steeper for women than for men, but the difference in slopes diminishes over time.[25]

It is worth noting, as Becker and Lindsay (1994) argue, that high-wage jobs tend to be more permanent, creating a positive relationship between tenure and wages. However, they justify the use of OLS to estimate the earnings equation, giving three reasons. First, they argue that the bias is small, even for large and heterogeneous samples. Second, comparisons between groups with similar tenure status should offer little scope for the bias to affect the coefficients associated with tenure. Third, there is no a priori reason to expect these biases to entail sex-specific effects; hence, such a bias should not affect any kind of gender tests.

Both sets of results show that our key variable, the number of occupational changes over the period, is negatively related to wages for men. This means that men who change occupations more often have lower wages than men with fewer changes. For women, the coefficient is generally positive in OLS but generally negative in the preferred form, IV/FGLS. This shows the importance of correcting for the correlation between tenure and the error component (individual effects) by using IV/FGLS.

Another critical result is that with the preferred form—IV/FGLS—the absolute value of the coefficient of the number of occupational changes declines between the periods 1972 to 1974 and 1990 to 1992. For men, occupation changers earned 13 percent less in the earlier period and 9 percent less in the later period, while for women the corresponding figures are a 31 percent reduction (though without a tenure variable included) in the early 1970s and a 5 percent decline in the early 1990s. The results also show that for men the earnings losses associated with occupational shifts actually rose between the early

Table 8.10 Estimates of Earnings Equations, Including Changes in Occupation, by IV/FGLS, 1972 to 1992

	Men				Women			
Variable	1972–1974	1978–1980	1984–1986	1990–1992	1972–1974	1978–1980	1984–1986	1990–1992
Constant	1.395	1.640	1.575	1.092	1.294	0.885	1.240	0.471
	(42.414)	(59.287)	(58.852)	(30.653)	(29.341)	(33.809)	(43.826)	(13.015)
Education	0.074	0.072	0.076	0.110	0.094	0.094	0.061	0.126
	(47.400)	(45.833)	(50.903)	(53.269)	(38.439)	(50.238)	(34.951)	(52.441)
Experience	0.040	0.032	0.017	0.012	-0.005	0.021	0.32	0.016
	(26.174)	(22.888)	(17.922)	(11.644)	(-2.336)	(15.800)	(21.027)	(17.725)
Experience^2/10	-0.007	-0.006	-0.002	-0.001	0.001	-0.005	-0.009	-0.002
	(-24.08)	(-18.35)	(-11.01)	(-7.366)	(1.269)	(-12.28)	(-21.27)	(-12.67)
Tenure	0.025	0.003	0.015	0.019	NA	0.008	0.025	0.022
	(3.937)	(4.045)	(13.726)	(17.583)		(9.931)	(19.939)	(20.048)
Tenure^2/10	-0.029	-0.001	-0.002	-0.003	NA	-0.003	-0.005	-0.005
	(-2.775)	(-3.062)	(-6.669)	(-9.346)		(-7.084)	(-10.43)	(-12.53)
Married	0.059	0.092	0.045	0.052	-0.006	0.092	0.028	0.121
	(5.323)	(10.755)	(5.770)	(5.129)	(-0.476)	(11.476)	(2.570)	(13.760)
Race	-0.071	-0.082	-0.112	-0.109	NA	NA	-0.102	-0.071
	(-11.98)	(-13.44)	(-18.43)	(-14.20)			(-16.03)	(-10.27)
Number of changes in occupation	-0.130	-0.162	-0.118	-0.092	-0.314	-0.072	0.001	-0.0542
	(-14.27)	(-18.09)	(-14.67)	(-10.11)	(-15.33)	(-8.281)	(0.084)	(-5.584)
Error structuture								
σ^2_μ	0.047	0.041	0.042	0.048	0.054	0.053	0.043	0.034
σ^2_ν	0.141	0.130	0.125	0.150	0.152	0.117	0.132	0.146
N	3,287	4,093	3,976	4,371	1,974	2,014	2,345	2,736

Source: Authors' compilation.
Note: T-statistics are reported in parentheses.
NA = Not available.

1970s and the late 1970s (from 13 to 16 percent) before declining in the mid-1980s.

The results for industry changes are shown in tables 8.11 and 8.12. The coefficient estimates and significance levels of the control variables in these regressions are remarkably similar to those for the occupation change regressions. Moreover, as in the occupation change regressions, when we use IV/FGLS instead of OLS, the coefficient of the tenure variable drops in all regressions (typically, by about half).

When we use the preferred IV/FGLS estimation procedure, we find that for men, industry shifts are associated with a 13 percent earnings drop in the 1972 to 1974 period. The earnings loss rises to 31 percent in the late 1970s and then falls to virtually zero by the early 1990s. For women, the earnings loss associated with industry changes also rises between the early 1970s and late 1970s (from 15 to 20 percent) and then falls to 13 percent in the early 1990s.

Conclusions

Our main finding is that the increased turbulence in the aggregate labor market in the 1980s relative to the 1970s—as indicated by the greater change in the (gross) distribution of employment both by occupation and industry—is echoed at the micro (individual worker) level. In particular, workers changed both occupation and industry more frequently in the period 1981 to 1992 than in 1969 to 1980, with the mean number of occupational changes rising from 1.8 to 2.1 and the mean number of industry changes from 0.8 to 1.2.

Another major finding here is that, although the descriptive statistics indicate that occupation and industry changers had, on average, greater *unconditional* growth in earnings over these two decades than nonchangers, once we control for personal characteristics (such as schooling, work experience, job tenure, marital status, and race), we find that workers who shift occupation or industry generally have *lower* earnings than nonchangers. Moreover, despite all the horror stories in the press suggesting that manufacturing workers are turning into hamburger flippers, both occupational and industry change has become generally less traumatic over time for both men and women. For men in particular the earnings loss associated with occupational change diminished from 13 percent in the period 1972 to 1974 to 9 percent in 1990 to 1992, and the loss associated with industry change dropped from 13 percent to zero. For both occupational and industry changes, the peak loss occurred in the late 1970s.

There are several other noteworthy findings. First, men tended to change occupation or industry more frequently than women did over the entire 1969 to 1992 period. Second, the logit regression results

Table 8.11 Estimates of Earnings Equations, Including Changes in Industry, by OLS, 1972 to 1992

Variable	Men				Women			
	1972–1974	1978–1980	1984–1986	1990–1992	1972–1974	1978–1980	1984–1986	1990–1992
Constant	1.136	1.456	1.067	0.789	1.066	0.795	0.717	0.412
	(19.155)	(33.701)	(23.671)	(14.958)	(19.867)	(19.146)	(14.198)	(7.895)
Education	0.076	0.078	0.101	0.117	0.099	0.098	0.100	0.129
	(33.428)	(33.184)	(39.105)	(39.326)	(32.581)	(32.404)	(29.928)	(37.825)
Experience	0.036	0.031	0.015	0.010	−0.008	0.017	0.024	0.010
	(14.747)	(14.888)	(9.576)	(6.824)	(−2.989)	(8.310)	(9.925)	(7.515)
Experience^2/10	−0.007	−0.006	−0.002	−0.001	0.002	−0.004	−0.007	−0.001
	(−14.63)	(−11.89)	(−5.658)	(−4.454)	(3.226)	(−6.770)	(−10.41)	(−6.257)
Tenure	0.053	0.007	0.024	0.036	NA	0.019	0.035	0.034
	(2.790)	(2.952)	(10.309)	(15.957)		(7.199)	(11.565)	(13.525)
Tenure^2/10	−0.004	−0.001	−0.004	−0.007	NA	−0.005	−0.005	−0.007
	(−0.141)	(−0.764)	(−5.078)	(−9.506)		(−3.938)	(−4.751)	(−7.340)
Married	0.176	0.132	0.107	0.115	0.017	0.040	0.032	0.025
	(7.286)	(6.730)	(6.428)	(5.635)	(1.075)	(2.857)	(1.988)	(1.845)
Race	−0.070	−0.082	−0.091	−0.111	NA	NA	−0.091	−0.077
	(−8.165)	(−9.205)	(−9.875)	(−10.35)			(−9.640)	(−7.819)
Number of changes in industry	−0.062	−0.126	−0.038	0.011	−0.037	−0.032	0.037	0.060
	(−8.067)	(−13.39)	(−5.074)	(1.294)	(−4.498)	(−3.534)	(4.078)	(6.062)
Error structure σ_v^2	0.191	0.167	0.167	0.199	0.206	0.170	0.175	0.179
N	3,287	4,093	3,976	4,371	1,974	2,014	2,345	2,736

Source: Authors' compilation.
Note: T-statistics are reported in parentheses.
NA = Not available.

Table 8.12   Estimates of Earnings Equations, Including Changes in Industry, by IV/FGLS, 1972 to 1992

	Men				Women			
Variable	1972–1974	1978–1980	1984–1986	1990–1992	1972–1974	1978–1980	1984–1986	1990–1992
Constant	1.382	1.701	1.497	0.995	1.110	0.946	1.307	0.481
	(39.486)	(63.484)	(57.932)	(28.247)	(28.684)	(36.603)	(44.115)	(13.030)
Education	0.077	0.073	0.078	0.110	0.099	0.092	0.065	0.127
	(49.221)	(47.522)	(53.486)	(53.775)	(44.331)	(48.401)	(35.093)	(51.730)
Experience	0.037	0.027	0.018	0.014	−0.003	0.016	0.030	0.016
	(23.191)	(19.856)	(18.752)	(13.432)	(−1.917)	(12.184)	(18.540)	(17.813)
Experience^2/10	−0.006	−0.005	−0.002	−0.002	0.001	−0.004	−0.008	−0.002
	(−21.75)	(−16.01)	(−11.37)	(−8.609)	(1.889)	(−9.909)	(−18.20)	(−12.73)
Tenure	0.019	0.002	0.014	0.021	NA	0.006	0.018	0.020
	(3.186)	(3.103)	(13.003)	(18.548)		(7.475)	(13.523)	(17.490)
Tenure^2/10	−0.003	−0.001	−0.002	−0.004	NA	−0.002	−0.003	−0.005
	(−0.269)	(−2.451)	(−6.228)	(−10.43)		(−5.562)	(−6.769)	(−11.28)
Married	0.051	0.074	0.052	0.059	0.007	0.102	0.024	0.113
	(4.556)	(8.809)	(6.857)	(5.831)	(0.585)	(12.492)	(2.113)	(12.551)
Race	−0.074	−0.092	−0.107	−0.113	NA	NA	−0.100	−0.068
	(−12.36)	(−15.26)	(−17.93)	(−14.78)			(14.89)	(−9.674)
Number of changes in industry	−0.126	−0.306	−0.0971	0.006	−0.152	−0.201	−0.169	−0.133
	(−13.43)	(−28.00)	(−11.25)	(0.563)	(−14.39)	(−19.80)	(−14.53)	(−10.53)
Error structure								
σ^2_μ	0.047	0.041	0.042	0.049	0.054	0.052	0.043	0.034
σ^2_v	0.143	0.126	0.125	0.151	0.152	0.117	0.132	0.145
N	3,287	4,093	3,976	4,371	1,974	2,014	2,345	2,736

Source: Authors' compilation.
Note: T-statistics are reported in parentheses.
NA = Not available.

indicate that older workers are less likely to change occupation or industry than younger ones. Third, the regressions show that better-paid men are less likely to shift occupation or industry than lower-paid ones, but the reverse is generally true for women. Finally, we find a strong positive relation between tenure and wages, and we also find that tenure is associated with a higher probability of staying in the same occupation or industry.

Though it is difficult to determine exactly what role was played by downsizing, circumstantial evidence suggests that the increased downsizing activity in the 1980s, as compared to the 1970s, at least as found for manufacturing, may have played a role in creating greater turbulence in the labor market in the latter period. The increased downsizing of the 1980s may have induced greater shifting of both industries and occupations among employed workers.

Chapter 9

What Have We Learned About Downsizing? Conclusions

W ITH OUR investigative journey now complete, it is worth pausing a moment to remember where we came in—and why. Roughly a decade ago, corporate downsizing was all over the news. Formerly rock-solid companies were announcing layoffs and restructurings, many American workers were feeling acute insecurity about their jobs, and the bleak employment picture was almost certainly the deciding issue in the 1992 presidential election. Two not very well documented impressions were in the air at the time: first, that the wave of downsizing was a new phenomenon of some sort; and second, that downsizing was something more than the normal job loss that accompanies a business cycle contraction. Later in the 1990s, as the economy first revived and then boomed, such concerns faded from the public consciousness. But they came back when the U.S. economy slowed abruptly in 2000 and then experienced a recession—the first in a decade—in 2001. These concerns are with us still.

The downsizing episode raised several questions. Was this phenomenon really something new? What cause or causes were behind it? Would it disappear or linger on when general business conditions improved?

Our analysis and the data we have gathered predictably depict downsizing as a phenomenon that is considerably more complex and whose elements are considerably more varied than seems generally to have been recognized. Downsizing is not merely a matter of a large number of firms reducing their labor forces substantially and thereby emerging "leaner and meaner." Indeed, often the developments are quite different from this. Moreover, the explanations of the accompanying changes in firm size are at least somewhat different from the standard explanations. In this chapter, we recapitulate our main re-

258

sults pertaining to three issues. First, to what extent have firms really tended to downsize? Second, what have been the consequences of such downsizing as actually did take place? And third, what are the influences that determined the movements in firm size that we observed? We then conclude with a few remarks on policy implications.

Developments in Firm Size: Have the Downsizers Downsized?

Our Newspaper Sample

The most striking feature of the data on very large firms is that many of the ones that announced sharp reductions in their labor forces soon ended up with at least as many employees as they had before they reported their intention to downsize. This finding shows up most clearly in the newspaper sample with which we began our discussion of the available evidence (chapter 2). That group of companies comprises all of the firms reported in the *New York Times* and the *Wall Street Journal* to have announced a downsizing program during the five years 1993 through 1997. As pointed out earlier, this group cannot be considered to be in any sense representative of the universe of firms that undertook a downsizing program in this period. But the newspaper sample is nevertheless pertinent here for two reasons. First, this sample consists of the business enterprises that are sufficiently well known to newspaper readers to be considered newsworthy. Thus, they are the sorts of companies on which the public perceptions about downsizing are surely based. Second, they are generally very large firms, and their employment decisions are likely to have the most substantial effects on the labor market. Incidentally, these enterprises make up a group that is not separated out in the general statistical sources.

In the newspaper-sample group, we found that almost exactly half of the firms had, not too many years later, a labor force at least as large as they possessed at the time of the downsizing announcement. Indeed, of this nondownsizing group, the majority actually upsized substantially, increasing their labor forces more than 10 percent. That does not mean that no labor forces were reduced. Rather, we often observed a temporal pattern in which an initial reduction in company jobs is followed by a greater number of hires.

There are at least three possible interpretations of the downsizing-upsizing sequence. It can happen when a company finds itself in temporary difficulties—facing decreased sales, a shortage of cash, or declining prices of its securities—and management decides that a temporary cut in spending on wages will help the company through the crisis, with the employment cut to be reversed when business conditions improve. Second, the downsizing-upsizing sequence may represent an attempt by management to increase efficiency that turns out to have been misguided. If serious effects on morale and critical labor shortages follow the job cuts, the firm may try to repair the damage by reversing its previous decision. Third, such churning of the company workforce may result from changes in the types of workers who best serve the needs of the firm. If a firm's technology becomes more complex and sophisticated, then a relatively uneducated labor force may no longer be adapted to the company's requirements. Downsizing may then be a first step in achieving the desired personnel changes—first, the relatively unskilled workers are fired, then they are replaced by employees better prepared to deal with the requirements of the new technology. The evidence suggests at least indirectly that each of these influences played some part in the extensive labor-force churning that we observed.

More Representative Data on Changes in Firm Size

Thus, our newspaper sample of firms already suggests that downsizing is not what it seems to be: the labor forces of many of the self-proclaimed downsizers actually grew larger, or at least they did not decline. This finding is even more strikingly evident in our analysis of the comprehensive data available from the federal government. Employing a rarely used data source, the U.S. Census Bureau's Enterprise Statistics, we found, first, that the downsizing that occurred in the manufacturing sector in the late 1980s and early 1990s was not a new phenomenon—downsizing has been going on in manufacturing since about 1967 (but probably not before). Second, and more to the point, the data showed that downsizing has been more or less restricted to the manufacturing sector. Outside of manufacturing, upsizing is far more common. Finally, we found that an extremely naive hypothesis goes a long way toward explaining where and when downsizing does and does not occur: firms in shrinking industries (as measured by employment) tend to downsize, while firms in expanding industries tend to upsize.

Thus, there was indeed *some* systematic downsizing in the late 1980s and early 1990s, notably in manufacturing, but it was not as significant as it may sound, for two critical reasons. First, manufacturing now employs less than 15 percent of the U.S. labor force, so it clearly tells only a limited part of the overall story. Outside of manufacturing, typical firm (or establishment) labor-force size tended quite consistently to increase. Second, while it is true that over the postwar period, and particularly in recent decades, the largest manufacturing firms tended to cut the number of their employees, *the opposite was true of the smaller manufacturing firms.* With big firms growing smaller and small firms growing larger, the script is clearly not one of universal decline, as the most obvious interpretation of downsizing might have us believe, but rather one of regression toward the mean.

Consequences of Downsizing: Profit, Productivity, and Payroll

There is no reason to doubt that those firms that did actually downsize, either temporarily or for longer periods, did so at least partly in order to increase profits. It has also been claimed that they downsized in an effort to increase productivity—that is, to reduce their workforces without cutting output, or at least without reducing output more than proportionately. But one can surmise that the claimed productivity goal was not a final objective but only a means to expand profits.

The systematic data in chapter 7 on the economic effects of downsizing in manufacturing as a whole show, on average, that where downsizing has occurred in this sector it has not contributed to productivity, contrary to what is frequently conjectured.[1] Second, downsizing has nevertheless served to increase profits. Third, it has also tended to depress wages and workers' total compensation. As a consequence, downsizing at both the establishment and firm level led to reductions in unit labor costs. Fourth, as this implies, a central effect of downsizing has apparently been a transfer of income from labor to capital—that is, from the workers to the owners. Fifth, despite its stimulus to profits, downsizing by a firm, curiously enough, has been associated with a decline in the price of its stocks, perhaps because investors take downsizing as management's response to prospects of trouble ahead. This picture of the consequences of downsizing is not something we had expected, but the evidence provides strong support for this interpretation of the phenomenon.

The disappointing finding that cutting the labor force is not a sure-fire way to increase the competitiveness of American enterprises, or an effective way of raising output per worker (which, in the last analysis, is the key to enhancement of standards of living), is in itself obviously important for evaluation of the downsizing phenomenon. The failure to add to productivity, taken in conjunction with its enhancement of profits, raises an obvious question. How can downsizing have raised profits without at the same time adding to productivity? If not from higher productivity, from where do the increased profits of the downsizers come?

The data support the answer to this question that was just suggested. They indicate that downsizing firms end up spending *less money on wages relative to output.* That is, while downsizing firms do not get more output per labor *hour,* they do obtain more output per labor *dollar.* That is just another way of saying that downsizing is profitable at least partly because it is an effective way to hold down wages. We may be led to say that this is the dirty little secret of downsizing.

Two other findings pertinent to the effects of downsizing emerged in chapter 8. We saw that workers changed both occupation and industry more frequently in the period 1981 to 1992 than in the 1969 to 1980 period, with the mean number of occupational changes rising from 1.8 to 2.1 and the mean number of industry changes from 0.8 to 1.2. We also found that workers who shifted occupation or industry generally had lower earnings than nonchangers, once we control for personal characteristics such as schooling, work experience, job tenure, marital status, and race. Although it is difficult to determine the exact role played by downsizing, circumstantial evidence does suggest that the increased downsizing activity in the 1980s relative to that in the 1970s, at least as found for manufacturing, may have played a role in creating greater turbulence in the labor market in the latter period. The increased downsizing in the 1980s may have induced greater shifting of employed workers among both industries and occupations. At the very least, there clearly was more restructuring and churning of the labor force during this period, even if the increased number of workers changing occupations was not attributable primarily to downsizing.

It may also be tempting to use some of the preceding observations to help explain another economic phenomenon that happened at about the same time: the dramatic slowdown in the growth of U.S. wages and compensation levels, below the remarkably rising trend that had prevailed for more than half a century before the 1970s (with, of course, the exception of the Great Depression). Our results, however, do not support this conclusion. As has just been recapitulated, reductions in labor-force size have hardly been the norm for American business firms. On the contrary, outside of manufacturing, rising firm size has more generally prevailed, and even in manufacturing it is mainly just the large firms that have tended to cut back on employment.

Explanations for the Observed Changes in Firm Size

To the extent that downsizing really does occur, there is surely no single influence that can be taken as the one and only cause. We began our investigation with a half-dozen hypotheses about the influences that could have led to a spreading of downsizing—and we added a seventh possibility along the way. The evidence is consistent with a role for several of our original hypotheses in determining whether firms will reduce or expand the number of their employees. But ultimately, our discussion focused on two primary determinants— one that seems to dominate shorter-run developments, the other playing the central role in the long run. The key short-run influence on downsizing appears to be the state of demand for the products of an industry, while the primary long-run determinant is, arguably, the character of technical change within an industry.

The econometric results of chapter 5 on the determinants of downsizing in manufacturing provided considerable support for the simple idea that expanding industries tend to upsize while contracting industries downsize. The results also lent some support to our hypotheses that technology has favored reduction in the largest enterprises (at least since 1967), and that falling profits put pressure on firms to downsize. We also found support for the idea that foreign competition, at least in terms of export markets, pushes firms to downsize. However, we did not find that unions are an effective impediment to downsizing, nor that faster capital (or information-technology capital) formation leads to downsizing by substituting capital for labor. Indeed, the evidence, if anything, indicated that unionized industries are *more* apt to downsize—perhaps to get rid of more expensive union labor. Moreover, the growth in information-technology capital does appear to have a significant negative effect on changes in the overall dispersion of employment among different size classes.

Regression analysis of the limited amount of data available in retailing and service industries also confirmed that both firms and establishments upsize more when their industry is growing faster—as suggested in chapter 3's theoretical discussion. We also found that upsizing is more pronounced in industries that compete heavily with imports (but surprisingly, not in export-oriented industries). On the other hand, neither technological improvement nor capital intensity nor profitability seemed to affect upsizing much in these sectors.

Thus, we conclude that there are two main determinants of changes in the number of employees in a representative firm. In the short run, the primary influence is the state of demand for the firm's products. In the long run, the key determinant is the state of technology.

Demand as Short-Run Determinant

The statistical evidence, as we have just seen, clearly assigns a primary role in downsizing to the market conditions facing the industry. When demand for its products is weak or declining, the industry's firms tend to reduce the number of their employees. When industry demand is abundant or rising, the labor forces of its firms tend to expand. The relationship is strong, statistically significant, and not matched by that between firm size and any other variable that is an obvious candidate for the role of determinant. This relationship is, of course, quite plausible, even obvious. But it is perhaps a bit disappointing that the story that emerges from our analysis is not more subtle. Surely it is what nonspecialists might have expected. And the data do indeed indicate that swings in the size of the typical firm's labor force simply mirror the demand for the products of the enterprise—prosperity creates jobs and recession destroys them, not only in the economy as a whole (as we knew) but in the representative firm as well.

Technological Developments: The Primary Longer-Term Influence

Our theoretical analysis, in contrast, points unambiguously to technology as the influence that must dominate the determination of the size of both firm and establishment labor forces in the longer run. Unfortunately, there is no easy way to test this conclusion statistically because technical change, regardless of the state of demand, sometimes forces competitive firms to expand their labor forces, and sometimes to decrease them. For example, technological innovations that enhance scale economies will force firms to grow larger even if there is a drop in demand for their product. The upshot will be an industry made up of larger enterprises whose number declines even more than the volume of industry output—because, as we know, competition does not permit significant inefficiency in production. So if the efficiency of larger firms grows relative to that of smaller enterprises, firm size must tend ultimately to increase, and the adaptation to the state of industry demand will take the form of a rise or fall in the number of these larger firms. The opposite will happen if technical change reduces the most efficient firm size in an industry.

Because technical change sometimes increases the most efficient firm size and sometimes decreases it, there is no clear way in which the relationship can be confirmed by a regression or some other obvious form of statistical analysis. One is left to the evidence of theory and anecdote. But that is no reason to reject the conclusion, which is strongly suggested by the magnitude and persistence of the differences in firm sizes in different industries. The labor forces of Ford or General Motors have been and remain far larger than those of a typical clothing manufacturer or the representative farmer, and in both prosperity and depression the railroads have remained far larger than the trucking firms with which they compete. All such examples, which are not difficult to multiply, clearly rest on technological determinants. And all are patently consistent with the very convincing theory that analyzes the influence of competitive market forces in imposing efficiency upon firms by requiring them to expand or contract toward the size necessary for cost minimization.

Is the Downsizing Phenomenon Long-Lasting or Transitory?

Earlier in the book we emphasized the question: Is downsizing a passing phenomenon, or does it represent a change that can be expected to endure, with all of the pressing policy problems that it may entail? The answer that we glean from the statistical evidence and the theoretical analysis is mixed. There is no reason to expect the reductions in labor force that are once again attracting much attention with the opening of the new century to endure for very long. But the mechanism that can lead to such movements can be expected to be with us for the foreseeable future. If we are right in concluding that, in the short run, downsizing is primarily determined by falling demand for the products of the affected industries or the economy more generally, we can confidently expect the downsizing pressures from this source to wax and wane along with business conditions, and there is no reason to foresee any imminent end to business fluctuations. Such intertemporal variations are surely exacerbated in the long run by the role of the state of technology in determining the size of the labor force in the representative firm in any industry or in the economy as a whole. Since, as has repeatedly been emphasized here, technical change sometimes increases the minimum efficient size of a firm's labor force and sometimes decreases it, we can be sure that this influence will sometimes lead to downsizing and sometimes to upsizing (but generally to restructuring and hence to churning of the labor force).

In sum, what is not transitory in this scenario is the role of demand for labor in the short run, and the role of the state of technology in the long run. These mechanisms can confidently be expected to continue playing their roles; consequently, downsizing can be expected to recur repeatedly in the future. But each such event can be expected to have a limited life, and to reappear only at some future date.

Policy Implications

In light of these conclusions, what can be suggested for public policy toward downsizing? The obvious answer, perhaps reassuring though surely not very exciting, is that no special programs appear to be called for, aside from measures to ease the transition of downsized workers to other jobs. First, as we have seen, the evidence provides no support for the conjecture that the economy is undergoing widespread and *protracted* reductions in the size of the typical firm's labor force. Widespread churning, regression toward the mean workforce size in manufacturing, and upsizing elsewhere do not suggest that the issue entails a substantial long-run threat to employment in the economy. Nor is there any reason why it should. As we have seen, falling firm size can be offset, or more than offset, by an accompanying increase in the number of enterprises.

Even in the short run, when declining demand during a recession does normally lead firms to cut jobs, the problem is macroeconomic, not microeconomic. In other words, the real problem is to be found in overall business conditions rather than in any developments *inside* the firm. That does not imply that nothing should be done about the growth in unemployment that follows such a pattern. The point, rather, is that reasonable policy designed to stimulate employment remains desirable but unchanged when joblessness is accompanied by a decrease in the size of the typical firm's labor force. This is no place to review the literature on employment policy, with all of its controversies. It suffices for us to conclude merely that the unemployment programs adopted on the basis of the available body of analysis appear to remain equally appropriate whether or not the economy's unemployment is accompanied by a marked decrease in the size of the labor forces of the economy's firms.

The longer-run developments in firm size that are induced by technical change do, in our view, call for public-sector measures. But here too nothing profoundly new emerges. Technical change itself should not be held back, for the reasons that have long led to rejection of Luddite approaches to protection of jobs. It is reported, for example, that for a long time in India, after it achieved its independence, the use of computers in the insurance industry was prohibited by government decree. Surely the protection this and other restrictive measures provided to clerks using pen and ink contributed little if anything to the economy's total employment, but it goes a long way toward explaining the country's continuing and spectacular poverty.

For the same reasons, it seems clearly ill advised to handicap or prevent the adaptation of firm size to the efficiency requirements of evolving technology. Such a restriction can also only contribute to poverty. At least in the long run, the benefits of efficiency in the operations of firms are widespread, and the creation of impediments to the adaptation of their sizes to the current technical requirements of efficiency hardly seems an appropriate way to serve the public interest.

What, then, is a defensible role of public policy toward downsizing in response to technical change? The answer, we believe, is support of those employees who suffer hardships in the process. Those whose skills have been rendered obsolete, or who simply have been made redundant, merit the support of a socially provided safety net.[2] Such an arrangement constitutes an insurance policy for the entire labor force, for one can never be sure where and when technical change will next lead to job terminations. Note that this problem arises even in cases of upsizing, if it is accompanied by churning of the labor force. Here we are led to turn, once again, to familiar solutions: programs of employee retraining, job counseling, job placement services, and income support for workers in transition between jobs—all of these are defensible measures for the purpose. Indeed, an effective program to make the job transition less painful may well speed technological progress by reducing worker resistance and management's hesitation about getting into conflict with the company's employees.

Our conclusion, then, is that when downsizing does occur, there is an appropriate and important role for public policy. But given what our analysis has indicated to be the prime influences that can lead to downsizing, the programs that are appropriate entail little that is new. The issue requires only a more determined and more effective execution of the policies called for by problems of unemployment.

Appendix:
Our Newspaper Search

The 292 Company Names Encountered in an Electronic Search of the *Wall Street Journal* and the *New York Times* for the Word "Downsizing," for the Years 1993 Through 1997

Finance and Insurance (48 Companies)

Aetna Inc.
American Express
American General Corp.
Australian National (Australia)
Banc One Corp.
BankAmerica Corp.
BankBoston Corp.
Bank of America Corp.
Bank of Boston
Bank of New York Co. Inc.
Banque Nationale
Barclays PLC/England (United Kingdom)
Bayerisch Hypotheken-und Wechsel-Bank (Germany)
Centel Corp.
Chase Manhattan Corp.
Chemical Financial Corp.
Cigna Corp.
Citicorp
Citizens Banking Corp.
Citizens Savings Bank
Connecticut Mutual Life Insurance Co.
Continental Bancorp-PA
Credit Lyonnais (France)
First Bank System
First Interstate Bancorp
First Union Corp.
Johnson & Higgins
Kidder-Peabody

Kohlberg Kravis Roberts & Co.
MassMutual Corp.
Mercedes-Benz Credit Corp. (Germany)
Merrill Lynch & Co.
Metropolitan Financial Corp.
Midlantic Corp.
Mitsui (Japan)
Morgan (J. P.) & Co.
NationsBank Corp.
Nationwide Insurance Enterprise
NatWest Bank (United Kingdom)
Northeast Bankcorp
PaineWebber Group
Peregrine Investment Holdings
Prudential Group Inc.
Shawmut National Corp.
Shearson Lehman Brothers Inc.
Thomas Cook Travel Money Services
Travelers Corp.
Wells Fargo & Co.

Telecommunications (15 Companies)

Ameritech Corp.
AT&T Corp.
Bell Atlantic Corp.
BellSouth Corp.
British Telecom PLC (United Kingdom)
Deutsche Telekom AG (Germany)
France Telecom (France)
GTE Corp.
MCI Worldcom Inc.
Nynex Corp.
Pacific Bell
Pacific Telesis Group
Sprint Corp. Consolidated
Telecom Italia Spa (Italy)
US West Consolidated

Airlines (9 Companies)

Air France (France)
American Airlines
Continental Airlines Inc.

Delta Airlines Inc.
Kiwi Airlines
KLM Royal Dutch Air (Netherlands)
TWA
USAir Inc.
US Airways

Oil and Gas (10 Companies)

Arco Pipeline Co.
British Gas (United Kingdom)
Chevron Corp.
Kerr-McGee Corp.
Mobil Corp.
Occidental Petroleum Corp.
Petro-Canada (Canada)
Tenneco Corp.
Texaco Inc.
Union Texas Petroleum Holdings Ltd.

Public Utilities (5 Companies)

Central & South West Corp.
Entergy Corp.
Niagara Mohawk Holdings Inc.
Pacific Gas & Electric
Peoples Natural Gas Co.

Metals Mining and Manufacturing (7 Companies)

Alcoa Inc.
National Steel Corp.
Phelps Dodge Corp.
Republic Steel Corp.
Reynolds Metals Co.
Timken Co.
USX-U.S. Steel Group

Aerospace, Aircraft, and Defense (22 Companies)

Alliant Techsystems Inc.
AlliedSignal Inc.
Boeing Co.
Eaton Corp.

General Dynamics Corp.
Goodrich (B. F.)
Grumman Corp.
Hughes Aircraft
Kaman Corp.
Litton Industries Inc.
Lockheed Martin Corp.
Loral Space & Communications
Martin Marietta Corp.
McDonnell Douglas Corp.
Northrop Grumman Corp.
Pratt & Whitney Aircraft
Raytheon Co.
Rockwell International Corp.
Thiokol Corp.
TRW Inc.
United Technologies Corp.
Westinghouse Electric

Food, Beverages, and Tobacco (26 Companies)

Anheuser-Busch Companies Inc.
Borden Inc.
Campbell Soup Co.
Coca-Cola Co.
Colgate-Palmolive Co.
Conagra Inc.
General Mills Inc.
Gerber Products
Green Giant Co.
Heinz (H. J.) Co.
Kellogg Co.
Kraft General Foods
Lewis Brothers Bakeries, Inc.
Masco Corp.
McDonald's Corp.
Miller Brewing
Pepsico Inc.
Pet Foods, Inc.
Philip Morris Companies Inc.
Pillsbury Co.
Quaker Oats Co.
Ralston Purina Co.
R. J. Reynolds Tobacco Holdings

Safeway Inc.
Sara Lee Corp.
Unilever Combined (United Kingdom)

Computers, Electronics, Data Services, and Software (28 Companies)

Apple Computer Inc.
Bell & Howell Co.
Contel Cellular Inc.
Digital Equipment
Dun and Bradstreet Corp.
Ericsson Italia (Italy)
Fujitsu Ltd. (Japan)
General Electric Co.
Grundig
Hewlett-Packard Co.
Honeywell Inc.
International Business Machines Corp.
Jostens Inc.
K-III Communications
LTX, Inc.
Motorola Inc.
NCR Corp.
Olivetti Spa (Italy)
Prodigy Communications Corp.
Proteon, Inc.
RCA Corp.
Siemens AG (Germany)
Square D Co.
Sunbeam Corp.
Tandem Computers
Texas Instruments Inc.
Toshiba (Japan)
Unisys Corp.

Pharmaceutical (13 Companies)

Bausch & Lomb Inc.
Bristol-Myers Squibb
Ciba-Geigy (Switzerland)
Lilly (Eli) & Co.
Marion Merrell Dow

Novartis AG (Switzerland)
Roche Holdings Ltd.
Sandoz (Switzerland)
Schering-Plough
SmithKline Beecham PLC (United Kingdom)
Sterling Winthrop (United Kingdom)
Upjohn (United Kingdom)
Warner-Lambert Co.

Autos, Other Vehicles, and Vehicle Parts (19 Companies)

BMW (Germany)
Caterpillar Inc.
Chrysler Corp.
DaimlerChrysler AG (Germany)
Electro-Motive
Ford Motor Co.
General Motors Corp.
Goodyear Tire & Rubber Co.
Honda Motor Ltd. (Japan)
Johnson Controls Inc.
Mazda (Japan)
Metallgesellschaft AG (Germany)
Michelin (France)
Nissan Motor Co. (Japan)
Paccar Inc.
Raba Railroad Carriage and Machine Works (Hungary)
Renault (France)
Sumi-Tomo Light Metal Industries (Japan)
TRW Inc.

Railroads (5 Companies)

Burlington Northern Railroad Inc.
Conrail Inc.
Norfolk Southern Corp.
Southern Pacific Rail Corp.
Union Pacific Corp.

Miscellaneous Manufacturing (64 Companies)

American Cyanamid Co.
American Home Products Corp.

American Tourister
Black & Decker Corp.
Bremer Vulkan Verbund (Germany)
Carrier Corp.
Carter-Wallace Inc.
Cooper Industries Inc.
Corning Inc.
Cranston Printworks
Crown Zellerbach
Deere & Co.
Deutsche Babcock AG (Germany)
Dial Corp.
Diebold Inc.
Dow Chemical
Du Pont (E. I.) de Nemours
Eastman Kodak Co.
Emerson Electric Co.
Fluor Corp.
FMC Corp.
Fruit of the Loom Ltd.
Georgia-Pacific Timber Co.
Gillette Co.
Grace (W. R.) & Co.
Hallmark Cards
Hercules Inc.
Hill Refrigeration
Hoechst AG (Germany)
Hoover Co.
Hudson Technologies
Ingersoll-Rand Co.
Interco Inc. (Florsheim)
ITT Industries Inc.
James River
J. Baker Inc.
Kimberly-Clark Corp.
Kobe Steel Corp. (Japan)
Lily-Tulip Inc.
Louisiana-Pacific Corp.
Medtronic Inc.
Moulinex, Inc. (France)
Nine West
Nippon Steel Corp. (Japan)
NKK Corp. (Japan)

Phelps Tool and Die of Kansas
PPG Industries Inc.
Procter & Gamble Co.
Scott Paper Co.
Sherwin-Williams Co.
Snap-On Inc.
Société Nationale Elf Aquitaine (France)
Springs Industries
Stanhome Inc.
Takashimaya (Japan)
Textron Inc.
Tupperware Corp.
VF Corp.
Weyerhaeuser Co.
Wheatstone Corp.
Whirlpool Corp.
Willert Home Products
Wynn's International Co.
Xerox Corp.

Retail and Miscellaneous Services (21 Companies)

Allen Management, Inc.
Begley Co.
Chemical Waste Management
Chiat-Day
Columbia/HCA Healthcare
Consolidated Press
Disney (Walt) Co.
Donnelly (R. R.) & Sons Corp.
Encyclopaedia Britannica Inc.
Image Bank Inc.
Joseph and Feiss
Kmart Corp.
Maculan Holdings AG (Austria)
Marriott International Inc.
Medical Imaging Centers of America
Michaels Stores Inc.
Sears Roebuck & Co.
Times Mirror Co.
WMX Technologies Inc.
Woolworth (F. W.)
Young & Rubicam Inc.

Newspaper-Search Downsizing Companies That Are Listed in Compustat Files

Compustat's Annual Industrial PST File (With Reported Date of Downsizing):

Insurance and Finance

Aetna Inc. (1990, 1991, 1992, 1993, 1994, 1995, 1996)
American Express (1994)
American General Corp. (1990–1991)
BankBoston Corp. (1996)
Bank of America Corp. (no date)
Bank of New York Co. Inc. (1990–1991)
Barclays PLC/England (United Kingdom) (no date)
Chase Manhattan Corp. (1990–1991, 1994, 1996)
Chemical Financial Corp. (1990–1991, 1994, 1996)
Cigna Corp. (1993)
Citizens Banking Corp. (no date)
First Union Corp. (1990–1991)
MassMutual Corp. (no date)
Merrill Lynch & Co. (no date)
Metropolitan Financial Corp. (no date)
Morgan (J. P.) & Co. (1990–1991)
Northeast Bancorp (no date)
PaineWebber Group (1995)
Wells Fargo & Co. (1996)

Telecommunications

Ameritech Corp. (no date)
AT&T Corp. (1980s, 1986, 1989, 1990, 1991, 1993, 1994, 1995, 1996, 1997 to 1998)
Bell Atlantic Corp. (1993–1996, 1997)
BellSouth Corp. (1986–1996)
British Telecom PLC (United Kingdom) (1993, 1995–1996)
Deutsche Telekom AG (Germany) (1996)
France Telecom (France) (no date)
GTE Corp. (1994)
MCI Worldcom Inc. (1995)
Telecom Italia Spa (Italy) (no date)

Airlines

Continental Airlines Inc. (no date)
Delta Airlines Inc. (1994)
KLM Royal Dutch Air (Netherlands) (1996)

Oil and Gas

Chevron Corp. (1986, 1993)
Kerr-McGee Corp. (1990–1991)
Mobil Corp. (1995)
Occidental Petroleum Corp. (1990–1991, 1994–1996)
Petro-Canada (Canada) (1990s)
Texaco Inc. (1990s)

Utilities

Central & South West Corp. (1990–1991)
Entergy Corp. (1990–1991)
Niagara Mohawk Holdings Inc. (1995)

Metals Manufacturing and Mining

Alcoa Inc. (1990–1991)
National Steel Corp. (1997)
Phelps Dodge Corp. (no date)
Reynolds Metals Co. (1997)
Timken Co. (1990s, 1996–1997)
USX-U.S. Steel Group (1980s, 1990s, 1990, 1991)

Aerospace, Aircraft, and Defense

Alliant Techsystems Inc. (1992–1993)
AlliedSignal Inc. (1990–1991, 1993, 1994)
Boeing Co. (1990–1991, 1993)
Eaton Corp. (1990–1991)
General Dynamics Corp. (1990–1991, 1990–1996, 1996)
Litton Industries Inc. (early 1990s)
Lockheed Martin Corp. (1990–1991, 1995)
Loral Space & Communications (no date)
Northrop Grumman Corp. (1994, 1995)
Raytheon Co. (1990–1991)
Rockwell International Corp. (1990, 1991, 1992)
TRW Inc. (1990–1991)
United Technologies Corp. (1990–1991, 1993)

Foods, Beverages, and Tobacco

Anheuser-Busch Companies Inc. (1990–1991)
Campbell Soup Co. (1990–1991, 1995–1996)
Coca-Cola Co. (1990–1991)
Colgate-Palmolive Co. (1993)
Conagra Inc. (1996)
General Mills Inc. (1990–1995, 1996)
Heinz (H. J.) Co. (1995–1996)
Kellogg Co. (1996)
Masco Corp. (Hardee Foods Unit, Roy Rogers Restaurants) (1996)
McDonald's Corp. (1990–1991)
Pepsico Inc. (1990–1995) (Frito-Lay Unit: 1996)
Philip Morris Companies Inc. (1993, 1996)
Quaker Oats Co. (1990–1991, 1996)
Ralston Purina Co. (1994)
R. J. Reynolds Tobacco Holdings (1989, 1990–1991, 1993, 1996)
Safeway Inc. (1990–1991)
Sara Lee Corp. (1990)
Unilever Combined (United Kingdom) (1996)

Computers, Electronics, Data Services, Electrical, and Software

Apple Computer Inc. (1993)
Bell & Howell Co. (1988)
Dun and Bradstreet Corp. (1995)
General Electric Co. (1988, 1990–1991, 1993, 1994, 1995, 1996)
Hewlett-Packard Co. (1990–1991)
Honeywell Inc. (1990–1991, 1993)
International Business Machines Corp. (1990, 1991, 1992, 1993, 1994, 1995, 1996)
Jostens Inc. (1993)
Motorola Inc. (no date)
NCR Corp. (mid-1990s, 1993)
Sunbeam Corp. (1996)
Texas Instruments Inc. (1990–1991)
Unisys Corp. (1990, 1991, 1995)

Pharmaceuticals

Bausch & Lomb Inc. (1996–1997)
Bristol-Myers Squibb (1994–1995)
Lilly (Eli) & Co. (no date)
Schering-Plough (1990–1991)

SmithKline Beecham PLC (United Kingdom) (1993)
Warner-Lambert Co. (no date)

Automobiles, Other Vehicles, and Vehicle Parts

Caterpillar Inc. (1990–1991, 1993–1996)
Chrysler Corp. (since 1988) (1990–1991)
DaimlerChrysler AG (Daimler-Benz AG) (Germany) (1993, 1996)
Ford Motor Co. (no date)
General Motors Corp. (1980s, 1987, 1990–1991, 1992, 1993, 1995, 1996)
Goodyear Tire & Rubber Co. (no date)
Honda Motor Ltd. (Japan) (1993)
Johnson Controls Inc. (1990–1991)
Paccar Inc. (1990–1991)
TRW Inc. (no date)

Railroads

Union Pacific Corp. (1996)
Norfolk Southern Corp. (1990–1991)

Miscellaneous Manufacturing

American Home Products Corp. (1990–1991)
Black & Decker Corp. (1990–1991)
Carter-Wallace Inc. (1995)
Cooper Industries Inc. (1990–1991)
Corning Inc. (1990–1991, 1996–1997)
Deere & Co. (1990–1991)
Dial Corp. (1990–1991)
Diebold Inc. (1996)
Dow Chemical (1990–1991)
Du Pont (E. I.) de Nemours (1990–1991)
Eastman Kodak Co. (late 1980s, 1986, 1990–1991, 1993, 1994, 1995, 1996, 1997)
Emerson Electric Co. (1990–1991)
Fluor Corp. (1990–1991)
FMC Corp. (1990–1991)
Fruit of the Loom Ltd. (1990–1991)
Georgia-Pacific Timber Co. (1990–1991)
Gillette Co. (1994)
Grace (W. R.) & Co. (1990–1991)
Hercules Inc. (1990–1991)

Hoechst AG (Germany) (1996)
Ingersoll-Rand Co. (1990–1991)
ITT Industries Inc. (1990–1991, 1993)
Kimberly-Clark Corp. (in Europe) (1996)
Louisiana-Pacific Corp. (1990–1991)
Medtronic Inc. (no date)
PPG Industries Inc. (1990–1991)
Procter & Gamble Co. (1992, 1993)
Sherwin-Williams Co. (1990–1991)
Snap-On Inc. (1990–1991)
Springs Industries (no date)
Textron Inc. (1990–1991)
Tupperware Corp. (no date)
VF Corp. (1990–1991)
Weyerhaeuser Co. (1990–1991)
Whirlpool Corp. (1995)
Wynn's International Co. (1993)

Retail and Miscellaneous Services

Columbia/HCA Healthcare (1995–1996)
Disney (Walt) Co. (1990–1991)
Donnelly (R. R.) & Sons Corp. (no date)
Kmart Corp. (1994, 1996)
Marriott International Inc. (1990–1991)
Sears Roebuck & Co. (1990–1991, 1993)
Times Mirror Co. (1990–1991, 1996)
WMX Technologies Inc. (1993)
Young & Rubicam Inc. (1994)

Compustat's Merged File (With Date of Reported Downsizing):

Insurance and Finance

Centel Corp. (1990–1991)
Continental Bancorp-PA (no date)
First Interstate Bancorp (1996)
Midlantic Corp. (1995)
Prudential Group Inc. (1994, 1995)
Shawmut National Corp. (1990–1991)
Shearson Lehman Bros Inc. (no date)
Travelers Corp. (1990–1991, 1992–1993)

Telecommunications

Nynex Corp. 1984, 1993, 1994, 1995, 1996, 1997
Pacific Telesis Group 1993

Oil and Gas

Arco Pipeline Co. (1991)
Tenneco Corp. (1990–1991)
Union Texas Petro Holdings Ltd. (1990–1991)

Metals Manufacturing and Mining

Republic Steel Corp. (1990s)

Aerospace, Aircraft, and Defense

Grumman Corp. (1987–1994)
Martin Marietta Corp. (1990–1991, 1993–1994)
McDonnell Douglas Corp. (1990–1991, 1993–1995)
Thiokol Corp. (no date)
Westinghouse Electric (1994)

Foods, Beverages, and Tobacco

Gerber Products (1990–1991)
Green Giant Co. (1993)
Kraft General Foods (1996, 1990–1995, 1993)
Pillsbury Co. (no date)

Computers, Electronics, Data Services, and Software

Contel Cellular Inc. (1990–1991)
Digital Equipment (1990–1991, 1993, 1994)
RCA Corp. (no date)
Square D Co. (no date)
Tandem Computers (1990–1991)

Railroads

Conrail Inc. (1990–1991)
Southern Pacific Rail Corp. (no date)

Miscellaneous Manufacturing

American Cyanamid Co. (1990–1991)
Carrier Corp. (1990s)
Crown Zellerbach (1980s, 1986–1989)
Hoover Co. (1990s)
Lily-Tulip Inc. (1983–1986)
Scott Paper Co. (1990–1991, 1993, 1994, 1995)
Xerox Corp. (1978, 1991, 1993, 1994, 1995, 1996)

Retail and Miscellaneous Services

Begley Co. (mid-1980s)
Chemical Waste Management (no date)
Image Bank Inc. (1991)
Medical Imaging Centers of America (1993)
Woolworth (F. W.) (1992–1993)

Compustat's Bank File (With Date of Reported Downsizing):

Insurance and Finance

Citicorp (1990–1991)
Nationsbank Corp. (no date)

Compustat's Full Coverage (Over the Counter [OTC]) File (With Date of Reported Downsizing):

Telecommunications

Pacific Bell (1992, 1994, 1996)
Sprint Corp. Consolidated (1993–1995)
US West Consolidated (1980s, early 1990s)

Airlines

American Airlines Inc. (1993, 1994)
USAir Inc. (1993–1994, 1995)

Aerospace

Kaman Corp. (no date)

Computers, Electronics, Data Services, and Software

Fujitsu Ltd. (Japan) (1993–1994)
Prodigy Communications Corp. (no date)

Pharmaceuticals

Novartis AG (Switzerland) (mid-1990s, 1996, 1997)
Roche Holdings Ltd. (1994)

Miscellaneous Manufacturing

Hudson Technologies (1993)

Retail and Miscellaneous Services

Michaels Stores Inc. (1997)

Food

Borden Inc. (1990–1991)

Railroads

Burlington Northern Railroad Inc. (1990–1991)

Newspaper-Search Downsizing Companies That Are Not Listed in Compustat (With Reported Date of Downsizing)

Insurance and Finance

Australian National (Australia) (1989)
Banc One Corp. (no date)
BankAmerica Corp. (1990–1991, 1993, 1995)
Bank of Boston (1990–1991, 1993)
Banque Nationale (France) (1996)
Bayerisch Hypotheken-und Wechsel-Bank (Germany) (1996)
Citizens Savings Bank (1994)
Connecticut Mutual Life Insurance Co. (1995)
Credit Lyonnais (France) (1995)
First Bank System, Inc. (no date)
Johnson & Higgins (1997)
Kidder-Peabody (1994, 1995)
Kohlberg Kravis Roberts & Co. (no date)

Mercedes-Benz Credit Corp. (Germany) (1996)
Mitsui (Japan) (no date)
Nationwide Insurance Enterprise (1994)
Natwest Bank (United Kingdom) (1990s)
Peregrine Investment Holdings (no date)
Thomas Cook Travel Money Services (1995)

Airlines

Air France (France) (no date)
Kiwi Airlines (1996)
TWA (1992)
US Airways (1997)

Oil and Gas

British Gas (United Kingdom) (no date)

Utilities

Pacific Gas & Electric (1993)
Peoples Natural Gas Co. (1995)

Aerospace

B. F. Goodrich (no date)
Hughes Aircraft (1994)
Pratt & Whitney Aircraft (1993)

Foods, Beverages, and Tobacco

Lewis Brothers Bakeries, Inc. (1993)
Miller Brewing (1996)
Pet Foods, Inc. (1990–1991)

Computers, Electronics, Data Services, and Software

Ericsson Italia (Italy) (no date)
Grundig (1996)
K-III Communications (no date)
LTX, Inc. (1985)
Olivetti Spa (Italy) (1989)
Proteon, Inc. (1986)

Siemens AG (Germany) (1996)
Toshiba (Japan) (1993)

Pharmaceuticals

Ciba-Geigy (Switzerland): *see* Novartis *in Industrial PST file*
Marion Merrell Dow (1993)
Sandoz (Switzerland): *see* Novartis *in Industrial PST file*
Sterling Winthrop (United Kingdom) (1995)
Upjohn (United Kingdom) (1990–1991)

Autos, Other Vehicles, and Vehicle Parts

BMW (Germany) (1996)
Electro-Motive (1994)
Mazda (Japan) (1993)
Metallgesellschaft AG (Germany) (1993)
Michelin (France) (1995)
Nissan Motor Co. (Japan) (1993)
Raba Railroad Carriage and Machine Works (Hungary) (1994)
Renault (France) (1997)
Sumi-Tomo Light Metal Industries (Japan) (1996)

Miscellaneous Manufacturing

American Tourister (1993)
Bremer Vulkan Verbund (Germany) (1996)
Cranston Printworks (1996)
Deutsche Babcock AG (Germany) (1996, 1997)
Hallmark Cards (1993–1994)
Hill Refrigeration (1995)
Interco Inc. (Florsheim) (1993)
James River (1990–1991)
J. Baker Inc. (1996)
Kobe Steel Corp. (Japan) (1996)
Moulinex, Inc. (France) (1996)
Nine West (no date)
Nippon Steel Corp. (Japan) (1996)
NKK Corp. (Japan) (1996, 1997)
Phelps Tool & Die of Kansas (1996)
Société Nationale Elf Aquitaine (France) (1995)
Stanhome Inc. (no date)
Takashimaya (Japan) (1993)
Wheatstone Corp. (no date)
Willert Home Products (1994)

Retail and Miscellaneous Services

Allen Management, Inc. (no date)
Chiat-Day (1993)
Consolidated Press (1991–1993)
Encyclopaedia Britannica Inc. (1995)
Joseph and Feiss (1993)
Maculan Holding AG (Austria) (1996)

Final 133-Firm Newspaper-Search Sample (Downsizing Companies Listed in Compustat for Which 1990 and 1998 Employment Data Were Available)

Aetna Inc.
Alcoa Inc.
Alliant Techsystems Inc.
AlliedSignal Inc.
American Express
American General Corp.
American Home Products Corp.
Ameritech Corp.
Anheuser-Busch Companies Inc.
Apple Computer Inc.
AT&T Corp.
BankBoston Corp.
Bank of America Corp.
Bank of New York Co. Inc.
Barclays PLC/England
Bausch & Lomb Inc.
Bell Atlantic Corp.
BellSouth Corp.
Black & Decker Corp.
Boeing Co.
Bristol-Myers Squibb
British Telecom PLC
Burlington Northern Railroad Inc.
Campbell Soup Co.
Carter-Wallace Inc.
Caterpillar Inc.
Central & South West Corp.
Chase Manhattan Corp.
Chevron Corp.
Cigna Corp.

Citizens Banking Corp.
Coca-Cola Co.
Colgate-Palmolive Co.
Columbia/HCA Healthcare
Continental Airlines Inc.
Cooper Industries Inc.
Corning Inc.
DaimlerChrysler AG
Deere & Co.
Delta Airlines Inc.
Diebold Inc.
Disney (Walt) Co.
Donnelly (R. R.) & Sons Corp.
Dow Chemical
Dun and Bradstreet Corp.
Du Pont (E. I.) de Nemours
Eastman Kodak Co.
Eaton Corp.
Emerson Electric Co.
Entergy Corp.
First Union Corp.
Fluor Corp.
FMC Corp.
Ford Motor Co.
Fruit of the Loom Ltd.
General Dynamics Corp.
General Electric Co.
Gillette Co.
General Motors Corp.
Goodyear Tire & Rubber Co.
Grace (W. R.) & Co.
GTE Corp.
Hercules Inc.
Hewlett-Packard Co.
Honeywell Inc.
International Business Machines Corp.
Ingersoll-Rand Co.
ITT Industries Inc.
Johnson Controls Inc.
Jostens Inc.
Kaman Corp.
Kellogg Co.
Kerr-McGee Corp.
Kimberly-Clark Corp.

Kmart Corp.
Lilly (Eli) & Co.
Litton Industries Inc.
Lockheed Martin Corp.
Louisiana-Pacific Corp.
Masco Corp.
McDonald's Corp.
Medtronic Inc.
Merrill Lynch & Co.
Michaels Stores Inc.
Mobil Corp.
Morgan (J. P.) & Co.
Motorola Inc.
National Steel Corp.
NCR Corp.
Niagara Mohawk Holdings Inc.
Norfolk Southern Corp.
Northrop Grumman Corp.
Occidental Petroleum Corp.
Paccar Inc.
Pacific Bell
PaineWebber Group
Pepsico Inc.
Phelps Dodge Corp.
Philip-Morris Companies Inc.
PPG Industries Inc.
Procter & Gamble Co.
Quaker Oats Co.
Ralston Purina Co.
Raytheon Co.
Reynolds Metals Co.
Rockwell International Corp.
Safeway Inc.
Sara Lee Corp.
Schering-Plough
Sears Roebuck & Co.
Sherwin-Williams Co.
SmithKline Beecham PLC
Snap-On Inc.
Springs Industries
Sunbeam Corp.
Texaco Inc.
Texas Instruments Inc.
Textron Inc.

Times Mirror Co.
Timken Co.
TRW Inc.
Unilever Combined
Union Pacific Corp.
Unisys Corp.
United Technologies Corp.
USAir Inc.
USX-U.S. Steel Group
VF Corp.
Warner-Lambert Co.
Wells Fargo & Co.
Weyerhaeuser Co.
Whirlpool Corp.
Wynn's International Co.

Notes

Chapter 1

1. See, for example, Abraham (1999), Caves and Krepps (1993), Farber and Hallock (1999), Hallock (1998), and Kalra, Henderson, and Walker (1994). Only Steven Abraham (1999) finds systematic support for the popular belief that downsizing announcements raised stock prices. John Abowd, George Milkovich, and John Hannon (1990) suggest that downsizing announcements had a larger effect on the *variance* of stock returns than on the average price.

2. There is by now a large empirical literature on how job stability did or did not change in the United States in the 1980s and 1990s. For one attempt to summarize and reconcile the disparate studies, see Neumark (2000). We add our own piece of evidence to this literature in chapter 8.

3. This fact is, of course, known well from, for example, the work of Steven Davis, John Haltiwanger, and Scott Schuh (1996).

4. "Top-coding" refers to the common practice, in statistical tabulations, of having an open-ended top category—such as "firms with 1,000 or more employees." Such a category includes firms with 1,000 employees, 10,000 employees, and 100,000 employees—leaving the investigator unable to distinguish one from the other.

5. See, for example, the symposium in the spring 1997 issue of the *Journal of Economic Perspectives,* featuring papers by Peter Gottschalk (1997), George Johnson (1997), Robert Topel (1997), and Nicole Fortin and Thomas Lemieux (1997). Dozens of other references could be cited.

6. This story is nicely told in Halberstam (1986).

7. For a comprehensive view, mainly in the context of wage inequality, see Burtless (1995).

8. One relevant reference is Krepps and Candell (1997), who find that increased import competition helps explain layoffs and plant closures.

9. For earlier research leading to more or less the same conclusion, see Baily, Bartelsman, and Haltiwanger (1996a), various of the AMA surveys, and Capelli (2000), which contains several additional references.

10. Compounding the difficulty, some industries (for example, durable man-
    ufacturing) are more heavily affected by cycles than are others (such as
    services).

11. Things have improved for labor in recent years. Real compensation per
    hour in the nonfarm business sector rose by an average of 2.5 percent
    per annum between 1996 and 2000, virtually matching the 2.6 percent
    annual average productivity gain.

12. This theme is elaborated upon in Blinder (2000).

13. Data are from the national income and product accounts. In addition,
    both Blanchard (1997) and Caballero and Hammour (1998) offer evi-
    dence supporting this hypothesis for Europe, although they characterize
    capital's gains as "getting even" for labor's gains in the early 1970s.

14. See, for example, Cochran (1999). For an extreme example of this hy-
    pothesis, see the popular book by James Glassman and Kevin Hassett
    (1999).

15. As noted in note 2, the scholarly literature on job instability is by now
    huge. For a specific study of perceptions of job security, see Manski and
    Straub (1999).

16. There is probably a great deal of reverse causation here: it is the less
    profitable firms that tend to adopt downsizing strategies.

Chapter 2

1. Nevertheless, our newspaper sampling cannot be deemed to meet any of
   the standard criteria for sample selection and is therefore in no sense
   representative of any part of the actual universe of downsizers or of
   those who claimed to be such. For that reason, we have deliberately not
   undertaken an elaborate study of the behavior and performance of the
   firms in the sample beyond what has happened to the size of their labor
   forces, but we do offer some evidence on these matters in this chapter.

2. We used the Lexis-Nexis database and the Dow-Jones News Service for
   the search.

3. Of course, we did not count articles in which the word "downsizing"
   was used in a different context (for example, the downsizing of automobile dimensions or the downsizing of museum art collections).

4. Of the 292 company names we encountered in the five-year search, 212
   are listed in Compustat. Sufficient data for the relevant years were available in Compustat's database for 133 of the firms. We note here that one
   of the (anonymous) readers of the manuscript of this book commented:
   "I am somewhat skeptical of the reliability of the employment levels in
   Compustat. Cross-checks of the employment levels in Compustat with
   databases at the U.S. Bureau of the Census (at the micro level) reveal
   that Compustat employment statistics are very noisy and do not match

up well with the census administrative, census and survey data on employment. (The census data may be noisy here as well but are likely more reliable.) Thus, unlike the financial data in Compustat, which is presumably more reliable given financial reporting requirements, the employment data in Compustat may be misleading." Accordingly, we warn the reader to interpret the pertinent part of our discussion with caution.

5. Standard & Poor's, Compustat (North America) annual files (Englewood, Colo.: McGraw-Hill, various years). We are grateful to Don Broach, data specialist in the Social Science Reference Center, Firestone Library, Princeton University, for his generous assistance with the Compustat database.

6. We are grateful to James Challenger and Jim Ciccone of Challenger, Gray & Christmas for releasing the data to us.

7. Some of the dramatic increases in job cuts in the last part of 2001 were associated with the September 11 terrorist attacks on the World Trade Center in New York City and the Pentagon in Washington, D.C.

8. Farber and Hallock's (1999) sample included 1,703 firm names and 3,878 job loss announcements culled from abstracts of annual editions of the *Wall Street Journal Index*.

9. American Management Association, 1601 Broadway, New York, N.Y. 10019–7420. See the AMA website at *www.amanet.org*. We are grateful to Eric Rolfe Greenberg, director of management studies at AMA, for providing us with the full set of surveys.

10. These surveys, which are biennial supplements to the Current Population Survey, were implemented in response to downsizing in the 1980s and have become an important source of data on job loss, particularly for long-tenure workers (those who were employed three years or longer in their previous jobs). Workers are considered to be displaced if they leave their jobs involuntarily, because of a plant closing, insufficient work or slack work, abolition of their position or their work shift, or for some other similar reason. The surveys are carried out by the U.S. Bureau of the Census for the Bureau of Labor Statistics.

11. For evidence on the general issue of the relation of job loss to general business conditions, see Farber (1998).

12. This figure does not take account of offsetting job creation—it is the *gross*, not the *net*, job loss.

13. If a firm's number of employees in 1998 was within (plus or minus) 10 percent of its number of employees in 1990, we judged it to have "remained the same."

14. This side of unemployment, in our view, is not sufficiently emphasized in the academic literature of economics, and the journalistic accounts appropriately help to redress the balance.

15. For example, Zoltan Acs (1999, 2) reports: "Between 1960 and 1983, the number of corporations and partnerships in the United States more than

doubled (from 2.0 million to 4.5 million), while the number of companies in Europe stagnated. It declined in Sweden, Denmark, the Netherlands, and Britain and increased only slightly in West Germany, France, Switzerland, and Italy." This trend continued in the United States in the 1990s: the number of corporations and partnerships reached 6.5 million in 1997 (U.S. Bureau of the Census 2000). And in Europe there were some signs of small-firm growth; see, for example, "European Startups to the Rescue," *Business Week*, March 12, 1998.

16. The ten companies are Sears, IBM, Kmart, General Electric, General Dynamics, Digital Equipment, McDonnell Douglas, Boeing, General Motors, and GTE.

Chapter 3

1. A substantial number of theoretical writings deal with the subjects of this chapter, particularly the relation between firm size and technical change. See, for example, Klepper (1996), Klette and Kortum (2002), and Pfann (2001).

2. There have been many studies of the influence of technology on the size and composition of a firm's labor force and related matters. See, for example, Aaronson and Housinger (1999), Davis and Weinstein (2002), Dunne and Schmitz (1995), and Robertson and Alston (1992).

3. The analysis goes back at least to the work of Don Patinkin (1947). Since then there have been many important contributions to the theory of size distribution of firms. For example, Robert Lucas (1977) has emphasized the influence of entrepreneurial ability and economies of scope, and Boyan Jovanovic (1982) and Ariel Pakes and Richard Ericson (1995) have dealt with the evolution of the size distribution of business firms under the influence of learning, selection and demand, and technology shocks. There is also the recent literature on creative destruction and its implications for churning, growth, and cycles in firm size; see, for example, Dale Mortensen and Christopher Pissarides (1999a, 1999b).

4. See, for example, Scherer and Ross (1990, 106–7). Frederic M. Scherer (personal correspondence, October 2001) cites petroleum refining, petroleum pipelines, steel manufacturing, automobile manufacturing, beer manufacturing, and fabric manufacturing as examples of industries in which empirical studies have shown such AC curves.

5. See Baumol, Panzar, and Willig (1988) for a discussion of this case. It should be emphasized that for the multiproduct firm, average cost cannot be defined or measured except by arbitrary apportionment of fixed and common costs or by adoption of an arbitrary index of the firm's total output.

6. Moreover, for reasons we need not go into here, the zone of possibly efficient firm sizes includes a substantial region below the M locus that is bounded by a hyperplane parallel to a lower supporting hyperplane, hh, of the M locus and lies closer to the origin than hh.

7. These remarks and those in the paragraphs that follow are related to what has been called "flexible specialization" in the large literature on organization of the firm.

8. Yet it is true that spending on information technology has become a very major budgetary item for most companies. Indeed, economies of scale in computer platforms are often cited to justify the claim that a proposed merger will provide significant cost savings.

9. Information technology may at the same time make internal control less costly and inefficient. This affects one of the classic arguments favoring reliance on markets—the observation that they economize on the need for information. Continued decline in the cost of acquiring, analyzing, and disseminating information should presumably reduce any inefficiencies entailed in internal control of a large bureaucratic corporation.

10. The model obviously assumes some stickiness in relative wages. Otherwise, the wages of the less-educated may fall sufficiently to offset the decline in the demand for those workers, though the usual supply-demand model leads us to expect a wage fall to moderate the rise in unemployment of the less-educated but not to offset it altogether.

11. And there is more to the story. The unemployed in these two groups may include a substantial number of persons who will never be employed again. Dismissed older workers whose skills are obsolete are reported to constitute a substantial share of "discouraged" workers and the permanently unemployed.

12. In the seventeenth and eighteenth centuries, ships did not even have the means to determine their longitude. As a result, writes David Landes (1999, 745), "too many were the ships that dashed aimlessly and fruitlessly about, too far this way, too near that, until scurvy and thirst killed off or incapacitated so many hands that the crew could no longer man the rigging and direct the vessel; and then the ship would float helpless with its population of skeletons and ghosts, another 'flying Dutchman.'" It is no wonder that Spain, the Netherlands, France, and Great Britain offered huge prizes to anyone who could invent a practical way to determine longitude at sea. The British prize, 20,000 pounds, was almost 150 times the annual income of the highest churchman in Scotland; see Rae (1895).

13. As we will see in the chapters that follow, our empirical analysis may not correspond perfectly either to the short run or to the long run and thus may not be ideally suited to the testing of either the hypothesis about the short-run role of demand or the hypothesis about the long-run influence of technology. The period of time covered by our data is substantial, but the regressions have not had built into them the substantial lags that would adapt them to investigation of the influences on firm size that take considerable time to work themselves out. Moreover, the influences that pertain to the short run, according to our hypotheses, are easier to observe and quantify than those that belong to the long run. It

is obviously easier to measure the volume of employment in an industry than to determine changes in the level of output that minimizes the firm's average cost, and it is even more difficult to carry out the corresponding calculations for real-life multiproduct firms. So, we conjecture that our empirical analysis has readily and clearly brought out the shorter-run relationships, but that it has been less successful in dealing with those of the longer run; it has shown the role of demand but not dealt directly with technology.

Chapter 4

1. A corresponding problem besets the Enterprise Statistics. For some firms, the industry classification may be arbitrary. And of course, not all of XYZ's employees work in manufacturing.

2. The Census of Retail Trade data (950 firms) agree with this figure almost exactly.

3. There is one further difference. In our tabulations using the Enterprise Statistics, we excluded firms and establishments with zero employees. These are included in the standard Economic Census data.

4. We have also used 1997 data for some limited purposes. Here, and in all comparisons, we include the 1963 to 1967 period, which is, of course, only four years.

5. Unfortunately, the lights are out for 1967, because Enterprise Statistics for that year did not tabulate data by establishment.

6. In applying this definition to our data, we purposefully violated strict mathematical parlance in one particular circumstance in order to reduce the number of ambiguous cases a bit. Suppose two cumulative distribution functions crossed only once, by no more than 0.1 percent, and then immediately crossed back—as in the numerical example given in the unnumbered table on page 296. In such cases, we treated the crossing as if it were a tangency and classified one as stochastically dominating the other even though that was not strictly true.

    This table should make the procedure clear. The numbers in the distribution B column are smaller than those in the distribution A column for firm sizes up to fifty employees, and then again for firm sizes of more than one hundred—suggesting that B stochastically dominates A. But the number in the distribution B column for fifty-one to one hundred employees exceeds that in the distribution A column by a minuscule margin. So in a strict mathematical sense, there is no stochastic dominance relation: the two distributions actually cross twice. However, since this crossing is of trivial magnitude, is immediately reversed, and could easily be accounted for by minor data errors, we decided to treat it as if it were a tangency rather than a crossing. Hence, we would have classified B as stochastically dominating A. Our application of this criterion was very strict, however, and entirely mechanical. We did not declare

Two Hypothetical Cumulative Distributions

Firm Size Category	Distribution A	Distribution B
Zero	15.6	12.5
1–10	42.4	39.0
11–20	72.4	71.0
21–50	97.5	96.9
51–100	99.21	99.29
101–250	99.8	99.7
251–500	99.9	99.8
501–1,000	99.97	99.94
Over 1,000	100.0	100.0

Source: Authors' compilation.

such a tangency unless there was only one such category (whether contiguous or not) and the difference between the two distributions was less than 0.10. Despite the strict application of this criterion, such pseudo-tangencies arose in forty-five cases—almost 14 percent of the total number of observations.

7. This suggests that 1992 to 1997 data, if we had them, would also show upsizing. Unfortunately, the Enterprise Statistics were not funded for 1997.

8. These are hotels (EIC 70), personal services (EIC 72), business services (EIC 73), automotive repair (EIC 75), miscellaneous repair services (EIC 76), motion pictures (EIC 78), and amusement and recreation services (EIC 79).

9. In this period, we add to the previous list: dental services (which becomes health services starting in 1982) (EIC 80), legal services (EIC 81), and engineering and architectural services (EIC 89). This last industry was no longer its own two-digit category after 1982, but we kept it in the sample anyway.

10. In addition to health services (see previous note), we add accounting, auditing, and bookkeeping services (EIC 89b, which switches to EIC 87.2 starting in 1987), and the catchall category "services, n.e.c." (EIC 89c, which switches to 89 starting in 1987).

11. The usable data come from trucking, water transportation, and transportation services.

12. It should be remembered that 1967 is missing for establishments, so we have only twelve observations.

13. This last sector joined the Enterprise Statistics only in 1992, so we have no data on *changes* from that source.

14. The earliest year covered is 1978, not 1977.

15. If we use establishment data instead, this inference is sharp only in retailing. The correlations between s and e and between n and e are roughly the same in manufacturing and services.

16. This was also amply justified by a Chow test with F-statistic 0.5 and p-value = 0.62.

17. We tried adding the initial *level* of firm size to each of the six equations as a rough test of regression toward the mean. (The percentage change in firm size should be a decreasing function of initial size.) But this additional variable was never significant at the 5 percent level.

18. In services alone, there is no trend.

Chapter 5

1. The 1997 Census of Manufacturing shifted from the old Standard Industrial Classification (SIC) to the new NAICS (North American Industrial Classification System). As a result, size distributions of establishments in 1997 are not directly comparable to those of earlier years. However, some bridge tables were provided for 1997 by the U.S. Census Bureau based on the old SIC scheme.

2. The earliest year covered is 1978, not 1977.

3. As noted in chapter 4, Enterprise Statistics are not available by establishment for 1967.

4. This statistic was suggested by an anonymous referee, whom we thank for the suggestion. This measure was also used by Davis, Haltiwanger, and Schuh (1996). See their book for further discussion.

5. The coworker mean could not be computed for 1997.

6. The Enterprise Statistics tabulate the size distribution according to employment by firm, not by establishment. The number of establishments owned by each firm in a size class is then summed to obtain the total number of establishments by (firm) size class. As a result, it is not possible to compute the size distribution of employment by size of establishment from these data. Moreover, Compustat does not provide summary data on firm size distributions by industry.

7. Because of missing data in the Enterprise Statistics, it is not possible to compute the size distribution of employment on the two-digit level from this source.

8. Results using the other two sets of weights involve second-order terms.

9. The Compustat data could not be used here since they are based on a rather arbitrary sample of companies.

10. It should be noted that the number of establishments and employment are much larger in the Enterprise Statistics than in the Census of Manufacturing. As we discussed earlier, the Enterprise Statistics classify establishments into industries according to the primary product of the firm to which they belong. As a result, the Enterprise Statistics include nonmanufacturing establishments that are part of manufacturing firms and exclude manufacturing establishments that are part of nonmanufacturing firms. Apparently the former is much larger than the latter.

11. As far as we could ascertain from a rather extensive literature search, there are relatively few papers or books on the economic determinants of downsizing. One exception is Krepps and Candell (1997), who find that increases in industry-level import competition, merger activity, and declines in industry demand account for a large fraction of layoffs and plant closures by firms or plants that are characterized by inefficiency (as they measure it). There is, on the other hand, a relatively extensive literature on the economic *effects* of downsizing (see chapter 7 for references).

12. There is the danger that "division bias" may be introduced by use of the change in average industry employment as an independent variable. The reason is that average establishment size is defined as the ratio of total employment to the number of establishments in an industry. Thus, a spurious correlation could conceivably be introduced between the percentage growth in mean establishment size and the percentage growth in employment. However, a comparison of the first two columns of table 5.10 suggests that the introduction of employment growth as an independent variable does not induce substantial changes in the other coefficient estimates. The coefficient signs remain unchanged. The absolute value of the coefficient of unionization declines, and its significance level falls from the 5 percent to the 10 percent level. The coefficient of R&D investment increases in absolute value and becomes statistically significant. The biggest change is for the coefficient of import intensity, which falls substantially in absolute value and becomes insignificant.

13. We also tested for the presence of period and industry effects and obtained the results reported in the unnumbered table on page 299: In only one instance is the addition of the full set of period dummy variables or industry dummy variables statistically significant. This is the case of the addition of period dummy variables to specification 2, for which the F-statistic is significant at the 5 percent level (but not the 1 percent level).

In other variants, we included the average period unemployment rate and the annual growth of economywide GDP (in constant dollars) as independent variables instead of period dummy variables. In neither case is the variable statistically significant. Because the results for both period and industry effects are so weak, we have ignored these effects in the subsequent regression analysis.

14. This is the one case in which we were so worried about simultaneity that we lagged the independent variable.

F-Tests for Period and Industry Dummy Variables in Table 5.10

F-tests (Table 5.10)	F-Statistic	Critical F-Value (.05 level)	Reject Null Hypothesis?
Specification 1			
Add period dummies	1.5664	2.30	No
Add industry dummies	0.8867	1.70	No
Add period and industry dummies	0.9588	1.65	No
Specification 2			
Add period dummies	2.6805	2.30	Yes
Add industry dummies	1.3047	1.70	No
Add period and industry dummies	1.5283	1.65	No

Source: Authors' compilation.

15. This is not too surprising since the correlation coefficient between PEP and FTEE is 0.993.

16. Because industry-level R&D data are generally unavailable before 1958, we cannot include the 1953 to 1958 period.

17. Employment distribution by size class for two-digit SIC manufacturing industries is not yet available for 1997.

18. Remember, there are no Enterprise Statistics for firms for 1997.

Chapter 6

1. The regressions reported later in this chapter are based on anywhere from 33 to 42 observations. In contrast, the comparable manufacturing regressions in chapter 5 used 116 or 140 observations.

2. See the data appendix to chapter 5 for a detailed discussion of the methods. Unfortunately, R&D expenditures proved to be a more powerful explanatory variable than TFP growth in manufacturing.

3. But note that we are not regressing a "trending" variable on a stationary one. Our right-hand variables are the ratios of exports and imports to output.

4. We experimented with keeping the TFP growth variable in the regression, but it was never significant when employment growth was included.

5. Once again, versions of regressions 3 through 7 were run with TFP growth replacing employment growth. The TFP variable was never close to being significant.

6. All growth rates used in the regressions are annualized.

Chapter 7

1. On the other hand, announcements of permanent staff reductions were associated with significant increases in the variation of abnormal total shareholder return around the announcement date.

2. The coefficient of the number of full-time equivalent scientists and engineers engaged in R&D per employee is also significant in every case, typically at the 1 percent level. The tables present results using R&D expenditures because it is more conventional.

3. Regression results (not shown) also indicate that contemporaneous changes in average firm or establishment size have no significant effect on TFP growth.

4. We also tested for the existence of industry effects, as well as period effects. On the basis of F-tests, we could not reject the null hypothesis of no industry (or period) effects at the 5 percent level.

5. In other specifications we included the period average Gini coefficient as a measure of the degree of concentration of the industry (since we lacked data on the four-firm or eight-firm concentration ratios). The coefficient of the variable, however, is not statistically significant.

6. This result also holds when time period and industry dummy variables are added to the regression equation (results not shown).

7. We did try to test for reverse causation by regressing the percentage change in average establishment size on TFP growth, R&D intensity, the unionization rate, the change in export and import intensity, the growth in total industry employment, the lagged profit rate, and the percentage change in the average market value of firms within an industry lagged one period. We find that the coefficient of the last of these variables is uniformly negative, though not statistically significant. This result is unexpected, since it suggests that when the stock value of a firm declines, it responds (after a lag) by increasing employment rather than decreasing it.

Chapter 8

1. The material in this chapter is drawn from Parrado and Wolff (1999).

2. See the next section for references to some of the literature, and see Farber (1997) for a review of the issues.

3. This is analogous to the use of the coworker (or employment-weighted) mean to evaluate the change in average firm size, a concept introduced in chapter 5 that reflects what happened to the size of firm or establishment of the typical worker.

4. This finding differs qualitatively from what we have inferred from our downsizing analysis in earlier chapters. This difference may be attribut-

able to the earlier time period studied here, and to the fact that the sample most likely includes many workers who shifted their employment on their own initiative.

5. In the study, we selected a sample of men (heads of households in the PSID) and women (heads of households and wives in the PSID) with continuous work histories.

6. See Jovanovic (1979) for a formal model of job matching, and Light and McGarry (1998), Garen (1989), Abraham and Farber (1987), and Altonji and Shakotko (1987) for empirical tests of the job-matching model.

7. Specifically, the disturbance term in the basic wage equation is positively correlated with job tenure. As Abraham and Farber (1987) point out, this may be explained by the correlation of tenure with an omitted variable representing the quality of the worker-job or worker-employer match.

8. In January of 1984, 1986, 1988, and 1990, the monthly Current Population Survey included a supplement with information from workers who had previously suffered a job displacement.

9. Each individual work history covers the time period January 1978 to December 1991.

10. In the 1981 to 1992 PSID data, the occupational variable is recorded at a three-digit level, while for the 1969 to 1975 and 1976 to 1980 periods, it is recorded at the one-digit and two-digit levels, respectively.

11. The industry variable is first recorded in the PSID in 1971. From 1971 to 1980, this series appears at a two-digit level, while from 1980 to 1992 it is at the three-digit level.

12. Other panel data, such as the Displaced Worker Survey, contain information from workers about both voluntary and involuntary job displacements.

13. This caveat is not relevant to changes in industry, since such a change also implies a change in firm.

14. In the three-year time periods, the mode is one, and this category accounts for between 18 and 23 percent of the total number of changes.

15. Topel and Ward (1992) and Light and McGarry (1998) report similar results for job changes.

16. These results are consistent with studies by Robert Hall (1982), Manuelita Ureta (1992), Kenneth Swinnerton and Howard Wial (1995), and Steven Allen, Robert Clark, and Ann McDermed (1993), who all argue that jobs in the United States are becoming less stable and that long-term employment relationships are becoming less important.

17. In three-year time periods, between 32 and 47 percent of workers changed occupations at least once. Dixie Sommers and Alan Eck (1977) report that 39 percent of adult men changed their three-digit (SIC code) occupation at least once between 1965 and 1970. We find in our sample that 45 percent of adult males changed one-digit occupation between 1972 and 1974.

18. Similarly, in three-year time periods, the modal number of industry changes is 1, and this category accounts for between 13 and 19 percent of the total number of industry changes.

19. Income figures are converted to 1990 dollars using the standard consumer price index (CPI-U).

20. They used ordinary least squares (OLS) to estimate earnings equations over the period 1981 through 1987.

21. James Markey and William Parks (1989), using the January 1987 CPS, find that age is the principal factor determining occupational mobility, with high mobility rates in young workers and low rates among middle-aged and older workers.

22. However, this result should be interpreted cautiously, because workers in the earlier sample have an average age of thirty-eight at the start of the period, and an average starting age of thirty-four in the later sample (see table 8.6).

23. The age and marriage effects found here are consistent with results on job mobility reported by Becker and Lindsay (1994), among others.

24. If T_{it}^M is the mean of tenure for individual i over the sample observations in period t, we can define the instrumental variable T_{it}^V to be the deviation of T_{it} from the job mean—that is, $T_{it}^V = T_{it} - T_{it}^M$ and $(T_{it}^V)^2 = T_{it}^2 - (T_{it}^M)^2$.

25. Becker and Lindsay (1994) also find that, among workers who remain in the same job, the tenure slope is steeper for women than for men.

Chapter 9

1. Not all downsizing studies are consistent with this result. For example, the Baily, Bartelsman, and Haltiwanger (1996a) study of U.S. manufacturing in the 1980s indicates that productivity increased for both downsizers and upsizers, and our newspaper sample of firms also suggests that.

2. This is, of course, hardly a new recommendation in the economics literature. Writers as far back as J.-B. Say (1821, 87, note) have proposed the use of public works to ease the problems of workers temporarily displaced by technical change: "Without having recourse to local or temporary restrictions on the use of new methods and machinery . . . a benevolent administration can make provision for the employment of supplanted or inactive labor in the construction of works of public utility at the public expense, as of canals, roads, churches, or the like."

References

Aaronson, Daniel, and Kenneth Housinger. 1999. "The Impact of Technology on Displacement and Reemployment." *Economic Perspectives* (Federal Reserve Bank of Chicago) 23(2): 14–30.

Abowd, John M., George T. Milkovich, and John M. Hannon. 1990. "The Effects of Human Resource Management Decisions on Shareholder Value." *Industrial Relations Review* 43: 203–36.

Abraham, Katherine G., and Henry S. Farber. 1987. "Job Duration, Seniority, and Earnings." *American Economic Review* 77: 278–97.

Abraham, Steven E. 1999. "Layoff and Employment Guarantee Announcements: How Do Shareholders Respond?" Working Paper. Oswego: State University of New York, Department of Economics.

Acs, Zoltan J. 1999. "The American Evolution." In *Are Small Firms Important?: Their Role and Impact,* edited by Zoltan J. Acs. Boston: Kluwer Academic Publishers.

Akerlof, George A. 1982. "Labor Contracts as Partial Gift Exchange." *Quarterly Journal of Economics* 97(4): 543–69.

Allen, Steven G., Robert L. Clark, and Ann A. McDermed. 1993. "Pensions, Bonding, and Lifetime Jobs." *Journal of Human Resources* 28(3): 463–81.

Allen, Steven G., Robert L. Clark, and Sylvester J. Scheiber. 1999. "Has Job Security Vanished in Large Corporations?" Working Paper 6966. Cambridge, Mass.: National Bureau of Economic Research.

Altonji, Joseph G., and Robert Shakotko. 1987. "Do Wages Rise with Job Seniority?" *Review of Economic Studies* 54: 437–59.

American Management Association. 1994. *Survey on Downsizing and Assistance to Displaced Workers.* New York: American Management Association.

———. Various years. *Survey on Staffing and Structure.* Available at: *www.amanet.org.*

Baily, Martin Neil, Eric J. Bartelsman, and John Haltiwanger. 1996a. "Downsizing and Productivity Growth: Myth or Reality?" *Small Business Economics* 8(4): 259–78. Reprinted in *Sources of Productivity Growth,* edited by David G. Mayes. Cambridge: Cambridge University Press.

———. 1996b. "Labor Productivity: Structural Change and Cyclical Dynamics." Working Paper 5503. Cambridge, Mass.: National Bureau of Economic Research.

Bartel, Ann P., and Frank R. Lichtenberg. 1987. "The Comparative Advantage of Educated Workers in Implementing New Technology." *Review of Economics and Statistics* 69(1): 1–11.

Baumol, William J. 2002. *The Free-Market Innovation Machine: Analyzing the Growth Miracle of Capitalism.* Princeton, N.J.: Princeton University Press.

Baumol, William J., and Dietrich Fischer. 1978. "Cost-Minimizing Number of Firms and Determination of Industry Structure." *Quarterly Journal of Economics* 92: 439–68.

Baumol, William J., John C. Panzar, and Robert D. Willig. 1988. *Contestable Markets and Theory of Industry Structure.* Rev. ed. San Diego: Harcourt, Brace and Jovanovich.

Baumol, William J., and Edward N. Wolff. 1999. "Technical Progress and Sharply Lengthened Time 'Between Jobs.'" Annandale-on-Hudson, N.Y.: Levy Institute of Economics, Bard College (October).

Becker, Elizabeth, and Cotton M. Lindsay. 1994. "Sex Differences in Tenure Profiles: Effects of Shared Firm-Specific Investment." *Journal of Labor Economics* 12(1): 98–118.

Becker, Gary S. 1962. "Investment in Human Capital: A Theoretical Analysis." *Journal of Political Economy,* part 2, 70(5): 9–49.

———. 1975. *Human Capital: A Theoretical and Empirical Analysis.* 2d ed. New York: Columbia University Press.

Bernard, Andrew B., Jonathan Eaton, J. Bradford Jensen, and Samuel Kortum. 2000. "Plants and Productivity in International Trade." Working Paper 7688. Cambridge, Mass.: National Bureau of Economic Research.

Blanchard, Olivier J. 1997. "The Medium Run." *Brookings Papers on Economic Activity* 2: 89–141.

Blinder, Alan S. 2000. "Life Imitates Art: How the Economy Came to Resemble the Model." *Business Economics* (January): 16–25.

Borjas, George. 1981. "Job Mobility and Earnings over the Life Cycle." *Industrial and Labor Relations Review* 34: 377–88.

Borjas, George J., and Valerie A. Ramey. 1995. "Foreign Competition, Market Power, and Wage Inequality." *Quarterly Journal of Economics* 110(4): 1075–1110.

Burtless, Gary. 1995. "International Trade and the Rise in Earnings Inequality." *Journal of Economic Literature* 33(June): 800–16.

Caballero, Ricardo J., and Mohamad L. Hammour. 1998. "Jobless Growth: Appropriability, Factor Substitution, and Unemployment." In *Carnegie-Rochester Conference Series on Public Policy* 48(June): 51–94.

Capelli, Peter. 1998. "Explaining the Incidence of Downsizing and the Effect on Performance." Paper presented at the Russell Sage Foundation Conference on Changes in Job Stability and Job Security, New York (February 27–28).

———. 2000. "Examining the Incidence of Downsizing and Its Effect on Establishment Performance." Working Paper 7742. Cambridge, Mass.: National Bureau of Economic Research (June).

Capelli, Peter, Laurie Bassi, Harry Katz, David Knoke, Paul Osterman, and Michael Useem. 1997. *Change at Work.* New York: Oxford University Press.

Caves, Richard E. 1998. "Industrial Organization and New Findings on the Turnover and Mobility of Firms." *Journal of Economic Literature* 36: 1947–82.

Caves, Richard E., and Matthew B. Krepps. 1993. "Fat: The Displacement of

Nonproduction Workers from U.S. Manufacturing Industries." *Brookings Papers on Economic Activity: Microeconomics* 2: 227–88.

Challenger, Gray & Christmas, Inc. Various years. Job-cut announcements and annual press release. Accessed January 2003 at: *www.economy.com/freelunch*.

Cochran, John. 1999. "New Facts in Finance." Working Paper 7169. Cambridge, Mass.: National Bureau of Economic Research (June).

Collins, Alan, and Richard I. D. Harris. 1999. "Downsizing and Productivity: The Case of UK Motor Vehicle Manufacturing 1974–1994." *Managerial and Decision Economics* 20(5): 281–90.

Council of Economic Advisers. 2001. *Economic Report of the President, 2001.* Washington: U.S. Government Printing Office (January).

Davis, Donald R., and David E. Weinstein. 2002. "Technological Superiority and the Losses from Migration." Working Paper 8971. Cambridge, Mass.: National Bureau of Economic Research.

Davis, Steven J., John C. Haltiwanger, and Scott Schuh. 1996. *Job Creation and Destruction.* Cambridge, Mass.: MIT Press.

Dickens, William T., and Lawrence F. Katz. 1987. "Interindustry Wage Differences and Theories of Wage Determination." Working Paper 2271. Cambridge, Mass.: National Bureau of Economic Research (June).

Downs, Alan. 1995. *Corporate Executions: The Ugly Truth About Layoffs—How Corporate Greed Is Shattering Lives, Companies, and Communities.* New York: AMACOM.

Dunne, Timothy, and James A. Schmitz. 1995. "Wages, Employment Structure, and Employer Size-Wage Premia: Their Relationship to Advanced-Technology Usage at U.S. Manufacturing Establishments." *Economica*, new series, 62(245): 89–107.

The Economist. 2001. "The Long March: Special Report on Mass Customization." July 14, 63–65.

Espahbodi, Reza, Teresa A. John, and Gopala Vasudevan. 2000. "The Effects of Downsizing on Operating Performance." *Review of Quantitative Finance and Accounting* 15(2): 107–26.

Farber, Henry S. 1997. "The Changing Face of Job Loss in the United States, 1981–1995." *Brookings Papers on Economic Activity: Microeconomics* 1997: 55–128.

———. 1998. "Has the Rate of Job Loss Increased in the Nineties?" Working Paper No. 394. Princeton, N.J.: Princeton University, Industrial Relations Section.

———. 2001. "Job Loss in the United States, 1981–1999." Working Paper 453, Princeton, N.J.: Princeton University, Industrial Relations Section (June).

———. 2003. "Job Loss in the United States, 1981–2001." Working paper no. 471. Princeton, N.J.: Princeton University, Industrial Relations Section (January).

Farber, Henry S., and Kevin F. Hallock. 1999. "Have Employment Reductions Become Good News for Shareholders?: The Effect of Job Loss Announcements on Stock Prices, 1970–1997." Working Paper 417. Princeton, N.J.: Princeton University, Industrial Relation Section (June).

Federal Reserve Bank of Dallas. 1996a. "The Upside of Downsizing." *Southwest Economy* (November–December): 7–11.

———. 1996b. "The Economy at Light Speed: Technology and Growth in the Information Age—and Beyond." *1996 Annual Report*: 5.

Fortin, Nicole M., and Thomas Lemieux. 1997. "Institutional Changes and Rising Wage Inequality: Is There a Linkage?" *Journal of Economic Perspectives* 11(2): 75–96.

Gardner, Jennifer. 1995. "Worker Displacement: A Decade of Change." *Monthly Labor Review* 188(April): 45–57.

Garen, John E. 1989. "Job-Match Quality as an Error Component and the Wage-Tenure Profile: A Comparison and Test of Alternative Estimators." *Journal of Business and Economic Statistics* 7(2): 245–52.

Glassman, James K., and Kevin A. Hassett. 1999. *Dow 36,000: The New Strategy for Profiting from the Coming Rise in the Stock Market.* New York: Random House/Times Books.

Gombola, Michael J., and George P. Tsetsekos. 1992. "Plant Closings for Financially Weak and Financially Strong Firms." *Quarterly Journal of Business and Economics* 31(3): 69–83.

Gordon, David M. 1996. *Fat and Mean: The Corporate Squeeze of Working Americans and the Myth of Managerial "Downsizing."* New York: Simon & Schuster.

Gottlieb, Marvin R., and Lori Conkling. 1995. *Managing the Workplace Survivors: Organizational Downsizing and the Commitment Gap.* Westport, Conn.: Quorum Books.

Gottschalk, Peter. 1997. "Inequality, Income Growth, and Mobility: The Basic Facts." *Journal of Economic Perspectives* 11(2): 21–40.

Griliches, Zvi. 1969. "Capital-Skill Complementarity." *Review of Economics and Statistics* 51(November): 465–68.

———. 1979. "Issues in Assessing the Contribution of Research and Development to Productivity Growth." *Bell Journal of Economics* 10(1): 92–116.

———. 1980. "R&D and the Productivity Slowdown." *American Economic Review* 70(2): 343–47.

———. 1992. "The Search for R&D Spillovers." *Scandinavian Journal of Economics* 94: 29–47.

Halberstam, David. 1986. *The Reckoning.* New York: William Morrow.

Hall, Robert. 1982. "The Importance of Lifetime Jobs in the U.S. Economy." *American Economic Review* 72(4): 716–24.

———. 1995. "Lost Jobs." *Brookings Papers on Economic Activity* 1995(1): 221–56.

Hallock, Kevin F. 1998. "Layoffs, Top Executive Pay, and Firm Performance." *American Economic Review* 88(4): 711–23.

Harper, Barry. 1995. "Male Occupational Mobility in Britain." *Oxford Bulletin of Economics and Statistics* 57(3): 349–69.

Hart, Peter E., and Nicholas Oulton. 2001. "Galtonian Regression, Company Age, and Job Generation 1986–1995." *Scottish Journal of Political Economy* 48(1): 82–98.

Hellgren, Johnny, and Magnus Sverke. 2001. "Unionized Employees' Perceptions of Role Stress and Fairness During Organizational Downsizing: Consequences for Job Satisfaction, Union Satisfaction, and Well-being." *Economic and Industrial Democracy* 22(4): 543–67.

Hipple, Steven. 1999. "Worker Displacement in the Mid-1990s." *Monthly Labor Review* (July): 15–32.

Hirsch, Barry T., and David A. Macpherson. 1993. "Union Membership and Coverage Files from the Current Population Surveys: Note." *Industrial and Labor Relations Review* 46(3): 574–78.

Idson, Todd. 1999. "Skill-Biased Technical Change and the Employer Size-Wage Effects." Unpublished paper. Columbia University, New York.

Ilg, Randy E. 1996. "The Nature of Employment Growth, 1989–1995." *Monthly Labor Review* 119(6): 29–36.

Jacobs, Eva E., ed. 1998. *Handbook of U.S. Labor Statistics*. 2d ed. Lanham, Md.: Bernan Press.

Johnson, George E. 1997. "Changes in Earnings Inequality: The Role of Demand Shifts." *Journal of Economic Perspectives* 11(2): 41–54.

Jovanovic, Boyan. 1979. "Job Matching and the Theory of Turnover." *Journal of Political Economy* 87: 972–90.

———. 1982. "Selection and the Evolution of Industry." *Econometrica* 50(3): 649–70.

Jovanovic, Boyan, and Peter L. Rousseau. 2001. "Mergers and Technological Change, 1885–1998." Working paper no. 01-W6. Department of Economics, Vanderbilt University (August).

Kalra, Rajiv, Glenn V. Henderson, and Michael C. Walker. 1994. "Share Price Reaction to Plant-Closing Announcements." *Journal of Economics and Business* 46(5): 381–95.

Khalil, Elias L. 1997. "The Red Queen Paradox: A Proper Name for a Popular Game." *Journal of Institutional and Theoretical Economics* 153(2): 411–15.

King, Deborah A. 1996. *Learning to Live with Downsizing: Seven Powerful Lessons for Building a Bridge to Tomorrow*. Marietta, Ga.: EMI.

Klepper, Steven. 1996. "Entry, Exit, Growth, and Innovation over the Product Life Cycle." *American Economic Review* 86: 562–83.

Klette, Tor Jakob, and Samuel Kortum. 2002. "Innovating Firms and Aggregate Innovation." Working Paper 8819. Cambridge, Mass.: National Bureau of Economic Research.

Kletzer, Lori G. 1998. "Job Displacement." *Journal of Economic Perspectives* 12(1): 115–36.

Kokkelenberg, Edward C., and Donna R. Sockell. 1985. "Union Membership in the United States, 1973–1981." *Industrial and Labor Relations Review* 38(4): 497–543.

Krepps, Matthew B., and Amy Bertin Candell. 1997. *Industrial Inefficiency and Downsizing: A Study of Layoffs and Plant Closures*. New York: Garland.

Krueger, Alan B. 1998. "Thoughts on Globalization, Unions, and Labor Market Rents." Unpublished paper. Princeton University, Princeton, N.J. (April 28).

Krueger, Alan B., and Lawrence H. Summers. 1987. "Reflections on the Interindustry Wage Structure." In *Unemployment and the Structure of Labor Markets*, edited by Kevin Lang and Jonathan S. Leonard. New York and Oxford: Blackwell.

———. 1988. "Efficiency Wages and the Interindustry Wage Structure." *Econometrica* 56(2): 259–93.

Landes, David. 1999. "Finding the Point at Sea." *NAWCC Bulletin* 41(December): 745–53.

Leana, Carrie R., and Daniel C. Feldman. 1992. *Coping with Job Loss: How Individuals, Organizations, and Communities Respond to Layoffs*. New York: Lexington Books.

Leibenstein, Harvey. 1966. "Allocative Efficiency vs. X-Efficiency." *American Economic Review* 56(June): 392–415.

Lewis, H. G. 1963. *Unionism and Relative Wages in the United States.* Chicago: University of Chicago Press.

———. 1986. *Union Relative Wage Effects: A Survey.* Chicago: University of Chicago Press.

Light, Audrey, and Kathleen McGarry. 1998. "Job Change Patterns and the Wages of Young Men." *Review of Economics and Statistics* 80(2): 276–86.

Lucas, Robert E., Jr. 1977. "On the Size Distribution of Business Firms." *Bell Journal of Economics* 9: 508–23.

Maddison, Angus. 1995. *Monitoring the World Economy, 1829–1992.* Paris: Organization for Economic Cooperation and Development.

———. 2001. *The World Economy: A Millennial Perspective.* Paris: Organization for Economic Cooperation and Development.

Mansfield, Edwin. 1965. "Rates of Return from Industrial Research and Development." *American Economic Review* 55(2): 310–22.

———. 1980. "Basic Research and Productivity Increase in Manufacturing." *American Economic Review* 70(5): 863–73.

Manski, Charles F., and John D. Straub. 1999. "Worker Perceptions of Job Insecurity in the Mid-1990s: Evidence from the Survey of Economic Expectations." Working Paper 6908. Cambridge, Mass.: National Bureau of Economic Research.

Markey, James P., and William Parks II. 1989. "Occupational Change: Pursuing a Different Kind of Work." *Monthly Labor Review* (September): 3–12.

Masters, Stanley H. 1969. "An Interindustry Analysis of Wages and Plant Size." *Review of Economics and Statistics* 51(3): 341–45.

Mellow, Wesley. 1981. "Employer Size and Wages." Working Paper 116. Washington: U.S. Department of Labor, Bureau of Labor Statistics (April).

Miller, Robert A. 1984. "Job Matching and Occupational Choice." *Journal of Political Economy* 92(6): 1086–1120.

Mincer, Jacob, and Boyan Jovanovic. 1981. "Labor Mobility and Wages." In *Studies in Labor Markets,* edited by Sherwin Rosen. Chicago: University of Chicago Press.

Mohnen, Pierre. 1992. *The Relationship Between R&D and Productivity Growth in Canada and Other Major Industrialized Countries.* Ottawa, Can.: Canada Communications Group.

Mortensen, Dale T., and Christopher A. Pissarides. 1999a. "Job Reallocation, Employment Fluctuations, and Unemployment." In *Handbook of Macroeconomics,* vol. 1B, edited by John B. Taylor and Michael Woodford, vol. 15 of *Handbooks in Economics.* Amsterdam, New York, and Oxford: Elsevier Science, North-Holland.

———. 1999b. "New Developments in Models of Search in the Labor Market." In *Handbook of Labor Economics,* vol. 3B, edited by Orley Ashenfelter and David Card, vol. 5 of *Handbooks in Economics.* Amsterdam, New York, and Oxford: Elsevier Science, North-Holland.

National Science Board. 2000. *Science and Engineering Indicators—2000.* Arlington, Va.: National Science Foundation.

National Science Foundation. 1996. *Research and Development in Industry*, NSF96-304. Arlington, Va.: NSF.

Neal, Derek. 1995. "Industry-Specific Human Capital: Evidence from Displaced Workers." *Journal of Labor Economics* 13(4): 653–77.

———. 1999. "The Complexity of Job Mobility Among Young Men." *Journal of Labor Economics* 17(2): 237–61.

Neumark, David. 2000. "Changes in Job Stability and Job Security: A Collective Effort to Untangle, Reconcile, and Interpret the Evidence." Working Paper 7472. Cambridge, Mass.: National Bureau of Economic Research.

New York Stock Exchange. 2000. *Shareownership 2000, Based on the 1998 Survey of Consumer Finances.* Accessed in January 2003 at: *www.nyse.com.*

Orazem, Peter F., and J. Peter Mattila. 1986. "Occupational Entry and Uncertainty: Males Leaving High School." *Review of Economics and Statistics* 68(2): 265–73.

Pakes, Ariel, and Richard Ericson. 1995. "Markov-Perfect Industry Dynamics: A Framework for Empirical Work." *Review of Economic Studies* 62(1): 53–82.

Parente, Daniel. 2000. "Industry-Specific Capital and the Wage Profile: Evidence from the National Longitudinal Survey of Youth and the Panel Study of Income Dynamics." *Journal of Labor Economics* 18(2): 306–23.

Parrado, Eric, and Edward N. Wolff. 1999. "Occupational and Industry Mobility in the United States, 1969–1992." Research Report 99-20. New York University, C. V. Starr Center.

Patinkin, Don. 1947. "Multiple-Plant Firms, Cartels, and Imperfect Competition." *Quarterly Journal of Economics* 61(2): 173–205.

Pfann, Gerard A. 2001. "Downsizing." Unpublished paper. Bonn, Germany: Forschungsinstitut zur Zukunft der Arbeit (Institute for the Study of Labor) (June).

Pietrykowski, Bruce. 1999. "Beyond the Fordist/Post-Fordist Dichotomy: Working Through the Second Industrial Divide." *Review of Social Economy* 57(2): 177–98.

Polsky, Daniel. 1999. "Changing Consequences of Job Separations in the United States." *Industrial and Labor Relations Review* 52(4): 565–80.

Pugel, Thomas A. 1980. "Profitability, Concentration, and the Interindustry Variation in Wages." *Review of Economics and Statistics* 62(2): 248–53.

Rae, John. 1895. *Life of Adam Smith*. London: Macmillan.

Robertson, Donald, and James Symons. 1990. "The Occupational Choice of British Children." *Economic Journal* 100: 828–41.

Robertson, Paul L., and Lee J. Alston. 1992. "Technological Choice and the Organization of Work in Capitalist Firms." *Economic History Review*, new series, 45(2): 330–49.

Rodriguez, Daniel, and Madeline Zavodny. 2000. "Are Displaced Workers Now Finished at Age Forty?" *Federal Reserve Bank of Atlanta Economic Review* 85(2): 33–47.

Rosen, Sherwin. 1972. "Learning and Experience in the Labor Market." *Journal of Human Resources* 7: 326–42.

Rosenberg, Nathan. 1982. *Inside the Black Box: Technology and Economics.* Cambridge: Cambridge University Press.

Rudolph, Barbara. 1998. *Disconnected: How Six People from AT&T Discovered the New Meaning of Work in a Downsized Corporate America.* New York: Free Press.

Say, Jean-Baptiste. 1821. *A Treatise on Political Economy.* London: Longman, Hurst, Rees, Orme, and Brown.

Scherer, Frederic M., and David Ross. 1990. *Industrial Market Structure and Economic Performance.* 3d ed. Boston: Houghton Mifflin.

Shaw, Kathryn L. 1986. "Occupational Change, Employer Change, and the Transferability of Skills." *Southern Economic Journal* 53: 702–19.

Shiller, Robert J. 2000. *Irrational Exuberance.* Princeton, N.J.: Princeton University Press.

Sicherman, Nachum, and Oded Galor. 1990. "A Theory of Career Mobility." *Journal of Political Economy* 98(1): 169–92.

Sommers, Dixie, and Alan Eck. 1977. "Occupational Mobility in the Labor Force." *Monthly Labor Review* (January): 3–26.

Standard & Poor's. Various years. Compustat (North America) annual files. Englewood, Colo.: McGraw-Hill.

Swinnerton, Kenneth A., and Howard Wial. 1995. "Is Job Stability Declining in the U.S. Economy?" *Industrial and Labor Relations Review* 48(2): 293–304.

Topel, Robert H. 1997. "Factor Proportions and Relative Wages: The Supply-Side Determinants of Wage Inequality." *Journal of Economic Perspectives* 11(2): 55–74.

Topel, Robert H., and Michael P. Ward. 1992. "Job Mobility and the Careers of Young Men." *Quarterly Journal of Economics* (May): 439–79.

Ureta, Manuelita. 1992. "The Importance of Lifetime Jobs in the U.S. Economy, Revisited." *American Economic Review* 82(1): 322–35.

U.S. Bureau of the Census. 2000. *Statistical Abstract of the United States: 2000.* 120th ed. Washington: U.S. Government Printing Office.

———. 1958–1992. Enterprise Statistics. Available at: *www.census.gov.*

———. Various years. Census of Manufacturing. Available at: *www.census.gov.*

U.S. Department of Commerce, Bureau of Economic Analysis. Various years. *National Income and Product Accounts.* Available at: *www.bea.gov.*

———. Various years. *Fixed Reproducible Tangible Wealth.* Available at: *www.bea.gov.*

———. 1993. *Fixed Reproducible Tangible Wealth in the United States, 1925–1989.* Washington: U.S. Government Printing Office (January).

U.S. Department of Labor, Bureau of Labor Statistics. 1979. *Handbook of Labor Statistics 1978.* Bulletin 2. Washington: U.S. Government Printing Office.

———. 1990. *Handbook of Labor Statistics 1989.* Bulletin 23. Washington: U.S. Government Printing Office.

———. Various years. Office of Employment Projections, output and employment database.

Weiss, Leonard W. 1966. "Concentration and Labor Earnings." *American Economic Review* 56(1): 96–117.

White, H. 1980. "A Heteroskedasticity-Consistent Covariance Matrix Estimator and a Direct Test for Heteroskedasticity." *Econometrica* 48(May): 817–38.

Wilson, R. Mark, and Carole Green. 1990. "Occupation, Occupational Change, and Movement Within the Income Distribution." *Eastern Economic Journal* 16(3): 209–20.

Wolff, Edward N. 1996. "Technology and the Demand for Skills." *OECD Science, Technology, and Industry Review* 18: 96–123.

Wood, Adrian. 1994. *North-South Trade, Employment, and Inequality: Changing Fortunes in a Skill-Driven World*. Oxford: Clarendon Press.

———. 1995. "How Trade Hurt Unskilled Workers." *Journal of Economic Perspectives* 9(3): 57–80.

Worrell, Dan L., Wallace N. Davidson III, and Varinder M. Sharma. 1991. "Layoff Announcements and Stockholder Wealth." *Academy of Management Journal* 43: 662–78.

Index